AF478229

The Middle
Kingdom
under the
Big Sky

The Middle Kingdom under the Big Sky

A History of the Chinese Experience in Montana

MARK T. JOHNSON

University of Nebraska Press
Lincoln

The University of Nebraska Press is part of a land-grant institution with campuses and programs on the past, present, and future homelands of the Pawnee, Ponca, Otoe-Missouria, Omaha, Dakota, Lakota, Kaw, Cheyenne, and Arapaho Peoples, as well as those of the relocated Ho-Chunk, Sac and Fox, and Iowa Peoples.

Publication of this volume was assisted by The Virginia Faulkner Fund, established in memory of Virginia Faulkner, editor in chief of the University of Nebraska Press.

Library of Congress Cataloging-in-Publication Data
Names: Johnson, Mark T., 1974–, author.
Title: The Middle Kingdom under the big sky: a history of the Chinese experience in Montana / Mark T. Johnson.
Description: Lincoln: University of Nebraska Press, [2022] | Includes bibliographical references and index.
Identifiers: LCCN 2021038215
ISBN 9781496230997 (hardback)
ISBN 9781496231918 (epub)
ISBN 9781496231925 (pdf)
Subjects: LCSH: Chinese—Montana—History. | Chinese—Montana—Social conditions. | Montana—Race relations. | Montana—Ethnic relations. | BISAC: HISTORY / United States / State & Local / West (AK, CA, CO, HI, ID, MT, NV, UT, WY) | SOCIAL SCIENCE / Ethnic Studies / American / Asian American Studies
Classification: LCC F740.C5 J64 2022 | DDC 978.6/004951—dc23
LC record available at https://lccn.loc.gov/2021038215

Set in Adobe Garamond Pro by Mikala R. Kolander.

To my family: Your support, encouragement,
and motivation made this possible.

CONTENTS

Figures

Maps

"Here he lies; his life cut short; his death avenged." This cryptic epitaph, found in Helena, Montana's Benton Avenue Cemetery, tells of John R. Bitzer's demise in January 1870. Armed with this intriguing inscription, I sought information at the Montana Historical Society (MHS) to see what more I could discover about Bitzer's death and the resulting vengeance. A fascinating story emerged of violence and vigilantism on the frontier as well as the diversity of the American West. Ah Chow, a Chinese resident of Helena, shot Bitzer in a domestic disturbance, the circumstances of which are still uncertain. The resulting events illustrated the pressures on the large Chinese community in Montana at the time, estimated to have been 10 to 15 percent of the territory's total population.

Discovering that the Bitzer story connected with the Chinese history of the region was serendipitous for me. At the time, I taught history at Concordia International School in Shanghai, China. I saw the Bitzer-Ah Chow story as an opportunity to connect my students in China to the history of Big Sky country. Hoping to explore this topic in new ways, I inquired with the specialists at the MHS Research Center as to whether they had any Chinese-language sources. They pointed me to a large collection featuring close to one hundred letters, business ledgers, maps, and prescriptions for Chinese traditional medicine. Though not related to the Bitzer-Ah Chow incident, I believed these documents held tremendous potential to deepen collective knowledge of the Chinese experience in Montana. While much is known about Chinese people's involvement in the American West, most studies have been conducted using only English-language sources. The large cache of untranslated Chinese documents seemed an exciting opportunity to add a significant contribution to broader understandings of the Chinese experience in Montana and the West.

There had been previous attempts to translate the collection. In 1988, the MHS reached out to a linguist at the University of Montana who, in noting that the letters dealt with family affairs, remarked, "I do not think they possess any true historical value." I disagreed and sought creative ways to use connections from my work in China to translate the documents. This proved harder than expected as the letters were written in difficult-to-decipher calligraphy and in the traditional form of writing Chinese characters. After the Communists' 1949 victory in the Chinese Civil War, the People's Republic of China simplified Chinese writing to increase literacy across the nation. As a result, most of my Chinese students, their families, and the Chinese-language teachers at my school could read only about 30 percent of the documents in the MHS collection. Undeterred, I sought a solution. Working with community members, we called on families from Hong Kong and Taiwan, where the educational systems still teach traditional characters. Additionally, volunteers of a certain age who had received their education before the simplification of the writing system assisted in the process. With this multigenerational, transnational team assembled, we began several projects to contribute to a deeper understanding of Montana's diverse history.

In the summer of 2012 I traveled from Shanghai to Helena with a team of student researchers. This on-site team digitized documents and sent the files to the translation team of sixteen students and fourteen teacher, parent, and grandparent volunteers working in Shanghai. To achieve the most accurate translation possible, two teams translated each document independently, with the results compared and cross-referenced for the final translation. As the translation team processed the documents, the team working at the MHS used the archives to corroborate evidence from other MHS collections and the Chinese-language collection itself and put the translated sources into the broader contexts of Montana, western, and world history. The translator from 1988 was correct—the letters did recount family matters. I disagree, however, with the assessment that they did not possess "any true historical value." As chapter 2 details, the letters illuminate the tremendous cultural pressures on the Chinese who came to Montana and show the extensive communication system that linked family members separated by thousands of miles who remained apart for decades at a time.

Every foray into the archives produced sources that helped me interpret the Chinese experience in Montana in new ways. These sources include the 1905 special census for the Chinese in the Montana and Idaho region. Seemingly unknown to most who have examined the experience of Chinese residents in the region, this document allowed a detailed examination of the location and movement of individuals throughout the region and showed trends of activism and resistance to efforts to expel the Chinese from the West, as explained in chapters 3 and 5. Chinese Montanans became leaders in resistance efforts within the United States and influenced events in China as well. Notably, documents emerged from MHS collections regarding the Chinese Empire Reform Association, a fascinating group started by exiled Chinese reformers to influence the ruling Qing dynasty (1644–1912), as described in chapter 4. These connections between Montana's Chinese residents and significant events in Chinese and world history continued with a 1905 boycott of American goods that reverberated across Montana, as shown in chapter 5.

While much of the previous coverage of the Chinese experience in Montana focused on the late nineteenth century, newly discovered sources allow this project to extend its analysis through the 1950s. During the archival exploration of what remained from the state's Chinese community, another collection emerged. Much larger than the first group of letters, "The Wing Hong Hum Papers" contain more than two hundred letters in Chinese and close to one hundred documents in English. The letters detail the ordeals of the Hom/Hum family. In the early 1930s Wing Hong Hom came to Butte, Montana, where he worked to support family members back in China and planned to facilitate the relocation of his younger brother, Wing Goon, to Butte. Due to the chaos engulfing China throughout the 1930s and 1940s, with the ongoing civil war between the Nationalists and Communists and the Japanese invasion causing widespread destruction, however, Wing Goon became stranded in Hong Kong. As detailed in chapter 8, the Hom family struggled to navigate constantly changing American immigration policies influenced by officials' fears of Communist infiltration. To interpret this much larger collection, I built upon the initial framework of the transnational translation project, returning to Montana in 2014 with another research team while a translation team worked in Shanghai.

One of the most exciting aspects of these translation projects was the forging of cross-generational connections. Students worked with teachers, parents, and grandparents to use their language abilities to unlock century-old mysteries. There was a wonderful symmetry in seeing a school community comprised of families brought to Shanghai by transnational economic trends work to illuminate the transnational history of how Chinese migrants peopled and developed frontier Montana.

This book seeks to deepen understanding of the Chinese history of the region by recovering immigrants' stories in their own words and by examining their experiences in Montana through a global lens. These collections provide insight into the pressures the Chinese community faced from family members back in China and from other Montanans as economic and cultural disturbances complicated efforts to accept them as residents of the state. Additionally, the documents reveal how political movements that advocated for reform in China connected to and were inspired by Chinese Montanans. By recovering the voices of Chinese Montanans and acknowledging them as active participants in the development of the state and region, this book will help readers understand how this group both shaped and was shaped by events in the American West and China.

This project began with a request from my mother-in-law, Lucille O'Leary. In 2010 she found John R. Bitzer's tombstone in Helena's Benton Avenue Cemetery and suggested that I look into the story of "his death avenged." Bitzer's demise connected to Montana's large Chinese community, and unraveling that story led from one fascinating source to another. I appreciate Lucille's initial inspiration, continued interest in the many stages of this project, and good-natured prompting to finish it.

Working as part of the wonderful learning community at Concordia International School Shanghai allowed exploration of the history of Montana's Chinese residents in creative ways. Students, faculty colleagues, administrators, and families in the community supported these projects with enthusiasm and provided the necessary language abilities to tell the history of Chinese Montanans in their own words. Over the years, dozens of students and community members helped with Chinese language translations and cultural interpretations that made this project possible. The students, teachers, parents, grandparents, and community volunteers who helped with the translation and research included Nuna Atadja, Tonia Au Yeung, Mike Burns, Ashleigh Carroll, Chris Carter, Karen Chang, Charlene Chen, Mu Hua Chen, Sophia Chen, Ying-chu Chen, Jason Cheng, Sarah Cheng, Stephanie Fan, Monica Fung, Marcus Gong, Alex Gu, Samantha Guo, Yulan He, Clarissa Hsu, Frondia Hsu, Cathy Hsueh, Joan Hu, Jae Min Jang, Christina Jiang, Jessica Jiang, Kimberly Kuh, Jasmin Lam, Jessica Lee, Sharlene Lee, Emily Leng, Yiluo Li, Roxanne Lin, Li Liu, Michelle Liu, Steven Pan, Karen Pyi, Ying Ying Reed, Lauren Ren, Sylvia Richards, Yucca Rieschel, Joseph Schwalbach, Fiona Sha, Lei Shi, Quinn Shultz, Sandy Wu, Wendy Xu, Jun Yanagi, Yun Yang, Michelle Yee, Sabrina Yin, Irrey Zhang, Wei Zhao, Doris Zhao, and Zhen Zheng. The team that traveled from Shanghai to Montana to work in residence at the Montana Historical Society included Madison Boll, Madeline Crispell, Alex Szabo, Jonathan Tai, and Allen Wang. Madeline Crispell, Yucca Rieschel, Allen Wang, and Sabrina Yin deserve special recognition for helping with the original translation projects and for being fruitful collaborators for years after the initial projects concluded.

Financial assistance to conduct research and to support travel involved with the translation project came from many organizations. I appreciate the support from the Montana Historical Society through the Dave Walter Research Fellowship (2011) and the Special Projects Fellowship (2012) which allowed extended time at the archives where so many of the sources that made this study possible reside. Assistance for the research trips and work throughout Montana also came from Humanities Montana with an Opportunity Grant (2012), the Honor Society of Phi Kappa Phi with a Love of Learning Award (2012), and the National Council for the Social Studies with the Christa McAuliffe Reach for the Stars Award (2014). Assistance for travel to National Archives and Record Administration branches in Washington, D.C., College Park, Maryland, and Seattle, Washington, was generously provided by Brigham Young University and the Charles Redd Center with the John Topham and Susan Redd Butler Off-Campus Faculty Award (2018).

Over the years, I have delivered versions of several chapters to specialists in the field and interested audience members. I am grateful to those who offered feedback on early forms of the project delivered at the Montana History Conference, the Global Borderlands Symposium sponsored by Texas A&M University-San Antonio, the Historical Museum at Fort Missoula, Bozeman's Extreme History Project, the Mai Wah Society, and the University of Montana's Lockridge History Workshop. An earlier version of chapter 4 was previously published as an article titled "Becoming Chinese in Montana: The Chinese Empire Reform Association and National Identity among Montana's Chinese Communities," in *Montana:*

The Magazine of Western History in Winter 2015. The Western History Association has been a particularly supportive academic community for feedback and collaboration, with much of the finished product being developed and critiqued at annual WHA conferences. I appreciate the thought-provoking and insightful discussions from the commentators, audience members, and fellow panelists during these collaborations.

During my hundreds of hours at the Montana Historical Society Research Center, the knowledgeable, friendly, and diligent staff was key to every phase of the research process. Zoe Ann Stoltz has been vital to this project from the first investigation into the Bitzer tombstone in the summer of 2010 through to the present. The positivity and collegiality of Zoe Ann, Rich Aarstad, Jeff Malcomson, and the rest of the staff at the MHS made the long hours of research truly delightful. The same is true for colleagues like Pat Munday and Richard Gibson of Butte's Mai Wah Society, Ellen Crain at the Butte-Silver Bow Public Archives, and Ken Robison of Fort Benton's Overholser Historical Research Center. I appreciate the assistance and graciousness of Bob Berry in providing access to a rare piece of this puzzle that adds to our understanding of Chinese culture as experienced in Montana.

I am grateful to Jane Leung Larson who consulted over the years as I built my knowledge on the Chinese Empire Reform Association. Her generosity in sharing materials and her insights on various sources were key to understanding the efforts of the Chinese Empire Reform Association in the region. In providing translations of key Chinese Empire Reform Association sources, Chi Jeng Chang has been very helpful. Additionally, Jane brought to my attention the 1905 special census described in chapters 3 and 5, allowing for analysis of the fight against the Geary Act and the ability to trace trends of movement in the state's Chinese population.

I am grateful for the partnership of Clark Whitehorn with the University of Nebraska Press, who showed interest in the project and helped me navigate the publishing process. Erin Greb was a fantastic collaborator to have in creating the maps, especially the map featured in chapter 1 with the many layers of information featured in such a creative way. Friends and colleagues Cindy and Randy Farley and Jeffrey A. Johnson read the manuscript and gave encouragement and important suggestions for improvement. Liping Zhu and Robert Swartout were key to this project in two ways. First, their pathbreaking work on the Chinese in the Rocky Mountain region provided the foundation on which I built. Second, they gave crucial feedback to improve the manuscript. I appreciate their gracious sharing of wisdom gained through decades of research and leadership in this field.

Nicholas Kent has been crucial to the many projects that have culminated in this book. From an enthusiastic teaching partner who was a delight to bounce ideas off of to my boss, who approved and supported the ambitious transnational translation projects that empowered students as historians, Nick's support has been a joy to count on throughout these years. Similarly, dear friend Brian Collier's interest in this project from the early stages signaled to me that I was on the right track and should persist. Friends like Nick and Brian gave me the confidence and encouragement needed to push through to completion of this book.

During the more than ten years building to the completion of this project, my family has been tremendously supportive. My sons, Jack and Thomas, have been interested listeners, productive thought partners, and frequent companions on research trips. My wife Janet has been wonderfully supportive on this journey. The excitement I felt with each new archival discovery was matched by Janet's enthusiasm for these developments and willingness to participate in many long, one-sided conversations about interpretation of sources and narrative structure. Her engaged, tireless support made this all possible.

In Montana and throughout the American West, for non-Chinese census takers, newspaper reporters, and the common public, pronouncing and spelling Chinese names proved challenging. This presents a difficulty for historians in working with sources from the time period. At times, non-Chinese references to Chinese names denoted the same person in many ways. For instance, Quon Loy, leader of Butte's Chinese community, was referred to as Quong Loue, Quon Louie, and Quong Louis. In such cases I have preserved the original spelling that appears in the documents while standardizing references to individuals in the narrative text.

Typically for Chinese individuals, the family name precedes the given name. This indicates the primacy that families have in the culture. For instance, Kang Youwei was of the Kang family with the given name Youwei. Therefore, repeated references to him as Kang after his first introduction refer to his family name. When the individual's family name is obvious, I reference it after its first introduction. When it is difficult to determine which is the family and which is the given name, I use both.

Place names as given in documents from the time refer to the cities of Canton and Nanking. When quoting from source material, I maintain the original names, clarifying the modern transliterations of these locations as Guangzhou and Nanjing in parentheses.

The Middle
Kingdom
under the
Big Sky

ONE

Telling the History of Montana's Chinese Pioneers

It is the rightful boast of an American citizen, that his country is the
refuge of the oppressed of every clime, and theatre of action for the
energetic of every nation. No nobler character can be claimed by any
people. . . . We believe competition to be the soul of business, and,
whether foreign or domestic, we say, let it come.

—THOMAS DIMSDALE, *Montana Post*, August 19, 1865

With the discovery of precious metals in the early 1860s,
the world came to Montana. As the editor of the territory's first newspaper, Thomas Dimsdale understood the
draw of the region, its need for workers, and the benefits of a multicultural workforce to Montana's development. Himself an immigrant
from England, Dimsdale welcomed all comers, with one exception:
the Chinese. As his column from August 1865 continued, Dimsdale
believed the Chinese

compete with our workingmen, living sumptuously on what white
men would starve; they fill every little lucrative post; they follow in
the track of our pioneer miners, and rob our gulches of millions of
dollars, while everything they earn or steal goes to China. . . . The
Chinaman is a social horseleech, sucking up the poor man's very life-
blood, and, unlike him, returning nothing. . . . We hope the miners of Montana will tell "John" to retire with extreme rapidity . . . A
Chinese can never be made into a citizen, and we say get rid of any

human animal that is not susceptible of improvement or elevation. We should be *transported* to know that the last of them were *exported*.[1]

A later entry warned of "a large stampede of Celestials from Nevada and California [coming] for Montana."[2] More than just alerting readers of the number of Chinese immigrants coming to Montana, Dimsdale fanned racial animosity with stories claiming that Chinese men meant to despoil white women. Reprinting an article from a San Francisco correspondent, Dimsdale's newspaper cautioned against employing Chinese workers as house servants: "They play sad havoc with the morals of the young females . . . The girls . . . being in constant contact with the China boys, they became imprudent and were ruined. It is sickening to think of beautiful white girls being seduced by these copper-colored young scoundrels." Dimsdale penned an addendum to the lengthy article with an allusion familiar to all Montanans following the vigilante actions of the mid–1860s, implying in his editorial that lynching was the solution: "Is there no hemp in California?"[3]

In many ways Dimsdale's editorials encapsulate the Chinese experience in Montana both in terms of the oppression they faced and the complex global networks they inhabited. They were hated by many for their perceived labor competition and despised for their racial and cultural differences. Dimsdale encouraged Montanans to evict the Chinese from the region, or worse. Many agreed, leading to efforts to oust the Chinese including economic boycotts, the ever-present threat of violent expulsion, and legal restrictions that limited their choice of occupations and ability to integrate into society. Federal legislation against the Chinese intensified throughout the 1890s. The resulting raids, arrests, and deportations diminished the state's Chinese population. Dimsdale would have been "transported" with delight to see so many Chinese people "exported" had he lived to see these actions. Chinese cultural rituals also facilitated the population's "export," though not in the way Dimsdale intended or would have approved. Chinese religious practices adapted to conditions in the American West, with transnational networks tending to the needs of migrants both in life and in death, including by returning remains of those who died in Montana for reburial in China. The maintenance of cultural practices brought comfort to the Chinese residents of the region but also served as fodder for anti-Chinese forces predisposed to find fault with them.

As Dimsdale's screed noted, "A Chinese can never be made into a citizen." Cutting through the dehumanizing language that often compared the Chinese to rats, mice, coyotes, or, in this case, a horseleech, his editorial correctly characterized the legal reality. Until 1943, Chinese people could not become naturalized citizens. Even by the 1950s, when ethnically Chinese Montanans were recognized as citizens, racial animosity and cultural suspicion persisted, limiting opportunities for these individuals.

Dimsdale and others feared "a scouting party" sending reports to San Francisco and China. Meant to denigrate the Chinese and spread fear that would lead to their expulsion, Dimsdale's invective hints at the complex global networks the Chinese in Montana inhabited. Extensive written communications linked Montana's Chinese communities with those across North America and back to China. Wealth generated in the American West not only contributed to the region's development but also sustained thousands of families in southern China. Frequent letters to and from Montana's Chinese communities informed individuals of family occurrences, local upheavals, and labor needs. Changing conditions in southern China, advances in technology that eased travel between nations, and the labor needs of the American West linked the two regions in an evolving transnational network. These frequent communications kept the region's Chinese residents informed of and engaged with political events in their home country. Montana's Chinese population became involved with and, in many ways, leaders of movements that influenced China, the United States, and the relationship between the two nations. From a global boycott that influenced longstanding American policies to efforts to reinstate the Chinese emperor that saw the development of an armed militia of soldiers, Montana's Chinese residents shaped events across the transnational networks they inhabited.

It is unlikely that Dimsdale and other anti-Chinese forces appreciated the complexity of the networks that brought the Chinese to Montana and allowed them to influence global events. Anti-Chinese forces instead fixated on economic claims that these immigrants "rob our gulches of millions of dollars." It is true that mining initially drew many Chinese settlers to the region.[4] Chinese miners arrived in California shortly after the discovery of gold and followed precious metal strikes across the American West. Work in the gold and silver fields of North America built on a tradition of mining among the cultures of southern China. Since the early 1600s Chinese migrants had worked in mining industries throughout Southeast Asia. Chinese miners who sought wealth in the West brought several generations worth of cultural and technological knowledge. Chinese miners in the American West usually followed just behind the first wave of miners, often working areas that other miners had abandoned, believing the gold had "played out." To explain the success of Chinese miners, myths emerged that they lurked below cabins of white prospectors and collected gold dust that fell through the cracks. The truth was that cooperation, patience, diligence, and technologies honed over generations helped them extract wealth from mining fields throughout the American West.[5] Rather than compete against Chinese miners, legal efforts to restrict them arose in most western territories, with taxes levied against noncitizens and limitations on mine ownership designed to hinder their work in the field. Restrictions on Chinese people's access to mining claims emerged quickly in Montana. By 1872 Montana's territorial legislature banned the Chinese from owning mining claims. At times these restrictions were challenged, at times they were affirmed, but the general sentiment persisted throughout Montana's development, reducing economic opportunities for the Chinese in Montana.

Chinese settlers began to take up other work, providing key services for frontier mining communities. Early Montana pioneer Andrew Fisk noted in a diary entry from October 1866: "Was up to Helena City today. . . . It is the busiest place I ever saw. . . . There are a good many Chinese there and all of them (I guess) wash clothes for a living."[6] Fisk's remark as to the size of Helena's Chinese community was borne out by the fact that it comprised more than twenty percent of the city's population by the end of the decade. His casual observation of the economic niche filled by the Chinese belies their struggle to occupy even this segment of the economy.

As pressure, competition, and exclusion increased in mining, many of the Chinese transitioned to other occupations, including restaurant work, vegetable production, and general labor, providing important services for frontier communities. Chinese settlers often started laundries, which required little capital, provided an important service in the community, and were a good source of income for individuals with limited English language abilities.[7] The animosity the Chinese faced in mining, however, followed them to these other occupations. In 1866 anti-Chinese forces in Helena attempted a tactic that would be repeated elsewhere throughout Montana for the next five decades—a boycott of Chinese-run businesses to try to cut off the population's source of sustenance and force them from the region. White settlers launched similar efforts in Dillon, Deer Lodge, and Neihart in 1885, in Missoula in 1891, throughout the 1880s and 1890s in Butte and Anaconda, in Kalispell in 1902–1903, and in smaller towns across the region (see Appendix I: Anti-Chinese Actions in Montana: 1866–1909). In the first known case in Montana, anti-Chinese forces in Helena urged a boycott of Chinese-owned laundries in 1866, arguing that laundry work was one of "the few branches of honest livelihood" open to white women.[8] Not willing to passively submit to the boycott, Chinese leaders in Helena spoke out, noting, "We have at all times been willing to abide by all the laws of the United States . . . and are now willing to deport ourselves as good law abiding citizens of Montana Territory, and ask but that protection that the liberal and good government of this country permits us to enjoy. We pay all our taxes and assessments, and only ask that the good people of Montana may let us earn an honest living by the sweat of our brow."[9] In authoring this defense, Ye Sing, Hob Hee, and Ye Hob stood up for the role they sought to play in the developing society.

This statement represents one of the earliest sources from Montana's Chinese community itself. Too often, the voices of the Chinese in the American West are not present in the record because of

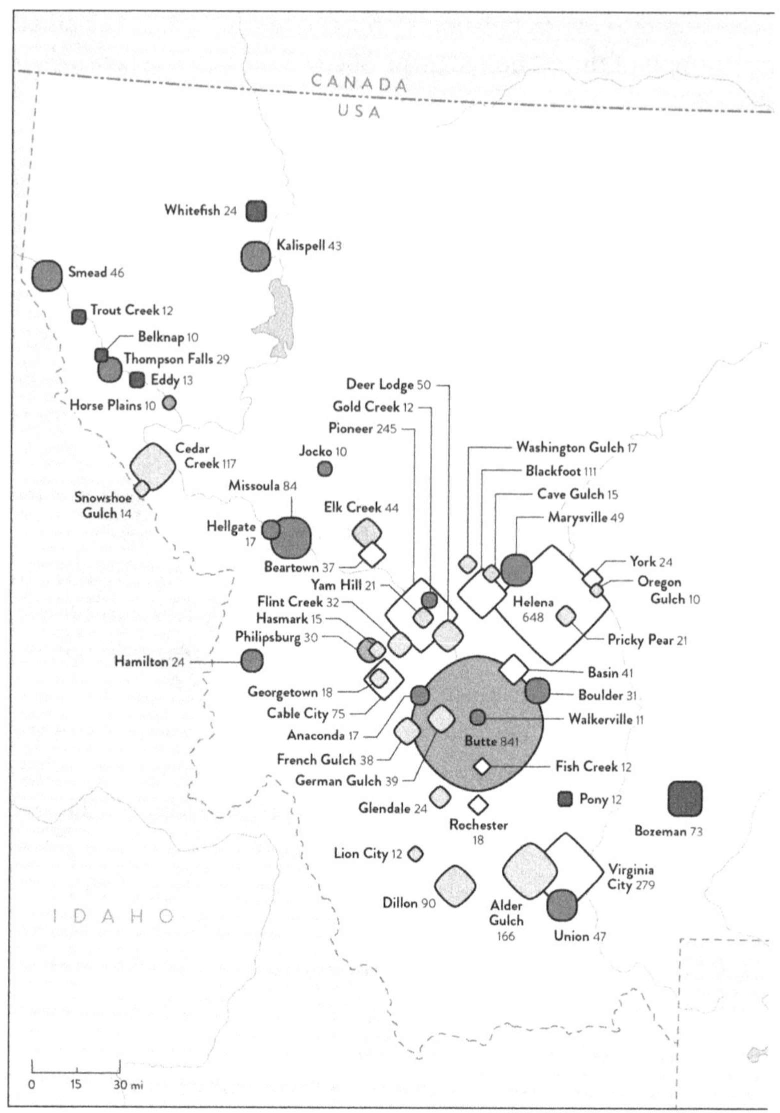

MAP 1. Locations in Montana having ten or more Chinese residents, 1870–1930. Figures are from the moment of highest population of Chinese residents per community based on census information from 1870, 1880, 1900, and 1930. Health Officer's Report 1891, Geary Act registration location as of 1894, and location of Chinese Montanans recorded on the special census of 1905. Unfortunately, detailed information from the 1890 census is unavailable as the records were destroyed by a fire in 1921. Map by Erin Greb.

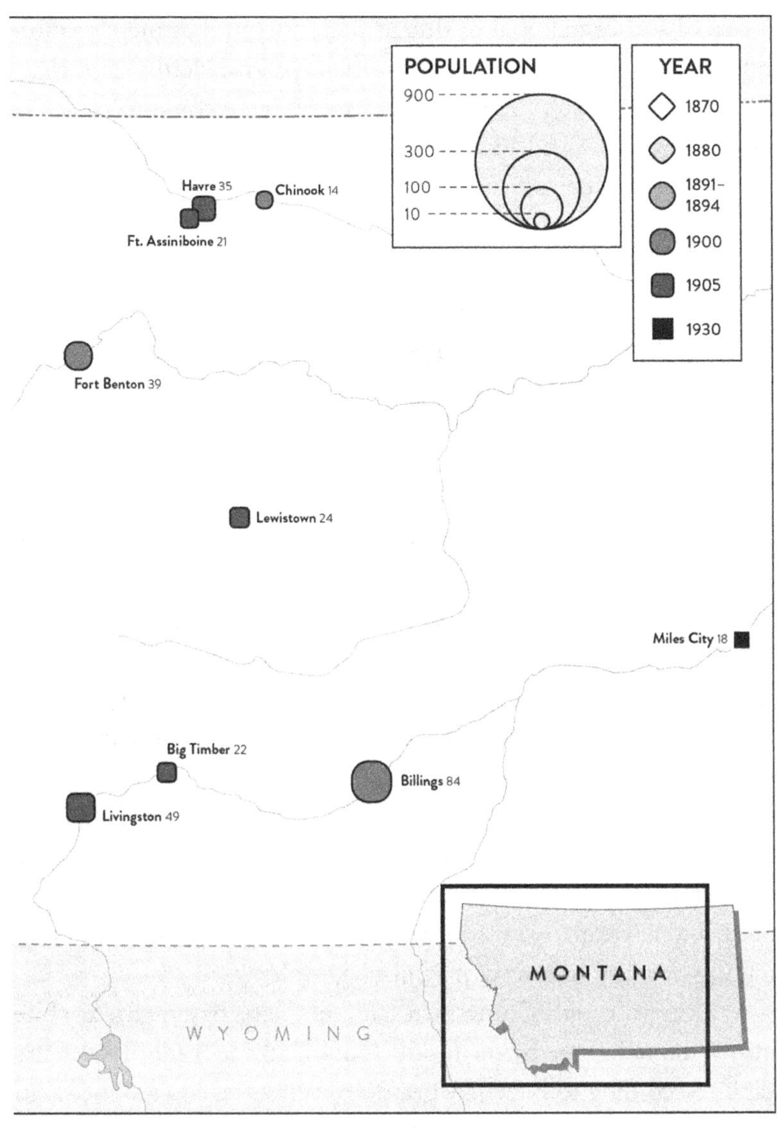

POPULATION
900
300
100
10
YEAR
1870
1880
1891–1894
1900
1905
1930
Havre 35
Chinook 14
Ft. Assiniboine 21
Fort Benton 39
Lewistown 24
Miles City 18
Big Timber 22
Billings 84
Livingston 49
MONTANA
WYOMING

a lack of source material or due to their portrayal as merely color-ful background to the region's history or passive victims of racially motivated frontier violence. When the Chinese come to us as the targets of oppressive legislation, mob action, or racist diatribes like Dimsdale's 1865 editorial, their identity is stripped and their human-ity demeaned. As with this moment of advocacy in 1866, however, throughout Montana's history Chinese Montanans fought for their rights, wielded agency in determined efforts to achieve their goals, and resisted hostility and oppression through ingenuity and com-munity mobilization.

In the case of the 1866 laundry boycott, the animosity abated due to Chinese residents' advocacy for their position in society and the importance of the services they provided. Yet with the ever-present threat of violence in a frontier community, confronting such hos-tile rhetoric directly could be dangerous. Early in 1870 an interac-tion in downtown Helena again threatened the Chinese populace, forcing community leaders to make crucial decisions that illustrate the difficult tensions they faced. By focusing with great specificity on this one event, the complex circumstances facing Montana's Chi-nese communities emerge. The events of early 1870 illustrate the ways that Chinese culture adapted to the realities of life in Montana, the difficult decisions involved in preserving key cultural traditions, the role gender played in the community's composition, and the nuance needed to navigate two worlds when one wrong step could lead sim-mering hostility to erupt into full-scale violence.

Walking through Chinatown late on a Saturday night, a white miner named John Bitzer found himself inside a Chinese man's cabin. According to Bitzer, he heard a disturbance, entered the cabin to investigate, and found a Chinese man named Ah Chow beating a woman. Bitzer claimed that he ordered Ah Chow to stop. The Chinese man left the room, returned with a pistol, and shot Bitzer. Wounded, Bitzer wrestled the pistol from Ah Chow, left the cabin, and stumbled to the Kiyus Saloon where he died fourteen hours later. A rival account, however, contended that Bitzer was in the Chinese man's cabin for less than honorable reasons, inferring that he was assaulting the woman in question and that Ah Chow shot

Bitzer in righteous defense of his home and the woman. Regardless of the circumstances, Ah Chow fled, likely to avoid the vigilante "justice" frequent in Montana throughout the 1860s.[10] By this point in Montana's short history, vigilantes had killed more than fifty people in six years.[11] With Bitzer dead and Ah Chow on the run, tensions were high in Helena.

Bitzer's mining partners issued a reward for their friend's killer, offering $300 for "delivering to us the body of Ah Chow . . . dead or alive." A detailed description accompanied the reward, with Ah Chow mentioned only in the past tense, perhaps to indicate the eventual result of the hunt: "Ah Chow, commonly called 'Jo,' used to drive a team of horses, hauling fire wood about town and drifting timbers up the gulch; was about 35 years of age, short and rather stout, cheek bones very prominent, and face uncommonly broad between the cheek bones; was affected with rheumatism, and had one arm in a sling; he also limped from the same cause; his arm was probably permanently affected. Is said to have a large sore on shoulder blade, or between the shoulders made by a hatchet."[12] As the search continued, stories in Helena's newspapers exposed divides within the community. Those convinced that Ah Chow was a ruthless murderer who should be caught and killed began to paint a lurid picture of him, with unsubstantiated claims emerging that he had killed several men, the number growing the longer he evaded capture. Others questioned Bitzer's version of events, hypothesizing that the trajectory of the bullet, which had entered Bitzer's groin and traveled upward through his stomach, indicated that Ah Chow had shot Bitzer while he was prone, assaulting the woman.

Those emphasizing Bitzer's innocence pressed the community to ferret out Ah Chow, believing his fellow countrymen were hiding him. The *Rocky Mountain Gazette* reported that "some of the principle Chinamen of the town held a meeting and resolved to give their aid in securing the arrest of the murderer." The author advised readers "not to place their entire reliance in the proffered aid of the Mongolians," urging readers to continue the hunt and possibly take matters into their own hands to deliver justice.[13] The Chinese in the region faced a difficult decision. If found to be aiding Ah Chow or not actively assisting in his capture, the violent rhetoric being used against him could easily turn into violence against the community.

The same day that the *Rocky Mountain Gazette* hinted readers should take efforts into their own hands, a second reward was issued for Ah Chow. Clearly, this reward emanated from the meeting of the "principle Chinamen of the town" referenced earlier. Given the widely disputed claims about the circumstances of the shooting and that many in Helena believed Ah Chow had acted justly, a question emerges as to the motivations of these merchants in aiding in the capture of Ah Chow. The $150 reward issued by the Chinese merchants was for anyone "who may arrest and deliver to the authorities the person of Ah Chow . . . or give some information as may lead to his arrest. Duck Ow, Ye Wan, Tong Hing"[14] The city's Chinese leaders wanted a peaceful resolution to the situation by allowing the facts to be determined in a court of law. In the early days of Montana, before a functioning legal system existed, vigilante justice was often used to keep order and to punish transgressors; some who were given a hasty trial; most who were not. By 1870, however, the territory had an established legal system, and many argued that Ah Chow should be apprehended, charged, and tried.

It is likely that the time of year factored into the merchants' decision as well. The deadly altercation between Ah Chow and Bitzer happened two weeks before Chinese New Year in 1870. Annual observances like this provided Chinese migrants living far from home with comfort and a sense of cultural continuity. Montana's newspapers frequently commented on the boisterous celebrations. As the *Montana Post* observed one year earlier, "Last night the Mongolians ushered in with fiery pyrotechnics and store clothes their New Year festivities."[15] Yet public celebration of the holiday might invite attention and violence if the Ah Chow situation was not handled in a manner suitable to Helena's dominant culture. The leaders of Helena's Chinese community calculated that it was in their best interests to assist in the apprehension of Ah Chow lest they run afoul of non-Chinese residents thirsty for vengeance for Bitzer's death. The Chinese faced the Ah Chow crisis with a mind to protect their population, nego-

tiating for the latitude to live and work in Helena and to be allowed
to preserve and practice key cultural traditions.

The fact that Chinese merchants served as leaders of the broader
community was a new development made necessary by conditions
in the American West. In traditional Chinese society, merchants
were a lowly class bearing little respect or responsibility, as scholars
and elders functioned as community leaders in village life. Migrants
seeking opportunities abroad, however, tended to be younger men
not trained as traditional Confucian scholars. In this void, merchants emerged as leaders, assuming responsibilities for the broader
community. A close examination of Tong Hing, one of the Chinese
merchants who issued the reward, shows the evolving role of Chinese merchants both for their community of countrymen and as a
go-between with the white community.

Tong elevated his standing among his countrymen by filling roles
usually shouldered by scholars and community elders. In 1875, for
instance, Tong Hing paid the considerable sum of "$1,000 for zinc
coffins in which to ship the remains of his dead countrymen to the
sacred soil of China," fulfilling an important cultural duty.[16] Additionally, to be allowed to work and thrive in Montana's emerging
economy, Tong needed allies in white society. Newspapers noted
Tong as "the big chief of the Chinese in this city." In 1872 Tong enter-
tained prominent members of Helena's white community during the
Chinese New Year festivities, serving as a key link between Helena's
white and Chinese residents. He was noted for his "urbanity and
courtesy," quite high praise at a time when many Montanans condemned the Chinese as lower than the mice and rats they supposedly
ate.[17] Following a series of fires that devastated Helena, Tong Hing
was the only nonwhite member on the city's Committee of Safety
tasked with fire prevention and implementing new building codes.[18]
Straddling both worlds, Tong Hing's funding of the reward for Ah
Chow's capture was calculated both to smooth tensions brought
about by the immediate crisis and to advance his desired position
as an emerging leader of the Chinese community and a businessman white Montanans could trust.

By issuing a reward that sought "information as may lead to his arrest," the Chinese merchants hoped that Montana had moved past its vigilante beginnings and that the functioning court system might allow Ah Chow to explain his version of events that left John Bitzer dead. Yet, even with an operational court system, would Ah Chow get a fair trial in Montana Territory in 1870? Section 13 of the Montana Criminal Practice Act stated that "no black or mulatto person, or Indian or Chinese, shall be permitted to give evidence in favor of or against any white person."[19] The issue was tested in 1868 when courts declared testimony from a Chinese man assaulted by a German butcher inadmissible because "testimony of the Chinaman was not allowed on the ground that he was not a citizen of the United States."[20] However, other noncitizen residents of the territory could testify. Whether or not Chinese people could become American citizens was an open question in the 1860s. In fact, in 1867 a Chinese man named Ah Chung applied to become a citizen, perplexing the court, which noted "the question as to his eligibility to become an American citizen is a novel one . . . whether the Mongolian race can justly claim to be classed with white citizens is a controverted point."[21] Ultimately the courts determined that the Chinese could not become naturalized citizens, a restriction that remained in effect until the repeal of the Chinese Exclusion Act in 1943. Thereafter, attempts to curtail the rights of the Chinese were usually slightly veiled by noting certain privileges were open to citizens or those who could become citizens, intentionally excluding the Chinese without needing to say as much. An additional rationale that excluded Chinese witnesses' testimony from being considered in court was a view that, due to their non-Christian belief system, they did not understand or value the meaning of a sworn oath.[22] Nonetheless, Chinese community leaders hoped that if Ah Chow were captured alive, authorities might hear his side of the story with objectivity.

Whether or not Ah Chow would have been afforded a fair trial will never be known. Helena's infamous hanging tree showed the results of the weeklong search for Ah Chow on the morning of January 25. Hundreds of residents from Helena came out to see his lifeless body. Pinned on his back was a sign reading "Beware! The Vigilantes still live!" Indeed, X. Beidler, one of the leading vigilantes in the mid-

1860s, was the man who caught and lynched Ah Chow. Beidler collected $600 for the deed, $300 from Bitzer's mining partners, $150 from the Chinese merchants, and an additional $150 from the excited crowd that gathered to see the gruesome spectacle.[23] Not all agreed with the lynching, however. Beidler received a note signed by "200 Anti-Vigilantes" that warned "we shall live to see you buried beside the poor Chinaman you have murdered."[24] This would not be the case as Beidler was eventually buried in Helena's Forestvale Cemetery, the resting place of many of Montana's illustrious founding fathers. Just outside the well-kept grounds of Forestvale Cemetery is China Row, a windswept, cactus-ridden burial ground intended for Helena's Chinese residents. Yet Ah Chow's remains do not reside in China Row, nor were they sent back to China for proper burial. Though Tong Hing took on the responsibility to organize funeral rites of deceased countrymen, he dared not attend to Ah Chow's remains for fear of crossing those still angry with the Chinese community. Tong and the others were reluctant to draw attention to themselves following Ah Chow's lynching. As noted above, the reward from the Chinese merchants was for Ah Chow's arrest and delivery to the authorities of Ah Chow, not dead or alive. Tong and the others knew better than to quibble on this point, however, and remitted the full amount to Beidler, hoping to put the trouble behind them and celebrate the New Year free from the threat of violence.

Ah Chow's body swung from the hanging tree for three days, left there "as a lesson to the other Chinese of the city."[25] It seems that only one person from the Chinese community made the trek to mourn Ah Chow—the woman at the center of the deadly disturbance. Piecing together information on her necessitates the difficult task of sifting through fragmentary documents either with sources missing or so vaguely rendered by white authorities that individual identities and histories are lost. As is the case with much of the telling of the Chinese history of the American West, in the absence of evidence, myth emerged to fill voids in the historic record.

Returning to the original encounter that led to Bitzer's death, questions emerge as to the status of the woman involved. Very few Chinese women made the voyage to America due to cultural practices that preferred sending men out for work. The migration pattern encouraged Chinese men to marry in their local village. Leaving a spouse behind helped ensure that the man would fulfill his societal obligations by sending money home and returning to the village after having made his fortune in America.[26] Additionally, American officials suspected all Chinese women who did immigrate to be prostitutes. In truth, a large percentage of Chinese women in the West did work as prostitutes, and red-light districts often bordered and were part of the Chinese section of settlements. Is this enough to identify the woman as a prostitute and Ah Chow as her handler? Was Bitzer a customer?

Some accounts at the time referred to her as Ah Chow's wife. These references alone are hardly enough to conclude with certainty that they were married. Turning to the records, Montana newspapers listed arrivals to the territory, but often indicated anyone of Chinese nationality simply as "Chinaman" or "Chinawoman" making the tracking of specific individuals almost impossible through this method. In February 1867, however, the *Montana Post* showed a "Mrs. Ah Chow" arriving to the territory. Is this mention and one interpretation of the deadly Bitzer-Ah Chow confrontation enough to establish that the woman was Ah Chow's wife?

Newspaper retrospectives often reflected community memory on the bygone mode of "justice" and recount early settlers' memories of the hanging tree. One of these remembrances gives a clue to the relationship between the woman in question and Ah Chow. In 1938 W. T. Thompson recalled his pioneer life in Helena as a schoolboy. Thompson reflected on Ah Chow's lynching, more specifically, the actions of a Chinese woman: "[T]he Chinaman's wife used to bring food every day . . . I guess she was feeding his spirit. The body remained hanging for three days as a lesson to the other Chinese of the city. . . . On the fourth day they cut down the body and gave it burial. The wife placed a lot of food on the grave which was quickly eaten by some of the youngsters."[27] Given that the tree was approximately one mile from Chinatown and the extreme cold temperatures—dipping as low as thirty-eight degrees below zero—during the time in question, that the woman made the daily trek to conduct ritual observances for Ah Chow's spirit seems to indicate a spouse's devotion. With these sources and inferences, it seems logical to conclude that she was indeed Mrs. Ah Chow. Yet through all of this, her actual name remained elusive.

Incomplete, missing, or destroyed records frustrate the search for clear answers about her identity and voice. The day of Bitzer's death, his mining partners brought the woman to where the body resided for the coroner's inquest. The scene must have been intimidating for her with Bitzer's body presented, flanked by his supporters, no allies of her own, and likely with limited English abilities to understand what they asked. According to Bitzer's mining partners, she gave the same account that Bitzer had about the events that led to the shooting. In the lengthy article that places her at the coroner's inquest, just as the column begins to give details about her, the original copy is damaged beyond use. All known microfilm images of the newspaper are similarly flawed since they were made from the same damaged source. Attempts to find the records of the coroner's inquest proved futile, with the record likely destroyed in a fire at the Montana Historical Society in 1874. With a territorial census taken later in 1870, it seemed possible to work backwards to try to uncover her identity. The census, which took place in July, proves useful for overall numbers of Chinese people across the territory, including their gender, age, and occupation. Census takers, however, had little patience for trying to communicate with Helena's Chinese residents. Though the government advised that census enumerators "adapt their inquiries to the comprehension of foreigners," funds to hire interpreters were not provided.[28] While a few are given by name, most are simply listed either as "John" or as "Chinaman," "Chinawoman," or in the case of a six-year-old child, "China Boy."[29] Furthermore, in newspapers of the time, Chinese Montanans were often not referred to by name. Rather they were called "Celestials," "Mongolians," "chinks," or "John Chinaman," frequently shortened to just "John" as a stand-in for any Chinese man. Not only were these Chinese Montanans stripped of their identity by census takers and newspaper reporters, but the lack of detail caused by this cultural divide creates a void in the historic record, frustrating attempts to construct a complete picture of Chinese communities.

In the absence of records that document the Chinese experience in the American West, myth often takes hold. Several books purport to know the name of the Chinese woman in question, referencing her as "Jasmine." Having researched these events quite thoroughly and never seeing the name "Jasmine," as well as feeling that the name was a bit anachronistic, I dug more deeply. What I found was a website for a bed and breakfast in the Helena Valley that told interesting local stories to entertain guests. The story of Ah Chow was a particularly engaging tale on the site, especially the dilemma of his wife, noted as "Jasmine" on the page. The owner of the bed and breakfast sought to give authority to the information on the page, noting, "I researched all my stories at the Historical Society where I had access to the original yellowed, fragile papers." Having myself spent considerable time with all the "yellowed, fragile papers" I could get my hands on, but never having seen the woman called "Jasmine," I reached out to the author of the blog to inquire as to what source unlocked the identity of the woman in question. The author responded that she had made up the name to give depth to the story, despite having given indications of firm sourcing with the reference to archival research.[30] This name of "Jasmine" has since made its way into several books, from popular history to more scholarly accounts of the vigilante movement in the region.

In telling this history, popular accounts tend to romanticize, mythologize, and exoticize the Chinese settlers of Montana. This tendency is seen not only in this case of "Jasmine," but in the frequent focus on opium dens, prostitution, wars between secret societies, and supposed "Chinese tunnels" rumored to exist beneath many Montana towns.[31] Academic analysis of the population so key to the region's development has focused on broad coverage of push-pull factors of migration, statistical analysis of tax and census records, or archeological investigations of what little evidence remains from the large Chinese communities that helped build Montana. To be sure, much can be learned about the Chinese communities, lifestyle, and locations through these studies, and, yes, opium use, prostitution, and wars between secret societies did occur.[32] Additional approaches focus on the many laws issued against the Chinese. These include

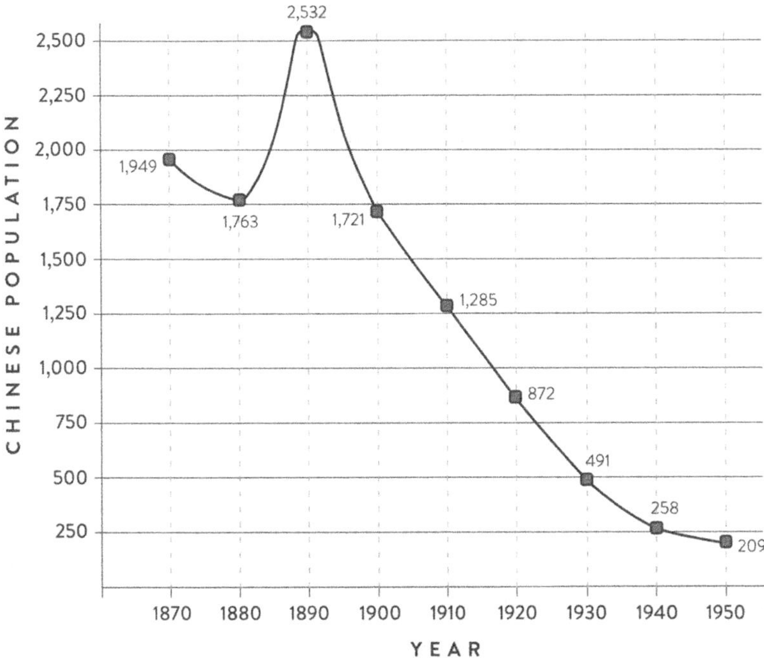

1. Chart showing total number of Chinese residents in Montana, 1870–1950. Chart by Erin Greb.

local restrictions such as attempts to ban the Chinese from owning mining claims, special taxes levied against Chinese-run laundries, laws against opium use, prohibitions on marriage outside their race, and national laws of Chinese exclusion. While these are important parts of the story of the Chinese experience in Montana, focusing on these restrictive laws tells us more about the groups advocating for these restrictions than about the Chinese community itself. Emphasizing the excluders brings their motives and methods to the fore while portraying the Chinese as passive set pieces to whom things happened.

These approaches, which swing between the analytical and sensational, suffer from a lack of inclusion of the thoughts, goals, considerations, motivations, and struggles of the Chinese in Montana in their own words and through a cultural understanding of the two worlds they inhabited. Both the academic coverage of the topic and the popular telling of the story have struggled with the same issue—a perception that there is an absence of sources from the historic Chinese community and a language barrier that impedes deep understanding of what were thought to be the few existing sources in Chinese.

Even when sources do exist, layers of cultural misunderstanding cloud their meaning. Thus we return to the name of the woman in question. After wading through the "Jasmine" issue, I encountered documents that referred to the woman by a name likely to be closer to her authentic identity. She was called Ah Choy.[33] This was likely not her full name, however, nor was Ah Chow likely the proper name of her husband. In southern and central Chinese cultures, "Ah" is a common diminutive expression. When used before a name it indicates familiarity when addressing close friends. In records across the American West, Chinese workers frequently are referred to by names such as "Ah Chow," "Ah You," "Ah Hung," and "Ah Ki."[34] This is probably due both to non-Chinese thinking these were the names of their neighbors and the Chinese seeing little need, or lacking the language ability, to have their proper names recorded. Within Chinese communities, members would have known specific family names that indicated geographic and clan affiliations.

An illustration of the continued obscuring of the identities of the Chinese in Montana is seen when comparing the 1870 and 1880 census with a record of most of the state's Chinese population taken in 1905. Upon first examination, the 1880 census appears to provide far more detail than the 1870 report, which listed most of Montana Territory's Chinese residents as "Chinaman" or "Chinawoman." By 1880 census enumerators had moved past this terminology, though they were still unable to find out key details about the Chinese people that they recorded. A close examination of the 1880 census for Helena shows that "Ah" was used as part of the name for 44 percent of the Chinese living in the city.[35] Again, the language barrier between Chinese residents and census enumerators clouds researchers' ability to ascribe an accurate identity to these individuals. A precise sense of who the Chinese people of the region were could only be attained if the language barrier was overcome. This became possible in 1905, though the instrument used to record the names of the Chinese of the state actually sought to secure their deportation. In 1905 immigration officials conducted a document check, referred to as a special census. This inspection targeted the region's Chinese population to see if they complied with the increasingly stringent requirements for residence in the United States. Officials conducting the raids worked with a Chinese interpreter named Moy Don Shing. With Moy's language abilities and cultural knowledge, it is likely that the names recorded on the 1905 special census come much closer to their actual identity. Of the 1336 Chinese residents of Montana examined during the spring of 1905, "Ah" is used for only five percent, indicating that those knowledgeable about Chinese language, culture, and clan affiliation could more precisely identify and catalog individual identities.[36] During the time of Ah Chow's lynching, however, the identities of the Chinese as reported in non-Chinese sources are obscured through overgeneralized and stereotypical references.

As Ah Choy tended to Ah Chow's spirit after his lynching, the question emerges as to his final resting place. Some claims hint that Ah Chow was buried at the base of the hanging tree. Other indications are that his body was moved to the city cemetery, underneath the playground of the present-day Central Elementary School. Still others believe his remains were moved to Benton Avenue Cemetery, interred in the same final resting place that houses Bitzer's remains.[37] In fact, Bitzer's distant relatives took an interest in his death, funding a new tombstone for Bitzer in 1997 that reads: "Here He Lies; His Life Cut Short; His Death Avenged." Wherever Ah Chow's remains reside, it is most certain they are not venerated by ancestors and, thus, in the beliefs of his native region, his spirit wanders as a hungry ghost rather than resting contented and bringing good fortune to descendants.

By broadening the lens of analysis from the tense circumstances present in Helena in 1870 to the wider geographic and chronological scope of their experiences in Montana, we can imagine similar pressures facing Chinese communities across the region. Rather than remaining passive and submitting to ill treatment, Montana's Chinese population mobilized to resist oppressive restrictions on their free movement, occupations, and cultural practices, becoming leading forces in global movements to advocate for better treatment in America and for a stronger homeland to which they could return.

Through the discovery, translation, and interpretation of several large collections of Chinese-language sources relating to Montana's Chinese communities, new insights emerge about this population so key to Montana's development. By recovering their experiences in their own words and by understanding the Chinese experience in Montana through a global lens, Montana's Chinese pioneers emerge as active participants in their environment, taking initiative to shape their lives and the development of Montana through motivated pursuit of individual and community goals, all the while navigating pressures from China and the surrounding non-Chinese community in their new home. Through the recovery of their voices, we see the Chinese in Montana as they saw themselves: not as an anonymous "Chinaman" on the 1870 census, stripped of identity and agency, but as filial sons and daughters preserving and adapting cultural practices to the conditions on the frontier and as reformers, activists, and leaders connected with and influencing global events far beyond Montana.

TWO

Pressures on Butte's Chinese Residents, 1880s–1920s

From the earliest days of non-Native settlement in Montana, Chinese pioneers played a key role in the region's development. Yet this population so crucial to Montana's history remains underrepresented in historical accounts. While some aspects of this topic have received focus from scholars, coverage of this influential group has rarely included the voices and experiences of the Chinese themselves. As noted with working to tell the story of Ah Chow, lack of source material from Chinese Montanans impedes deeper understanding of their experiences across the American West. In his work to analyze and contextualize archeological remnants of Chinese communities across Montana, Christopher Merritt notes the difficulty in telling the history of this population:

> Lack of primary source data hinders the historical study of the Chinese in Montana and, realistically, most other regions of the diaspora. Due to their generally low social status, significant language barriers, and inherent racial stereotyping, Chinese populations do not fill the pages of historical documents. Furthermore, few primary historical accounts from their perspective in Montana or China have been identified to date. . . . The most unfortunate part of the Chinese story is that by the twenty-first century the majority known about this population is from anecdotal stories in Montana's press and biased primary resources.[1]

Because of this perceived lack of sources, answers to questions about the Chinese in Montana have been wanting. What hopes and motivations did they bring? To what extent did they achieve their goals? What pressures did they face? In what ways did they continue their cultural practices, and in what ways did they adapt to the realities of life so far from home? How fully did they integrate into Montana society?

A rare glimpse into the lives of the Chinese families stretching from southern China to Montana is now possible. Through translation and analysis of a large collection of letters from the 1880s to the 1920s, the pressures and difficulties facing Montana's Chinese community, as well as their motivations and goals, become clear. The letters are from family members in southern China to a man named De Quan working in Butte, Montana. Ranging from the 1880s through the 1920s, these letters attest to the difficulties of life in China and reveal how family connections persisted despite being separated by thousands of miles and going decades without contact.

While the story is incomplete, it appears that De Quan came to Butte in the late 1880s. Often called the "Richest Hill on Earth," Butte's population and economy boomed in the late-nineteenth century due to the large veins of high-quality copper ore running under the city, a vital resource for the emerging electrical grid of the nation. Mining and its related industries provided the economic basis for the large and growing city. Local sentiments, however, prohibited the Chinese from working in mining in Butte. The city's large number of Chinese residents worked in other occupations, mainly in restaurants, laundries, or vegetable gardens. De Quan's exact occupation is unknown, though it is likely that he worked in one of the city's many Chinese-run laundries or restaurants. The letters are preserved to this day thanks to the efforts of Butte resident Hal Waldrup, who worked as the caretaker for the Wah Chong Tai and Mai Wah buildings, remnants of Butte's once thriving Chinatown. As Butte's Chinese population dwindled throughout the 1940s and 1950s, community members stored artifacts in the remaining buildings. By the 1980s the buildings had fallen into disrepair, threatened by leaks, vandalism, and frequent break-ins. Convinced of the importance of the contents of the buildings, Mr. Waldrup consulted preservation-

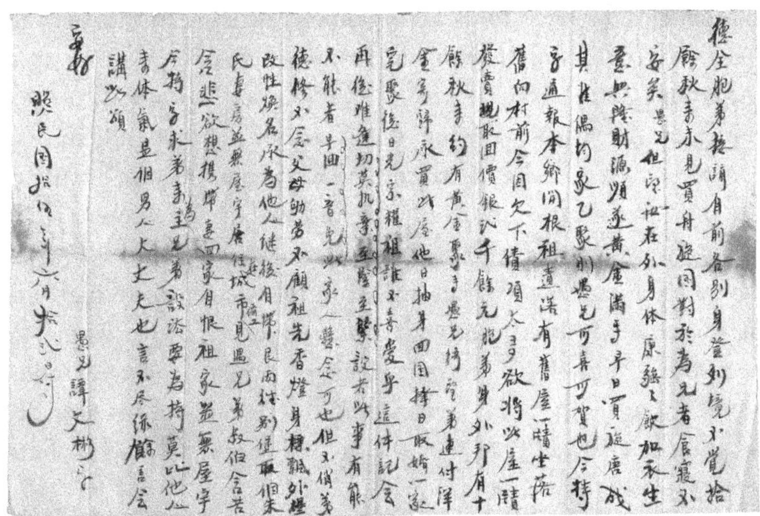

2. A letter from family in southern China to De Quan, a resident of Butte, Montana, ca. 1920s. Chinese Collection. Letter (in Chinese) File, acc 87–5.31, Montana Historical Society Research Center Archives, Helena MT.

ists from the Butte-Silver Bow Archives and the Montana Historical Society. By 1987 preservationists had moved the contents of the buildings to Helena where they remain housed in the collection of the Montana Historical Society. The transnational translation project that I launched with the help of several colleagues and students in 2012 shed new light on these unique documents.

Written in rural China, these letters traveled thousands of miles to Butte. After being haphazardly housed in dilapidated buildings, they were eventually transferred to the Montana Historical Society and, thankfully, preserved, though much has been lost.[2] The translation team identified the recipient of the letters as De Quan, the Mandarin pronunciation of the characters of his name. As a speaker of Taishanese, however, he would likely have been referred to as Tak Chun or Duck Chun and his family name may have been Tom or Hom/Hum. Unfortunately, no combination of these names appears in census records, tax listings, local papers, or other sources. It is possible, as described below, that his entry to the United States was illicit, and he used an assumed identity to circumvent American policies designed to exclude Chinese workers. In that case, he may have been referred to as one name by relatives communicating from China but appeared in immigration and official records under another name.[3] Despite the questions that persist about De Quan, the letters from his family members offer a clear picture of the pressures on the Chinese living and working in Montana. De Quan was caught between Chinese cultural expectations to support his family financially and an insistence that he return to marry to produce children to continue the family line. At the same time, he needed to calibrate his movements across borders and be mindful of the increasingly harsh restrictions that threatened his presence in America and ability to earn the money needed to help his family in China survive.

A variety of factors combined to intensify the pace of emigration from southern China. During the late eighteenth and early nineteenth centuries, dramatic population growth in southern China nearly doubled the population in Guangdong province, placing pressure on the region. Agricultural production struggled to feed the populace. Natural disasters worsened the situation. Economic and political unrest led to numerous uprisings, most notably the Taiping Rebellion (1850–1864), causing disruption across southern China. Following the defeat of the Qing dynasty in the Opium Wars (1839–1842), foreign incursions into the region created opportunities for those close to Guangzhou, Fuzhou, and Hong Kong. However, these changes disrupted traditional economies throughout the region. While migrants had traditionally left the region for work, the Qing state, which conceived of China as the Middle Kingdom—the center of the world, arrogantly viewed emigrants as disloyal and undeserving of the government's protection while abroad.[4] For centuries the Qing banned emigration, threatening death to those who migrated and returned. With the Qing dynasty weakened through internal rebellion and defeats in foreign wars, the government not only failed to protect its citizens abroad, but it also did little to alleviate poor conditions at home. Emigration increased dramatically in the mid-to-late nineteenth century as southern Chinese workers continued to seek economic opportunities throughout South

Asia while also being drawn to Australia, South Africa, and increasingly, after the discovery of gold in California in 1848, North America. Technological advances in steam ship transportation aided the movement of people in these transnational networks by reducing the time and cost of crossing the Pacific.

Most of the Chinese who came to America were from the southern Chinese province of Guangdong.[5] More specifically, the majority these migrants were from one county known before 1914 as Xinning (Sunning) and since as Taishan. Lacking easily navigable waterways or rich agricultural conditions and geographically distant from urban markets that boomed with the growth of colonial economies, the population of Taishan looked outward for opportunities. Estimates throughout the 1860s indicated that close to 60 percent of the Chinese who immigrated to America came from Taishan, increasing to 83 percent from the 1870s through the 1920s.[6]

References throughout the letters confirm that De Quan's family lived in Taishan. The movement of people and the effects of colonial incursion caused the economy and agriculture of the region to suffer. Local uprisings, rebellions, and banditry worsened the situation: "Ever since the disturbances caused by the Red [Turban] bandits and the Hakka bandits, dealings with foreigners have increased greatly. The able-bodied go abroad. The fields are clogged with weeds. . . . Daughters are often drowned rather than raised."[7] Families increasingly relied on money earned overseas for survival.

Workers abroad struggled against mistreatment, racism, and outright violence as they labored to send financial remittances home to support families in Taishan. As mistreatment of Chinese laborers increased, the Qing court felt a growing need to protect its overseas citizens. The court began dispatching diplomats to areas where Chinese migrants resided to establish treaties with foreign nations and to advocate for better treatment of Chinese workers, though with little success. As the financial resources accrued by the overseas Chinese became apparent, Qing officials recognized the benefits of changing policy to welcome investment in domestic industries and allow workers who could bring technological skills to aid in the nation's development to return. Thus, in 1893 the Qing court repealed the

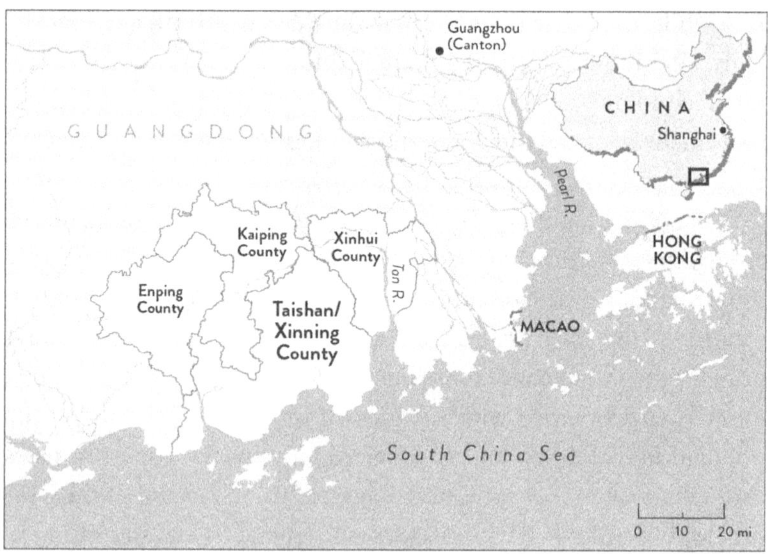

MAP 2. Southern China. Map by Erin Greb.

ban on emigration, recognizing the reciprocal relationship between the state and its citizens abroad. This change facilitated an infusion of capital from overseas labor and aided in the economic development of southern China.[8]

In 1893 the Guangxu Emperor, ruler of the Qing dynasty, commissioned a study of southern China out of a concern for the region from which most of the nation's citizens emigrated and a realization of the hardships they faced both at home and abroad. Zhao Tianxi, a civil administrator for the Qing government, analyzed conditions in Taishan. His study reported on conditions in Taishan and also produced a detailed map of the county that indicated physical features, cities, towns, and villages.

One of two known copies of this map made its way to Butte, Montana, and is now housed at the Montana Historical Society.[9] It is likely that this large map of the county that most Chinese migrants called home was displayed on the wall of a communal gathering place in Butte. As Zhao's geographic study described the region, "The terrain of the whole county rises at the center and falls ruggedly at the south and north. The mountains are steep, the currents of rivers are rapid, sands block the rivers, and some rivers are dry. The boats can

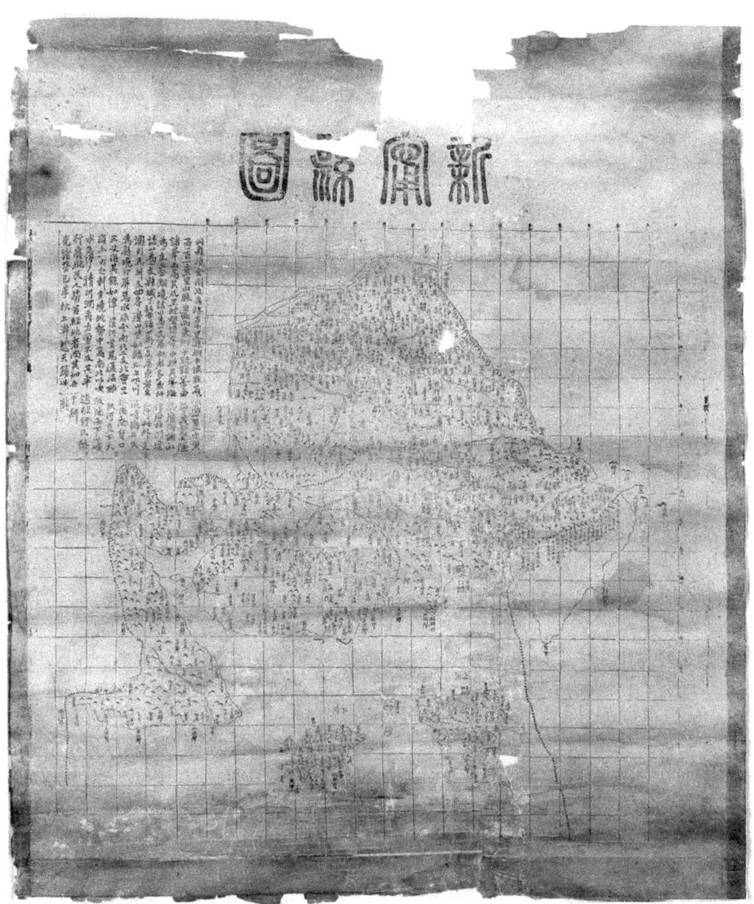

3. Map of Taishan County, 1893, commissioned by the Guangxu Emperor. UPMC 157 87:2–6, Montana Historical Society Research Center Archives, Helena MT.

only sail less than half way. People go back to the land when the rivers are muddy. The people who carry things on their shoulders walk very hard, but those who only walk on land suffer even more."[10]

The study indicated that two-thirds of the population made at least some of their livelihood through agriculture; poor conditions, however, made it increasingly difficult for farming to sustain the population.[11] An additional report from 1893 noted that in Taishan, "Annual harvests provide food enough for only half the year; the rest of the time foreign rice must be bought. It is lamentable that when the ships occasionally cannot [sail] fires in kitchens immediately stop burning."[12] Letters from family members reported these conditions to De Quan, with his brother noting, "I am at home working and hating the high price of rice. Every yuan can only buy 3–4 liters of rice." He added, "I wanted to let you know that the cost of living, including oil and rice, is getting expensive."[13] The local population survived because of money earned abroad. This reliance increased during the early twentieth century. From the turn of the century to the beginning of World War II, annual remittances exceeded money earned through agriculture in Taishan. A study conducted from 1934 to 1935 revealed the importance of wages earned outside of southern China, estimating that remittances sent from overseas workers comprised 75 to 80 percent of the income of families with members working abroad.[14]

Families in Taishan became increasingly interconnected with global economic trends. Men from Taishan took on the obligation, as stated by one migrant, to "climb thousands of mountains and cross tens of thousands of rivers for no other reason than the livelihood and happiness of the family."[15] To maximize opportunity, families varied their earning potential through geographic and occupational diversification. Male family members in their prime working years went out to different locations, taking up whatever money-making opportunities they could while remaining closely connected to the family structure back in Taishan through exchanging letters and remitting money to support the family. If economic conditions changed in one location, the diversified labor systems around the world enabled the family's diffused earning network to persist. For instance, in the letters to De Quan, two male relatives reported working close to the home village in Taishan, one "at a dumpling restaurant. The wage per month is three yuan which is just enough for me to keep a living," and the other "as a farmer in our hometown in order to care for and sustain our aging mother."[16] Other family members took opportunities farther from home. Letters informed De Quan that his brother "De Nu went to work in Hong Kong," while another brother, De Yong, "just returned to Luzon island [Philippines] in May to make money."[17] With De Quan in America, the family's varied economic structure maximized earning potential while minimizing risk from an overreliance on any one region.

De Quan's family, like thousands of others in Taishan that were separated by great distances and often apart for decades at a time, remained bound together by a strategy that aimed to achieve local goals through globalized labor. As the letters emphasized repeatedly, these goals included raising the status of the family by increasing financial holdings through the acquisition of land and houses in the village, caring for aging family members, most notably De Quan's mother, and furthering the family line by bearing children who would continue to boost the family's wealth and status. Furthermore, beyond the present world, it was imperative to produce descendants who would honor tradition by venerating ancestors by properly conducting ritual observances.[18]

The letters to De Quan speak directly to his obligation to family members and the necessity for him to uphold traditional expectations. The strong Confucian influences throughout southern China created reciprocal relationships that bound De Quan to elders, relatives, and ancestors. The collection of letters to De Quan repeatedly stress his obligations to the family, most notably through remittances of money earned in Montana. Letters indicate that the money De Quan earned was needed for everything from funding a family member's marriage, to buying false documents to gain entry to the United States for a sibling. "Ye Ju still has not married . . . the price is very expensive. It will cost more than one hundred dollars. Please send money as soon as you get this message," read one letter. Another request pleaded with De Quan, "Please get a birth certificate for younger brother Wu Qin so that he can go to Gold Mountain to earn money."[19] By far the most frequent requests to De Quan related to purchasing houses and property. In 1895 letters from his older brother report: "I do not have a single cent. I cannot figure out any other solution [to purchase the house]. Brother, please let me know if you intend to send the money back. . . . Is it possible to send back three to four hundred of silver to pay the first stage of the house building costs?"[20] While we have no letters from De Quan himself, as these would likely be in Taishan if they still exist, the back and forth indicates that while he frequently sent considerable sums of money, these funds barely covered the subsistence of the large family he supported. As his brother noted, "We still do not have our own house, but there is a property for sale near the bamboo forest . . . Please write us back as soon as possible and let us know if we should buy it."[21]

The lengthy span of time covered by the letters shows the evolution of the ways that the Chinese in the American West communicated with and financially supported family members in Taishan. A complex system kept the migrants interconnected with their family as money, goods, and letters flowed back and forth across the Pacific. As the number of migrants from China rose during the 1870s, shipping increased to meet this demand. At the height of this period, ships from Hong Kong made the cross-Pacific journey twice a month. Even after the Chinese Exclusion Act went into effect in 1882, shipping between China and the United States continued, thus making the flow of the letters and remittances described in this chapter possible. To transmit money and communications from workers like De Quan to family in Taishan, three methods evolved, each with its own benefits and drawbacks. First, money could be delivered by the returning worker or sent with a relative or friend who returned from America. It seems that the family used this system at times, with a letter from the 1880s noting, "We picked up the relatives that were on board. The two brothers brought their letters from you and Hai Xuan."[22] The trust in the integrity of the person was a benefit of this method, but the relatively infrequent nature of travel made it only sporadically useful. Second, for a 5 percent fee, a worker could hire a courier to deliver the money to family members.[23] A 1923 letter indicates that De Quan used this system at times: "Yesterday, I received uncle's letter couriered over by Uncle Feng Yi of the village behind us. It contained ten dollars. Both letter and money were well received."[24] This process allowed for sending money on a more regular basis, or as family needs required, but there was no guarantee the messenger would deliver the money.

The most frequently used method of transferring money was through a Gold Mountain firm (*jinshanzhuang*). These firms evolved to meet the large demand to send money and goods to and from China. They relied on ties with migrants from particular areas of China; De Quan used firms that specialized in transmitting remittances to Taishan.[25] Along with the funds, the firms sent letters with specific instructions regarding who to deliver the money to and how to distribute the remittance. A letter to De Quan from 1900 reports that the money arrived and that his instructions were followed: "I have received uncle's letter, and I understand the things you wanted me to do. I have exchanged the one hundred dollars you sent to my mother to 97850 Hong Kong dollars, based on the exchange rate of January 12. As you ordered, I gave uncle De Nu 80 dollars and gave uncle De Xiu 20 dollars."[26]

Throughout the Rocky Mountain region, access to the services of Gold Mountain firms came through Chinese grocery stores that facilitated the remittance process. For Chinese workers, earning money was only part of the process. With shared living arrangements and the constant threat of violence, the Chinese in the West developed ways to keep their savings safe. In addition to providing goods from home, Chinese grocery stores also served as banks and facilitated transfer of money. As part of the Gold Mountain firm system, merchants used the remittances to buy goods, pooling capital from several remittances to maximize profits. These goods, which included commodities and, at times, gold and silver, were then sold in Hong Kong, with the amount from the initial investment set aside for the intended individuals.[27] Finally, the Gold Mountain firm used messengers to transmit the money to branches in regional cities and villages close to the final destination. Family members were notified through word-of-mouth that a letter had arrived. De Quan used Chinese grocery stores in Butte to facilitate his remittance process. In the collection of his letters housed at the Montana Historical Society, only three envelopes remain. These include the addressee's names in English, with notations in Chinese characters indicating the true recipient was De Quan. Two of these envelopes are addressed to Kim Chong Tai and one is addressed to Quong Tuck Wing. Both were important members of Butte's Chinese community, coordinating services for countrymen throughout the region. It is likely that family members addressed letters meant for De Quan to these Butte merchants because they had more stable living arrangements, were well known throughout the community, and facilitated distribution of communications to the intended individuals. For De Quan's family this system seemed to be the most frequent and effective manner of receiving funds. Letters informed De Quan of the receipt of funds. One reported, "We received your letter with 50 dollars," while another explained, "Brother, we received the 72.80 silver dollars you sent from Gold Mountain during mid-July. Please do not worry about that anymore."[28] Occasionally, the process broke down, as noted in a letter from 1908: "The end of last month, I received your letter that had 50 yuan attached, so don't worry; but last year, I didn't receive 25 yuan from Guang Ying Tai bank that you mentioned. When you see this letter, please tell me whom to ask for the money."[29]

When the system worked, family members appreciated the funds and relied on this support for survival. Relatives continually reinforced the pressure to earn, however, noting throughout the letters, "We hope you make money through your gold and silver."[30] While the funds may have been converted at one point in the process to gold and silver, De Quan's earnings from work in Butte's laundries likely came in more meager forms, saved through his thrift to provide for the never-ending requests and needs. The pressures persisted, with both acknowledgement of the funds received and requests for more: "We received your one hundred silver yuan on April 7. . . . However, it is not enough and we still owe some money."[31] Throughout De Quan's decades of residence and labor in Montana, it is possible that his family members increased their holdings, but their requests continued with even more insistence. As one such letter read, "I am writing today to tell brother that, in our village, Kai Gen's ancestors left a piece of land with an old house on it. They want to sell it now because they owe too much debt. Brother has been working outside the country for many years, I presume that you have some money on your hands. I am writing today to tell brother to decide on buying the house. In the future, we have to think about each other. Be a man, my brother."[32]

The insistence to "be a man" spoke to the cultural expectations on De Quan and others like him. As family life in Taishan evolved to meet the transnational realities connecting Taishan and Montana specifically and China and America more broadly, cultural expectations did not fade, they adapted.[33] Throughout the letters, family members repeatedly insist that De Quan return to get married and have children: "You left our country for more than twenty years. Our family eagerly expects you to come back according to the original plan. It will be best that you can get married here. You can have offspring for our forefathers and glorify our family. It is a fundamental family tradition."[34] Producing descendants who would inherit and further increase family wealth as well as tend to ritual observances to honor ancestors' spirits were firm cultural expectations.[35] For De Quan and others like him, to marry meant returning to China for a brief time and hoping to produce children that were often born after their father had returned to Gold Mountain for work. Finding suitable marriage partners in the United States was difficult due to clashing cultures and laws intentionally designed to limit the establishment of Chinese families on American soil.

Various factors limited marriage opportunities for Chinese men in the United States. At first, a general societal reluctance both from Americans and the Chinese made marriage across ethnic groups unlikely. An 1873 report of a marriage between a white man and a Chinese woman in Blackfoot, Montana, angered the local populace. "When a white man voluntarily ties himself to a Chinawoman, and thereby becomes her lawful husband," read one account, "we consider it not only an extraordinary, but a barbarous act. . . . The citizens of that town, it is said, are greatly incensed at the base outrage perpetrated in their midst and threaten the offender against public morals and decency with a coat of tar and feathers . . . It is the only instance recorded in Montana of intermarriage with the 'Heathen Chinee,' and it is hoped that it will be the last."[36]

Montana later codified this sentiment with anti-miscegenation laws, in effect from 1909 through 1953, that prohibited marriage between people of Chinese ethnicity and whites. While marriage between Chinese men and women was allowed, the significant gender imbalance in Chinese communities in the American West severely limited the availability of eligible partners. Several factors caused the gender imbalance in Chinese communities in the American West. Cultural traditions holding that men could emigrate for work while women remained home, tending to duties in the village, made Chinese communities in the West predominantly male. For instance, in Montana, the ratio of Chinese men to women in 1870 was 14.2 to 1. The Page Act of 1875, a precursor to the more extensive Chinese Exclusion Act of 1882, sought to bar entry of Chinese women on the assumption that they were prostitutes, resulting in the ratio of Chinese men to women in Montana widening to 20.5 to 1 by 1880.[37]

Further complicating marriage prospects in the early twentieth century was the issue of citizenship. The Expatriation Act of 1907 stipulated that any woman who was a U.S. citizen would lose her citizenship if she married a non-citizen. After several decades of Chinese presence in America, some family groups had taken root, largely due to windows in exclusion that allowed merchants to bring family members to the United States. With children born in America automatically gaining citizenship, these women stood to lose their citizenship if they married a Chinese man, who was, by legal definition, incapable of becoming a citizen. For Chinese American women, this reality of renouncing one's citizenship if married to a noncitizen remained in effect until 1931.[38] Taken as a whole, the restrictions barring Chinese women from entry, the anti-miscegenation statutes common to western states, and the renunciation of citizenship as a disincentive to marry noncitizens all but achieved the goal stated by Washington representative Albert Johnson, who urged further restrictions on immigration: "The necessity arises from the fact that we do not want to establish additional Oriental families here."[39]

Yet, due to cultural tradition, Chinese immigrants' insistence to produce children to inherit family wealth and tend to ancestors' spirits never abated. Chinese men working in America returned to marry and have children, only to leave family members behind as the family unit adapted to the needs of the transnational realities linking Taishan and America. Chinese communities across the American West have often been referred to as "bachelor societies" due to their male-dominated demographics, but the idea that all Chinese men working in America were bachelors misunderstands the evolving family unit. For instance, in Montana in 1900, 41 percent of Chinese men were married, a number that increased to 44 percent by 1930. In 1930, however, more than 90 percent of Chinese married men were not living with their spouse.[40] Instead of thinking of the male-dominated Chinese communities in the American West as "bachelor societies," it is more accurate to view them as part of split-household families.[41] As Taishan became enmeshed with global trends, this family structure evolved and functioned as a continuation of the strategy to diversify family earning power. It also reinforced the production of descendants as a cultural imperative both for worldly transmission of wealth and otherworldly maintenance of spiritual responsibilities.

In addition to being constantly exhorted to send more money, return and get married, and to tend to an array of responsibilities, relatives also pressured De Quan through counterexamples of those who disappointed the family. De Quan's younger brother De Xiu also went to America to work, but letters indicate that De Xiu was not attentive to his duties. In 1895 a family member wrote, "I still cannot find where brother De Xiu is. No news and no money. As soon as you get information about De Xiu please write to tell us so we will not worry too much."[42] By the turn of the century De Xiu had resurfaced, but he still proved a disappointment. In a letter urging De Quan to send money to purchase property, a family member suggests, "I hope you won't be like De Xiu, who does not care for his parents and his ancestors' incense. He wanders outside and changed his name, and bears descendants for other people. When he meets his brothers and other relatives, he is sorrowful and ashamed."[43] The implication for De Quan was clear—you have duties that extend beyond yourself.

Further obligations required of a properly filial son weighed on De Quan as well. No mention is ever given of his father, indicating that he must have died before De Quan's departure for America. The letters do contain repeated references to the matriarch of the family. Letters from 1895 inform De Quan of his mother's ailing health: "Our kind mother is in very old age and towards the last few years of her life. If you have made your fortune, please come back home. This way you can repay mother the grace of her parenting and our brothers could sit together, chat, and enjoy being together."[44] The letter goes on, however, to request four hundred silver dollars for house construction. Thus, De Quan was pressured to return while being simultaneously bombarded with appeals for more money. Family members seemed to think that De Quan was wealthy, writing "you have a great flow of income from your very good business, so you do not need to worry much," and that "your hands are covered in gold."[45] Yet records indicate that he had incurred substantial debts, seemingly going into debt to subsist in Montana in order to send as much money home as he could. These continual tensions of his family's requests and their reliance on the money he earned, also in addition to their insistence that he return to fulfill traditional expectations, weighed heavily on De Quan. One letter from his mother, written in 1908, has survived. It illustrates both a mother's concern and the pressures facing a son far from home with substantial responsibilities to others: "Last month I was very sick, but luckily, the illness is cured. However, I'm not completely recovered yet, thus money would be helpful. . . . I only wish for your health, but please work hard. Don't waste your time wandering around in casinos or red-light districts. When you get money, regardless of the amount, return home immediately. After that, you may return to work again."[46]

Several years later, family members continued applying the dual pressure of requesting money and informing De Quan of his mother's condition. "Mother is so old and weak now," one letter noted. "When you have enough money to purchase a boat ticket, I hope that you can come home to visit and comfort her. It is our biggest wish to see you come home."[47] Unfortunately, De Quan was not able to return in time. A letter from De Xiu, who had returned home penniless after years of irresponsibility, informed De Quan: "Our mother had been sick since last June. Sadly, she passed away the evening of September 18 last year. Sorry that I didn't let you know earlier; please forgive me. When mother was sick, we deposited money for her treatment. It was not enough and we still owe. We received your one hundred silver yuan on April 7. I am also thankful for the twenty silver yuan you sent to me. Since we still owe money to others, could you please send us more so that we can clear our debts."[48] In another letter, De Xiu complains to De Quan, "How I hate that mother has no money for burial!"[49] In both letters informing De Quan of his mother's passing, De Xiu also requests money for business proposals, inferring that De Quan must continue working far from home no matter the familial pressures to return. Separated from family by thousands of miles, unable to return home, and needing to continue sending as much money as he could, life was not easy for De Quan nor the thousands of his countrymen working to balance responsibilities to their home region with opportunities in Montana.

Living and working far from home, De Quan and his fellow countrymen relied on each other for sustenance. Native-place organizations, known as *huiguan*, formed to provide mutual support, sharing of cultural traditions, and camaraderie for Chinese people from the same region who spoke the same dialect. The huiguan provided members with temporary lodging upon arrival, assistance finding work, places for worship and fellowship, and provision for returning the remains of those who died in America. Additionally, the huiguan mediated disputes between members or across rival clans or associations, as one Chinese resident of Butte remembered: "Many disputes arose between associations. In case of a dispute within our own association, it would be settled here. The elders—businessmen and those men who have lived in Butte longest—would hear the facts from the parties in dispute. The council of elders would decide who was right and who was wrong."[50] It is likely that De Quan was part of the Ning Yeung huiguan, largest of the native-place organizations, as it represented migrants from Taishan.[51]

Those not choosing to join native-place organizations had another opportunity to gather for mutual support, social services, camaraderie, and the preservation of Chinese culture far from home. The Zhigongtang—known as the Chee Kung Tong in Cantonese—or "Active Justice Society" was open to all Chinese men willing to swear secrecy and allegiance to the organization's goals. This group came to be known throughout the West as the Chinese Freemasons, though the organization had little connection to European Freemasonry.[52] It seems the secretive nature of both organizations and the emphasis on rituals and on moral development brought many to believe the Zhigongtang was a Chinese version of Freemasonry. Some members of the Zhigongtang even emphasized these similarities, furthering the belief in the supposed connection. It is likely that the Zhigongtang members coopted the language and title of Masonry hoping the vague connections between their organization and traditional Freemasonry might provide protection in an often-hostile context.[53] For instance, as Cornelius Hedges, an influential Montana Mason, noted in 1897, "We have a Chinese Lodge of Freemasons. They honor us with frequent invitations. They do us no harm and probably do some good in their way. Our Chinese Lodges extorted from us a certificate that they were not 'highbinders.'"[54] Chinese Montanans commonly called on non-Chinese allies for letters attesting to their good standing throughout the 1890s, when legislative efforts to expel them from America increased.

For their part, non-Chinese Masons seemed interested in the supposed connections between the Zhigongtang and traditional Masonry. They were likely drawn to romanticized notions of the mystical wisdom of the Chinese and the secret connections thought to be shared by these organizations, which gave their own rituals increasingly mysterious and potent auras. The tendency to exoticize the Chinese experience in the West distances these communities from our modern understanding through layers of myth rather than through true understanding of the Chinese roots of the experience of such organizations.

References to Chinese Masons became shorthand for any ritualized activities in the Chinese communities. Newspapers often referenced Chinese claims, rendered in pidgin English, that they were "allee samee 'Melica man—Flee Masons."[55] While most newspapers repeated the overgeneralized description of such organizations as Chinese Masons, continuing to imply a linkage with traditional Freemasonry, the Deer Lodge *New Northwest* explained the history and goals of the Zhigongtang with surprising accuracy. The 1886 article noted that the Zhigongtang had a decidedly revolutionary purpose rooted in Chinese politics. The Zhigongtang was dedicated to the restoration of the Ming dynasty, which had been supplanted by the Qing dynasty in the seventeenth century. Founded by Manchu conquerors invading from the north, the Qing had ruled since 1644. The Zhigongtang vowed to overthrow the Qing and return ethnically Chinese rulers to power.[56] Indeed this goal linked Zhigongtang branches with Chinese revolutionaries. Most notably, Sun Yat-sen, whose efforts eventually toppled the Qing dynasty, was a member of the Zhigongtang. Sun traveled throughout the American West, visiting Chinese communities to seek support for his anti-Qing efforts. His efforts brought him to locales in California, Colorado, and Nevada where the Zhigongtang was particularly powerful.[57] While Montana had several branches of the Zhigongtang, notably in Virginia City, Helena, Butte, and Missoula, the organization was never as prominent in Montana as in other Chinese enclaves in the American West. Sun likely avoided Montana in these travels due to the relative weakness of the Zhigongtang and the strength of the rival Chinese Empire Reform Association, which sought to strengthen the Qing dynasty and had widespread support across the state.

The Montana branches of the Zhigongtang likely drew membership less because of the stated goals of revolution against the Qing and more because of the social services they provided to members. Much like the huiguan, though not tied to native place, clan, or dialect, the Zhigongtang provided camaraderie, mutual aid, burial services, and structure for moral self-improvement. This last element featured prominently in the organization's values, as seen in an important artifact from the Virginia City Zhigongtang branch, a large banner displaying the thirty-six oaths members would recite and the twenty-one regulations that governed their behavior.

These pronouncements sought to maintain secrecy, promote order, transmit cultural values, and strive for the moral improvement of members and Chinese communities. Members were told they must "defend the secrecy of their lodge" and were prohibited from assisting any Chinese people who belonged to a rival organization. The group told them they must not "covet the wife or sisters of brethren because of their beauty, . . . occupy by force the property of

4. Virginia City's Chinese Masonic Temple banner detailing rules of behavior for members. Canvas, ink, March 3, 1876, X1982.01.46, Montana Historical Society Collection, Helena MT.

your brethren, . . . [or] deceive your brethren through fast talking." The oaths also established rules for proper handling of weddings and funerals, giving members assurance that their remains would be returned to China for burial.[58] Punishments for transgressions included 306 strokes with a cane and ritual executions for those who divulged the secrets of the society.[59] The latter led to symbolic death in the society as described that "great placards announcing his disgrace [displayed] throughout the Chinese quarter, and as soon as news becomes known the guilty man is completely ostracized by his old associates, and in fact, by all the society."[60] It seems the positive benefits of membership were likely more present and motivating than the threats of punishment. Like the huiguan, Zhigongtang members helped each other by providing mutual support and assistance in finding work, and by holding each other to high moral standards so as to improve themselves and Chinese society.

With numerous huiguan representing Chinese people across America, eventually these groups merged into a federation to represent all of the Chinese in the United States known as the Chinese Consolidated Benevolent Association, or more commonly the Chinese Six Companies. As reported by one Chinese American, "These six companies were first organized for benevolent purposes . . . providing their people with the necessities of life until employment could be obtained for them. . . . now [they adjudicate] personal differences of the members of the companies. They act in place of the courts of the state. When a Chinaman has a grievance he reports it to his company, who in turn reports the case to officials of the six companies. A committee of residents of Chinatown is selected, to whom the matter is left for arbitration."[61] The Six Companies mediated disputes between huiguan, provided charity and mutual aid for members, and offered general protection for the Chinese in America. With the Qing government slow to engage in international diplomacy, the Six Companies took on the responsibility to advocate for the Chinese in America. In this role, representatives of the Six Companies petitioned authorities when Chinese people were mistreated and lobbied the government when anti-Chinese legislation was being considered.[62] In this last role, ever-changing American laws that restricted the status of the Chinese in America kept the Six Companies quite busy advocating for people like De Quan and his countrymen.

In the 1840s and 1850s Chinese workers came freely to California in the search of gold. The Burlingame Treaty of 1868 welcomed Chinese workers to America to aid in the construction of the transcontinental railroad. After railroad construction finished, however, complaints about Chinese workers competing with whites for jobs grew. Anti-Chinese rhetoric increased throughout the 1870s and 1880s, often coinciding with economic downturns. At times this rhetoric flared into violence, most notably with the anti-Chinese riot in Denver in 1880 and violent outbursts against the Chinese in Rock Springs, Wyoming, and across the Pacific Northwest from 1885 to 1887. These acts of violence at the local level often influenced legislation at the national level. For instance, the anti-Chinese riots in Denver influenced the passage of the Chinese Exclusion Act in 1882.[63] The violence across the region in 1885 was largely motivated by local sentiment that the 1882 act was ineffective, prompting enhanced restrictions.[64]

In 1882—building on the Page Act of 1875, which limited the migration of Chinese women—Congress passed the Chinese Exclusion Act. This legislation restricted entry of Chinese laborers while allowing entry for some exempt classes including merchants, diplomats, students, teachers, and travelers. Viewing the Exclusion Act as racially motivated and unfair in its singling out of one nationality, many Chinese people continued to seek financial opportunities in America, defying the restrictions through numerous methods including illegally crossing the border or purchasing the identities of exempt individuals. Purchased identities included those of classes allowed into the United States, or those belonging to American-born citizens or their children. Many Chinese immigrants known as "paper sons" gained entry in such a way. During the exclusion era from 1882 until the repeal of the restriction in 1943, an estimated three hundred thousand Chinese people entered America, many by assuming false identities through the paper son system and many through illegally crossing borders. Those who chose illicit routes felt justified in circumventing a system so obviously racially motivated to enter a nation that, just years earlier, had welcomed them for their diligence. Whether or not the laws had changed, dire conditions in southern China necessitated earning money in America. As one migrant stated: "The reason we Chinese come to the United States is because of extremity at home, we have no other method by which we can keep our bodies and souls together. Should we be blocked in this . . . will our calamity not be inexpressible?"[65]

American officials worked to prevent illicit entry by Chinese paper sons by developing numerous methods to detect fraud. Most notably, officials questioned immigrants extensively about the details of the identity they claimed. These sessions included intense questioning about their family line, burial placement and orientation of graves of relatives back home, neighbors in their home village, the number of steps from their house to the village well, and other details so minute that even if the person were who they claimed to be answering the questions would be difficult. As part of the paper son system, coaching papers could be purchased to study the assumed identity and to prepare for the interrogation.[66] As noted with the uncertainty regarding De Quan's actual identity, it is likely that he slipped through immigration restrictions either by purchasing the papers of someone exempt from exclusion or that he claimed U.S. birth.

Responding to these illicit entries, Congress enhanced restrictions with the 1888 passage of the Scott Act prohibiting the return of all Chinese laborers who had left the country and attempted reentry.[67] These workers, many in America legally, having gained entry before the passage of the 1882 Exclusion Act, had returned to China in accordance with the cultural expectations described earlier. Efforts that intensified exclusion like the Scott Act were an ever-present consideration for workers like De Quan and may have been a significant factor in his long absence from his home village. If he had entered America under an assumed identity, he may have been hesitant to have that identity questioned at points of reentry, or the dictates of the Scott Act may have convinced him that the risk of being barred from returning were too high.

De Quan and others like him, working in Montana to support extended families in Taishan, were caught between Chinese cultural expectations to support relatives financially and the difficulties of navigating border crossings to tend to cultural expectations. These stresses grew considerably throughout the 1890s as increasingly harsh anti-Chinese legislation changed policies from exclusion to expulsion, not merely stopping potential migrants at ports of entry but projecting enhanced control over migrants in the interior of the nation or wherever the Chinese were found.

THREE

Chinese Resistance to the 1892 Geary Act

As 1892 approached, marking the end of the ten-year life of the Chinese Exclusion Act, Congress took up the issue of its replacement. Persuaded by anti-Chinese labor organizations in the American West to strengthen restrictions and exclusion, the resulting Geary Act created a system of surveillance to catalog and control the Chinese across the region. Supporters hoped it would aid in the mass deportation of the Chinese from the country. Led by the Six Companies, Montana's Chinese communities fought these changes, advocating for their right to reside in the United States and contribute both to its development and to their responsibilities back in China.

The intent of the Geary Act was both to end immigration of the Chinese into the United States and to expel them from within the nation's borders. Far more restrictive than the earlier Chinese Exclusion Act, the Geary Act broadened the definition of laborer, seeking categorical exclusion of this group, while also narrowing the classification of who qualified as a merchant, a group that had been exempt under the 1882 act.[1] Geary Act proponents were frustrated that the earlier act had not reduced the amount of people of Chinese origin living in the United States. In fact, the nation's Chinese population had stayed steady at around 105,000 over the ten years after the Exclusion Act went into effect. Officials noted this goal by stating, "That the intent of the law was, not only to prevent an increase in that class of Chinese in this country, but to gradually reduce the number already here . . . by the limitation placed upon the right to return."[2] Anti-Chinese agitators had hoped that exclusion would not only stop new immigrants from arriving, but also harass the Chinese in the United States to the point of departure. While the number of Chinese people stayed relatively constant on the national level, in Montana it increased considerably, from 1,763 in 1880 to 2,532 in 1890.[3] U.S. senator from Montana Wilbur F. Sanders articulated what many white westerners believed about the Chinese's ability to circumvent exclusion: "We have been mocked, and that is why we are dissatisfied."[4]

The Geary Act tightened immigration to allow entry to fewer categories of Chinese immigrants. It closed loopholes that some had used to circumvent exclusion. Furthermore, and most relevant to those who had gained residence, the Geary Act required all Chinese laborers in the United States to "apply to the collector of internal revenue of their respective district . . . for a certificate of residence." This requirement to attain a registration certificate, which mandated a photograph of the registrant, amounted to an internal passport or an early form of a green card. According to the act, those found without this registration certificate "shall be imprisoned at hard labor for a period of not exceeding one year and thereafter removed from the United States." If an individual could not attain a certificate or if it was lost or accidentally destroyed, he must prove "to the satisfaction of the court, and by at least one credible white witness, that he was a resident of the United States at the time of the passage of" the act.[5] With the prerequisites for being in America thus changed, Chinese immigrants bore a new, much greater burden of proof.

The Chinese in the United States reacted strongly against the Geary Act. While many may not have agreed with their selective exclusion over the last decade, they had adapted to the system. The increasingly harsh restrictions seemed unfair, racially motivated, and aimed at not only stopping further migration, but forcing out those who had been working in America for years. The Geary Act did not target individuals who had broken standing laws; instead, it criminalized a population that had already gained entry to the country by extending immigration control from ports and borders to the interior and by seeking to catch and deport those found out of compliance. Indeed, the mandate for a photograph indicated that the anti-Chinese forces pushing this requirement viewed all Chinese people as criminals. Prior to this point in American history, only convicted criminals were required to be photographed. Law enforcement officers studied collections of photographs of convicted offenders, called the "rogues' gallery," to track criminals and for helping victims identify the perpetrators of crimes. Requiring Chinese residents who had gained legal entry to the United States to have a photograph on file with government agencies clearly equated their ethnic identity with criminality.[6]

The supporters of the Geary Act worried little about how the Chinese viewed this new legislation. Many American politicians welcomed the strengthened action against the Chinese out of frustration that the previous laws, including the Page Act of 1875, the Chinese Exclusion Act of 1882, and the Scott Act of 1888 had failed to reduce their population as desired. After ten years of stated but ineffective exclusion, the Geary Act sought not just exclusion but expulsion. Senator Wilbur F. Sanders expressed sentiments that illustrate the true intent of the Geary Act: "It is not desirable that these people shall be multiplied in this country, but that they shall be diminished to extinction."[7] Combined with increasing violence against Chinese during the late 1880s, including the Rock Springs Massacre in Wyoming in 1885 and the Snake River Massacre on the Oregon-Idaho border in 1887, Sanders's rhetoric threatened dire consequences.

Pressures from the federal passage of the Geary Act combined with local empowerment of anti-Chinese forces put Montana's Chinese community in a precarious position. The state's Chinese population chose active resistance rather than passive submission. Along with their compatriots throughout the West, Chinese people in Montana took part in a coordinated campaign of strategic noncompliance, refusing to register as the law required. The Six Companies requested funds from the Chinese throughout the United States to help with a legal challenge to the Geary Act. The noncompliance of Montana's Chinese residents surprised many, with newspapers reporting: "The opposition of the Six Companies to the government in this matter has startled everybody by its bold defiance."[8] Montana's newspapers, however, interpreted the refusal to comply not as strategic resistance but passive acquiescence to heavy-handed demands from the Six Companies: "Those who do not pay will not be given papers to return to China. . . . The Six Companies command the Chinese not to register . . . under the penalty of death." Quon Loy, a leader of Butte's large Chinese community, countered this claim, noting "that any Chinaman can go home whenever he wants and that it is not necessary for him to secure any passport or other papers from the Six Companies or any other organization."[9] Quon indicated the support for the effort from Butte's Chinese community by emphasizing the voluntary nature of their participation.[10] Helena's *Daily Independent* printed the proclamation that circulated throughout Chinese communities. It did not include pressure of travel restrictions or threats to one's life. The Six Companies' proclamation presented the Geary Act as:

> An unjust law and no Chinese should obey it. The law degrades the Chinese, and if obeyed will put them lower than the meanest of people. . . . It is a cruel law. It is a bad law. We do not want the Chinese to obey it. We do not believe the Chinese will obey it. In making this law the people of the United States have treated the sworn treaties made with our country and our emperor with contempt. They have disregarded our rights and paid no attention to their promises, and made a law to suit themselves, no matter how unjust to us. No Chinese can read this law without a feeling of disgust. If any of our people think they are wiser than we are and would obey the law, if they would obey it for the sake of making money, let them stop. Do not do it. You will repent it if you do. . . . Again we warn you not to obey this law. It is not right, it is not just.[11]

This proclamation built on opposition to the Geary Act from Chinese communities across the nation and communicated a strategy of defiance.[12] The Six Companies hoped for assistance from white allies who agreed that the law was unjust. Charles Hartman, the U.S. representative from Montana, advanced a petition from Montana's Annual Conference of the Methodist Episcopal Church to the Committee on Immigration and Naturalization "asking the immediate

5. Quon Loy, often described as the leader of Butte's Chinese community, in 1901. Detail, Committee of the Chinese Empire Reform Association, Butte MT. PAC 95–22 MM 1, Montana Historical Society Research Center Photograph Archives, Helena MT.

repeal of the Geary law."[13] Illinois congressman Robert Hitt emerged as a leading voice against the Geary Act. He based his objections on the possible breakdown of trade with China in addition to protesting the act on moral grounds.[14] A key element that the Chinese opposed was the requirement of photographs. These images, one of which was required to be on record with the state revenue office and one of which was to be affixed to the registration certificate to be carried at all times, struck the Chinese as equivalent to mug shots: "A huge cry was then raised against furnishing photographs, the Chinese claiming the government was gathering a collection that might be referred to as a 'rogues' gallery."[15] Hitt agreed, speaking with passion about the registration and photograph requirements: "Never before in a free country was there such a system of tagging a man like a dog, to be caught by the police, and examined, and if his tag or collar is not all right, taken to the pound or drowned or shot. . . . men, innocent of offense, who must obtain this certificate, this ticket of leave, and carry it around with them in a free country."[16] Despite this opposition, most in Congress supported the Geary Act which became law on May 5, 1892.

Montana's Chinese expressed their disagreement with the Geary Act through noncompliance, a potentially risky strategy given the penalties for being found without a registration certificate. Newspapers across the state noted this noncompliance: "The Chinese of Butte are becoming more and more outspoken in their opposition to the Geary law."[17] Inspectors employed to implement and enforce registration conducted spot-checks to determine the level of compliance with the law. Captain Michael Hogarty—one of the so-called Chinese inspectors that surveyed the Chinese community in Helena—reported: "In a whole day's work the inspector ran across but two Chinamen who had certificates" despite the fact that Helena was home to more than three hundred Chinese people at the time. The article continued to express Hogarty's view that the Chinese did not and could not assimilate, and that they only sought financial gain to take back to China and had failed to contribute to the development of America. Hogarty stated that "he does not think that the Chinese are a very desirable class of citizens."[18] Hogarty's point about the suitability of Chinese as citizens was moot as they could not become citizens. The question arose, however, as to exactly what rights alien residents did have. In addition to the strategic noncompliance with the Geary Act, the Six Companies solicited funds from Chinese communities to support a legal challenge to the act, using the courts to assert the rights of Chinese in America.

While the Six Companies prepared a legal defense and awaited the impending deadline for the enforcement of the Geary Act, the defiance of the Chinese in Montana caught the attention of anti-Chinese elements in the state who felt emboldened to act at local levels following the passage of the act: "It is generally understood that the anti-Chinese crusaders in Butte and Anaconda are only waiting for the expiration of that time to make a vigorous effort to drive the Chinamen out of those towns."[19] Beginning in February 1893, as it became clear that the Chinese would not comply, anti-Chinese forces in Butte and Anaconda attempted economic action against the cities' large Chinese communities. A Butte resident editorialized his views on the Chinese, stating them even more strongly than Captain Hogarty had: "The Chinaman is no more a citizen than a coyote is a citizen, and never can be. . . . The Chinaman's life is not our life; his religion is not our religion. . . . His very existence in our midst is an insult to our own intelligence. Pestilence and disease follow in his wake. . . . Let him go hence. He belongs not in Butte."[20]

Emboldened by the spirit of the Geary Act and frustrated by the defiance of the Chinese, an anti-Chinese group formed, expressing its intent in the prolabor Butte *Bystander*. With workers across the country beginning to feel the first effects of the Panic of 1893, the group sought to eliminate labor competition, specifically in the laundry business, not because this was a vital industry to the region's working men, but because it was an economic niche held by the city's Chinese: "Resolved, That we, the people of Butte City, express our hearty approval of any lawful effort to rid our community of this undesirable pest. . . . Resolved, That a committee of 10 be appointed by the chairman, of the business men, and that said committee shall take vigorous means to make this movement a success and to act in conjunction with the anti-Chinese committee of the Silver Bow Trades and Labor assembly."[21]

The committee met several times, pressuring Butte and Anaconda residents to stop business with Chinese laundries. Attendance grew, with a large meeting in early March proclaiming: "Down With the Chinese: A Monster Meeting of Men at Evans Hall Last Night." At the meeting, city leaders, labor organizers, state legislators, and law-yers spoke to the large crowd, urging economic action against the Chinese: "Once more we have assembled to discuss the best means of ridding our several communities of the pig-tailed, almond-eyed Mongolian."[22] Support for the cause seemed high. Few alternative laundry services arose, however, undercutting the movement. As people continued to patronize Chinese-owned businesses, the effort waned, frustrating organizers: "The anti-Chinese committee, which met at the council chamber on Monday evening, showed a remark-able lack of attendance on the part of business men."[23] It seems the determination of the Chinese to resist the dictates of the Geary Act was stronger than the resolve of anti-Chinese forces to boycott. Yet this idea of an economic boycott against Butte's Chinese reemerged three years later.

Less than a month before the Geary Act was to go into effect, government officials reported only ten Chinese had registered in Montana, Idaho, and Utah, a region with an estimated Chinese population of more than five thousand. The deputy U.S. marshal who was to register Chinese residents in Butte found himself with plenty of free time. By late April 1893 the marshal had "not regis-tered a single Chinaman so far and it is altogether probable that the new law will go into effect on May 5, without one of them hav-ing secured the necessary certificate of residence permitting him to remain in the country."[24] Montana's Chinese led the call to fight the Geary Act through noncompliance. Next, with financial contribu-tions from Chinese across the nation, the Six Companies mounted the legal challenge.

The Geary Act's dictate that those found without proper docu-ments could be imprisoned, fined, and deported, all without due process, seemed to violate Constitutional protections. The Six Companies arranged a test case to challenge its constitutionality. Quon Loy of Butte voiced his views on the act, expressing that he: "doesn't believe the Geary law will be sustained . . . [and believes] that the Chinese have as much right here as any other foreign nationality and that they do not propose to comply with the Geary law unless they are absolutely compelled to."[25] The test case proceeded after May 5, 1892, the date the Geary Act was to go into effect. Fong Yue Ting, Wong Quan, and Lee Joe submitted themselves to the U.S. marshal in New York as having resided in the United States unlawfully because they had not registered as the law instructed. Each man had resided in the country for a considerable time, gaining entry under the terms of earlier treaties, notably the Burlingame Treaty of 1868. Two had refused to register. One had been unable to register because he could not produce a credible white witness to testify to his residency. The attorneys for the Chinese challenged the Geary Act's legality on several fronts. In general, attorneys claimed the act violated the due process of Chinese residents. The Geary Act, they argued, violated the Fourth Amendment as it subjected Chinese residents to detention and search and seizure without a warrant or probable cause. That the government could act against Chinese people accused of breaking the law without a grand jury indictment also violated the Fifth Amendment's requirement of such for capital or infamous crimes. In addition, the Chinese's lack of ability to summon witnesses on their own behalf, consult with an attorney, or examine evidence brought against them violated the Sixth Amendment. Finally, the penalty of imprisonment at hard labor followed by deportation violated the Eighth Amendment's prohibition of cruel and unusual punishment. Furthermore, the challenge presented by the attorneys of the Chinese defendants asserted that the Geary Act vested Congress with powers far beyond the intent of the U.S. Constitution. "No power is given to Congress by the Federal Constitution to remove friendly alien residents in a time of peace. Congress can pass no law unless the power to do so is given to it by some express power granted by the Constitution."[26] Attorneys for the defendants argued that the power to expel residents was different than the power to exclude potential immigrants at the border.[27]

Ultimately, the U.S. Supreme Court upheld the Geary Act with a 6–3 majority decision asserting that Congress held both the power to exclude immigrants at the border and to expel alien residents from the nation. For alien residents, specifically the Chinese, who were noncitizens and who could not become naturalized, "The provisions of the Constitution, securing the right of trial by jury and prohibiting unreasonable searches and seizures, and cruel and unusual punishment, have no application," stated Justice Horace Gray.[28] The court determined deportation was an administrative act, not a punishment. Therefore, as detention and deportation were not punishments for a crime, there was no need to allow due process or to follow the Constitution's dictates on search and seizure, issuance of grand jury indictments, permission of witnesses, or obtaining of warrants. Imprisonment for a year of hard labor before deportation was not, in the opinion of most justices, cruel and unusual punishment. Rather it was merely part of the administrative procedure of implementing immigration restrictions.[29]

Three justices dissented, arguing that the Geary Act represented a serious denial of due process and violation of the Fourteenth Amendment's requirement for equal protection under the law.[30] The majority recognized the protections that amendment granted but argued that Congress could decide if the residents' "removal is necessary or expedient for the public interest."[31] The conclusion reflected a trend in legal decisions involving Chinese petitioners across the nation. From the gold rush to the 1880s, both criminal and civil cases tended to be decided objectively and often favorably regarding the claims of Chinese litigants. Courts in most western states, however, experienced a shift in the 1880s. These decisions mirrored the trend of growing anti-Chinese attitudes amongst westerners.[32]

With the Geary Act upheld through *Fong Yue Ting v. United States*, the deportation of those who had not registered could commence. The tremendous number of Chinese who took part in the strategic noncompliance, however, threatened to overwhelm the administrative apparatus of the government. It is estimated that no more than 13 percent of the nation's Chinese residents registered by the May 5, 1893 deadline. Additionally, the Treasury Department's budget of

$25,000 to enforce the act was a fraction of the estimated seven million dollars needed to follow through on its requirements.[33] Uncertain of how to proceed, Congress eventually issued the McCreary Amendment in November 1893, which gave Chinese people an additional six months to register. Many in Congress opposed the extension and demanded immediate action against those who had not registered. The McCreary Amendment appeased anti-Chinese forces by further restricting who could be defined as a merchant, narrowing the exempt class considerably.[34]

During the struggles over the Geary Act, the Chinese government paid close attention to Congressional debates. A key question in these negotiations was whether control of migration between the two nations was determined by treaties between governments or unilaterally passed through legislation. Since the completion of the major railroad lines, which had been aided by Chinese workers welcomed in following the Burlingame Treaty of 1868, the Qing government had lost negotiating power and anti-Chinese forces from western states gained influence, leading to more restrictive and humiliating acts of legislation targeting the Chinese. For instance, the Scott Act of 1888 restricted freedom of movement for Chinese people who had established residency in the United States. Some returning Chinese who had been in the nation legally were stranded abroad with the passage of the Scott Act. As reported in the *Helena Independent*, a Chinese leader in the United States indicated—in reference to the Scott Act—that "our own government is placed in a humiliating position by that act, and from the tone of communications I am sure they realized their position."[35] During negotiations in 1894 the Qing government sought to placate the United States by voluntarily limiting new migration of laborers in exchange for an agreement to allow the "return of registered laborers, who may have gone back to China leaving property in this country of the value of $1,000 or more."[36] The resulting Gresham-Yang Treaty of 1894 also allowed the free movement of Chinese officials, students, and merchants, though this last category had been severely narrowed with the Geary Act and the McCreary Amendment. Restrictive provisions such as verification from white witnesses as to the individual's

in the willingness of the organization to take on similar conflicts. This left Montana's Chinese community isolated and unsupported in the late 1890s.

Compliance with the Geary Act did not end tensions in the state. Their loss in the Supreme Court case weakened Chinese residents' effort to advocate for their rights. Though a lack of full funding hindered the implementation of the law to its fullest extent, raids by government officials and deportations proceeded in Montana. As opponents of the Geary Act warned, local officials gained power that could be exercised arbitrarily. A retired government inspector admitted, "If you were Chinese, you could be arrested just off the streets, and you were made to prove your right to be here."[40] Shortly after the enactment of the new restrictions, a newly arrived Chinese resident of Montana suffered through the uncertainties of the regulations:

> A Chinaman named Toy Fou, being tried on a charge of being in this country without the necessary certificate . . . From several depositions of white men and Chinamen in Isleton, Cal., and the testimony of two Chinese witnesses on the stand it was ascertained that Toy Fou at the time it was necessary to secure certificates had been a merchant in the town of Isleton, and therefore it was not necessary that he should take out a certificate . . . Toy Fou came to Helena a year ago and since that time has not done any manual labor. It came to the notice of the Chinese inspector that he was without a license or certificate. Hence his arrest and trial.[41]

While Toy Fou was ultimately discharged rather than deported, his case illustrates that the letter of the law, which exempted merchants from the need to carry the certificate, mattered little with inspectors and government officials empowered to conduct document checks on any person of Chinese heritage. Toy Fou had carefully secured supporting evidence for his legitimate right to be in the United States. This evidence was often not enough. Officials questioned the veracity of the many layers of documentation provided by Butte resident Wong Que Fook: "He says that he was once a merchant in Boston. He has a paper to that effect. In 1897 he returned to this country from China and the paper bears the notation of Customs Inspector

Sanders of Port Townsend. There is suspicion the paper is a forg-
ery. . . . The officials think it strange that the Chinaman has been in
this country 22 years, yet he cannot speak the English language."[42]

As the cases of Toy and Wong indicate, even compliance with the
law and extensive documentation could be questioned to an extreme.
The enforcement of the provisions often fell to the arbitrary whims
of officials. Across the state, Chinese residents faced uncertainties,
harassment, and capricious enactments of the policies. An *Anaconda
Standard* report described one such situation: "Judge McPherson
had a Chinaman before him on Tuesday afternoon as a fit subject
for deportation . . . Wong Wee . . . tried to make believe he had lost
the valuable paper in Great Falls, Helena or some other town, but
of no avail, for he was sent to the county jail as a Chinese laborer,
with no rights at all."[43] The sentiment that Chinese laborers had "no
rights at all," combined with the view of the Chinese as "undesirable pests" led to vigorous action against Montana's Chinese population. While not fully achieving the stated goal of Senator Sanders
that the Chinese in Montana should be "diminished to extinction,"
population trends in the state show a decline. The Geary Act and
related restrictions severely impacted Montana's Chinese community, decreasing the population in the state from a high of 2,532 in
1890 to 1,721 in 1900. As will be discussed in Chapter 5, the most
vigorous enforcement of the new policies came during the period
from 1903 to 1906, resulting in a further decline in the population
to 1,285 by 1910.[44]

While many Chinese people throughout the state suffered persecution with little assistance from the surrounding non-Chinese
population, some had enough ties to the white majority to proac-
tively seek support, hoping to solidify their claims to residence and
to allow for travel between nations. For instance, Lee Sam Fong
sought support for his need to travel to China on family business
from the Episcopal Bishop of Montana who wrote: "Lee Sam Fong
is a reputable resident and property holder of [Helena]. He is married and has three children. He has a good business . . ." Lee knew
the need for white allies and had a history of seeking assistance. An
1890 document attested to the opinion that "Lee Sam Fong is an

7. Helena resident Lee Sam Fong's Geary Act certificate, March 19, 1894. SC 2747 "Immigration 1890–1912, 12/14." Montana Historical Society Research Center Archives, Helena MT.

old time Chinese resident of this city and a taxpayer and real estate owner. He is a square Chinaman, straight in all his dealings and perfectly honest."[45] Twenty-two prominent Montanans signed the document, including both a sitting and former state supreme court justice, a former governor, police chief, and the bishop. That Lee felt compelled to verify his good standing in the community two years before the mandate from the Geary Act required such certificates attests to the idea even longtime residents realized their precarious status. Lee relied on his standing in Helena society and his numerous connections outside the Chinese community; most Chinese people in the state did not have similar networks to call on for support.

Those who sought to comply with the new policies had difficulties when exercising their rights under the new restrictions. Great

Falls had a history of excessive hostility to Chinese people. From its founding, workers and city leaders maintained an informal commitment to exclude Chinese immigrants from the city. Various accounts note that the Chinese who tried to establish businesses were run out of town, with some stories claiming that they were thrown into the Missouri River. Noting that the city had no Chinese residents, an 1899 article recognized the oddity that "more Chinamen register at the highest price hotel in the [Great Falls] than does at any other $3-a-day house in the United States." This paradox was due to the increasingly extensive documentary evidence needed to both reside in the United States and to travel to China and hope to return to America. "To secure papers entitling him to return to the United States Hop Lee must travel a straight and narrow road, fenced in from end to end with tape of the most scarlet hue. If he lives in the district comprising Montana and Idaho he must apply to Collector of Customs Browne at Great Falls, at least one month prior to his departure. . . . But for this time, he carefully avoids Great Falls."[46]

Having to travel to the city in the region most hostile to them created great anxiety for Montana's Chinese residents. Playing on this difficult situation, the Park Hotel served as the only accommodation willing to house Chinese guests, and, given the hotel's proximity to the rail station and the necessary offices, overcharged them since they had no choice but to comply. Other businesses that made their home in the building took pains to indicate their anti-Chinese stance. For instance, advertisements for Nate Wertheim's tailor shop in the Park Hotel made clear to residents of the city his stance on Chinese laundry work: "We handle no almond-eyed, opium-tainted, washee washee goods."[47]

For the Chinese forced to travel to Great Falls to secure the proper documentation, no matter how short the stay in city was likely to be, applicants came prepared, bringing letters of support from white allies from their city of origin who attested to their good standing in the community. Great Falls residents noted: "Each Chinaman who comes here has securely fastened inside his garment a letter from some well-known resident of the city from which they come, stating that they are here on business and will get out of Great Falls as quick as Jim Hill's [railroad] timetable and benign Providence will allow them."[48] Even passing through Great Falls to other destinations could be dangerous, as a Chinese traveler discovered in 1898. A passenger traveling from Portland to Helena stopped in Great Falls awaiting the next train. Reports of a Chinese person in the city reached the officials in charge of Geary Act certificate compliance, who proceeded to

> round him up and asked him to exhibit the certificate and attached photograph . . . The Mongolian refused to accompany them and resisted arrest. He attempted to prevent their entering the depot, holding the door and fighting, but finally Mr. Trevillyan got the "come alongs" on his wrist and the Chinaman was dragged to the Park hotel. The "nippers" were cutting him severely and as he reached the corner near the hotel he weakened and, going down into one of the capacious pockets of his shirt, he produced his certificate. It showed that his name is Kin Tai and that he is a merchant of Portland. His appearance tallied with the description and he was accordingly released and the proceedings against him were quashed. The Chinaman will leave this morning for Helena . . . [and will] give some of the leading citizens of Helena pointers concerning the impression which a Great Falls policeman made upon his mind and his wrists.[49]

The case is interesting because Chinese merchants were not required to register, though inspectors cared little for this exemption, suspecting anyone of Chinese appearance to be illegally in the country. It is unlikely that Kin Tai produced a Geary Act certificate; instead, he may have produced documentation proving his status as a merchant and thus his right to be in the United States. Either way, the hostile environment of Great Falls and the suspicion of criminality toward anyone of Chinese heritage spread throughout the state.

After Chinese residents had faced almost a decade of the onerous requirement that they travel to Great Falls to secure documentation in order to visit China and return, regulations changed. By 1902 bureaucratic restructuring had altered but not necessarily eased the process. The case of Soo Hoo Tom of Billings illustrates the steps needed to visit China and return to the United States:

Soo Hoo Tom, is a Christianized Chinaman, who long ago discarded his queue and in other ways has conformed to the ways
and manners of the "Melican man," but for all that he must comply with the requirements of the exclusion act and in consequence
finds himself compelled to submit to an almost endless amount of
red tape because he is preparing to pay a visit to his native land. . . .
Tom must make affidavit, supported by the testimony of witnesses,
that he leaves here with parties indebted to him in a sum aggregat-
ing no less than $1,000.[50]

This element of the Geary Act extended exclusion by targeting
individuals who had gained legal entry and had certificates in accordance with the Act by making return to the United States increasingly difficult.

Inspectors charged with enforcing the Geary Act conducted raids
across the state, rounding up the region's Chinese people and checking
for documents, which could be arbitrarily discounted at the whim of
the inspector. Required in the mid–1890s, many of the state's Chinese
residents had lost their certificates over time, with dire consequences:
"Next to his pigtail, the most important possession of a Chinaman is
his certificate, without it he has no business being on earth, and his
troubles are many. Upon demand of a customs officer at any time he
must show his certificate, and if he has it not, woe be to him! Jail is
his portion, and until it is found again and his entire past life inquired
into, he becomes a sort of an international question mark."[51]

For the Chinese throughout the West, the issue of losing a certificate or of it being destroyed was a very real concern. Of the 1,336
Chinese rounded up and checked for the certificate in 1905, thirty
claimed to have lost their certificate or left it elsewhere as they traveled for work and ten claimed that their certificate was destroyed,
usually indicating it was lost in a fire.[52] There was a formal process to
replace a lost or destroyed certificate, but government officials worried that Chinese who had gained entry to the United States illegally may abuse the system to obtain a legitimate certificate. The case
of Butte resident Sue Nam illustrates the steps required to request
a replacement and government officials' suspicions of such efforts.

In June 1904 Sue Nam began the process to request a replacement for his certificate. He obtained a lawyer from Helena, provided new photographs, and produced a statement about the circumstances necessitating a new certificate. After having registered in San Francisco, Sue Nam went to work on a farm outside Suisun City, California. Sue claimed that a fire swept through the farm, destroying his certificate. After relocating to Montana, Sue began the process to replace the document. To do so Sue's lawyer communicated with Alfred Hampton, the official in charge of enforcing laws related to the Chinese in Montana. Hampton elevated the issue to offices in Washington, DC, for a decision. In some of the communications during this process, however, Hampton transposed letters in the applicant's name, rendering Sue Nam as Sue Man, highlighting the difficulty of the cross-cultural communication involved in these affairs. The discrepancy threatened to weaken Sue Nam's claim or to delay the process unnecessarily. After having his first request returned for such discrepancies, Sue submitted more paperwork, which was returned for lack of evidence. Seeking to answer the requests for more formal proof, Sue Nam and his attorney completed a lengthy affidavit attesting to the circumstances of the certificate's destruction. Even with his lawyer's assistance and the multiple pieces of evidence submitted, however, officials questioned the claim: "The Bureau has to advise you that unless Sue Nam can furnish some proof of the loss of the original registration certificate, no investigation can be conducted. His unsupported statement cannot be considered sufficient to justify such investigation."[53] Despite following the stated process and providing multiple layers of evidence sworn in official affidavit, officials rejected Sue Nam's requests, leaving him to reside in Montana as an undocumented resident under threat of deportation if found by the government's squad of Chinese inspectors.

H. D. Ebey, a Chinese inspector headquartered in Helena, traveled throughout the state with an interpreter, conducting raids on Chinese communities large and small. Ebey believed that "he was appointed for the purpose of making the expulsion feature of the Chinese exclusion laws as effective as the exclusion feature thereof."[54] During his travels, after he had "rounded up . . . 23 Chinamen in Lewistown,"

Ebey spoke to the *Fergus County Argus*. His comments give interesting insight into the humiliation that such roundups caused the Chinese in the state. When asked if he thought that similar restrictive actions would be taken against Japanese seeking to migrate to the United States or currently residing in the nation, Mr. Ebey replied that "Japan would never allow herself to be humiliated by an enactment to that end."[55] The government officials in charge of enforcing the Geary Act and its related laws clearly knew the humiliating nature of the requirements and the related raids. Their view of the weakness of the Chinese state in advocating on behalf of its people abroad facilitated further harassment of Chinese within the United States. This sentiment echoed the oft-repeated refrain that: "In intelligence, enterprise, and morals, the Chinaman is infinitely inferior to even the most ignorant of European immigrants. . . . If China ever takes a place among the other nations as an advocate of civilization and enlightenment and her people are prepared to accept the duties and responsibilities of American citizenship, then and not sooner will the door be thrown open and the exclusion law become a thing of the past."[56] Montana's Chinese population faced humiliating roundups, economic boycotts, and increasingly violent rhetoric from their non-Chinese neighbors. Coupled with a lack of effectual support from the Qing government in advocating for its people abroad, the Chinese in the Montana were in danger of being pushed out.

During this decade of increasing restriction, exclusion, and expulsion in America, events back in China caused an interesting coming together of unlikely allies. Wilbur F. Sanders, for instance, would stand up for Butte's Chinese people. The most highly educated Confucian scholars, meanwhile, would visit ordinary Chinese workers in Fort Benton, Livingston, Butte, Helena, and Billings. What emerged in the late 1890s was a fascinating convergence of the interests and activities of ordinary Chinese laborers in the American West with court politics and debates about the direction of China's future. The continued weakening and humiliation of the Qing dynasty led to a call for modernization and westernization that resonated among Chinese populations throughout the world, none more so than the Chinese communities in Montana.

FOUR

The Chinese Empire Reform Association

At roughly the same time that Chinese communities in Montana struggled with the implications of the Geary Act, turmoil in China created an unlikely opportunity to strengthen protection for Chinese people around the world. Intricacies of Chinese court politics brought two of the most brilliant Confucian scholars in China's modern history into contact with laundry workers and dishwashers in small towns across Montana. Amid imperial court intrigues that resulted in executions and exile, what was seemingly a Chinese issue spilled over into migrant communities abroad. The resulting efforts of the Chinese Empire Reform Association became a global phenomenon in the period from 1899 to 1906, with the Chinese across North America and especially in Montana taking up active participation in Chinese politics from afar. The reform efforts focused on China's need to modernize and westernize and called on the experiences of the Chinese living overseas to use practical skills gained in America to spark the nation's rejuvenation.

Without a modern government to advocate on their behalf, the Chinese in America were targets of discrimination and violence. Little effective support came from the few Qing dynasty diplomats in America; instead, the nation's Chinese residents relied on the Chinese Six Companies to advocate for them. Yet during the fight against the Geary Act in the mid–1890s, this advocacy was not always successful. The influence of the Six Companies declined in the late 1890s following their defeat in the struggle against the Geary Act. Though some support came from local fraternal organizations such as the

Zhigongtang and *huiguan* networks, Chinese people in America were tested in their ability to persevere in the face of adversity and attempt to prosper.[1] Some hoped that if China modernized, learned from the advances of the West, and adopted innovations in technology, education, and political systems it could provide stronger protection for the Chinese in America.

The weakness of the Qing dynasty worried not just the overseas Chinese but their countrymen back home as well. Efforts at reform did occur, most notably the Self-Strengthening Movement from the 1860s to 1890s, which attempted to adapt western military innovations to Chinese needs following the nation's humiliating defeats during the Opium Wars of the mid-nineteenth century. These efforts, however, failed to position China to defend itself against the modern militaries of the western powers and a transformed Japanese state. Especially damaging was the nation's defeat in the Sino-Japanese War of 1894–1895. News of this loss inspired a radical protest from within that challenged China's age-old system. In 1895 thousands of candidates hoping to earn a civil administration position gathered in Beijing to sit for the imperial examination. Upon learning of the humiliating terms of the Treaty of Shimonoseki, more than six hundred candidates signed a petition urging the Qing to reject the treaty and to adopt far-reaching reforms to strengthen China and prevent further disgraces. The radical call for reform challenged the system of Confucianism, with its emphasis on tradition, hierarchy, respect, and deference. The leader of the movement, Kang Youwei, challenged the imperial examination system as outdated. Kang submitted numerous memorials to the emperor to this effect, and the petition signed by the patriotic scholars advanced to the court as well.[2]

The nominal leader of the Qing dynasty was the Guangxu Emperor who was open to such ideas. Yet the conservative Dowager Empress Cixi, who held power for much of the Guangxu Emperor's reign, checked his authority and firmly resisted such modernization efforts. She was gradually moving into retirement, however, allowing Guangxu to reign. He took note of Kang's memorial, granting him a rare private audience.[3] Kang took full advantage of this opportunity, encouraging the emperor to initiate widespread reforms, arguing that: "A survey of all states in the world will show that those states that undertook reforms became strong while those states that clung to the past perished. . . . if we can change, we can preserve ourselves; but if we cannot change, we shall perish."[4] Following the advice of Kang, his most prominent student Liang Qichao, and other reform-minded scholars, the emperor issued a flurry of imperial edicts enacting reforms in education, economics, military training, and foreign affairs. In quick succession from June through September of 1898, the Guangxu Emperor issued decrees dealing with such issues as "the sending of imperial clansmen to foreign countries to study the form and conditions of European and American government." The emperor also "advised the adoption of Western arms and drill for all the Tartar troops," established "Bureaus of Mines and Railroads," and ordered "Naval academies and training-ships."[5]

Few educated Chinese, however, had direct experience with the West and the technologies and systems that the Guangxu Emperor sought to implement. As Tan Sitong, a leading reformer, stated:

> In China, during the last several decades, where have we had genuine understanding of foreign culture? When have we had scholars or officials who could discuss them? If they had been able to discuss foreign matters, there would have been no [defeat of China by Japan]. What you mean by foreign matters are . . . steamships, telegraph lines, trains, guns, cannon, torpedoes, and machines for weaving and for metallurgy; that's all. You have never dreamed of or seen the beauty and perfection of Western legal systems and political institutions. . . . All they speak of are the branches and foliage of foreign matters, not the roots.[6]

To implement modernization, China needed a new class of administrators trained in the ways of the West. Unfortunately, a conservative reaction sabotaged the reforms that began in 1898 before such programs could take root.

Called the Hundred Days of Reform, the efforts of Guangxu, Kang, Liang, and others challenged the status quo and incited anxiety from those who stood to lose power. A group of conservative court officials backed by the still powerful Cixi launched a coup detaining the emperor and confining him under house arrest. The officials arrested and executed several reformers. Kang and Liang barely escaped but continued their efforts from exile. Montana newspapers noted the aftermath of the failed reform efforts, reporting that the Dowager Empress "has issued an imperial edict offering 100,000 taels for the capture of the 'modern sage' and his ally, Liang Chi'io-ch'ao [Liang Qichao], dead or alive; and in order to rout out every trace of Kang's existence from the sacred soil of China Li Hung Chang has been ordered to desecrate and destroy the tombs of his ancestors."[7] With Cixi back in power, China became increasingly anti-foreign. This trend ultimately contributed to the Boxer Rebellion (1899–1901), with rebels in the north of China struggling to oust foreigners, a cause eventually supported by the Qing court. Foreign armies put down the Boxer uprising, and the Qing dynasty's decline accelerated.

Exile did not diminish Kang and Liang's enthusiasm for reform. Instead, they simply sought support elsewhere—specifically, among the overseas Chinese. These Chinese workers had useful financial resources and direct experience with the industries and political systems of the West. These workers also had a vested interest in seeing China modernize, believing that if China became more powerful, their position in America would improve as well. The Chinatowns of the North American West became fertile ground for Kang and Liang to continue their efforts to reform China from afar. Seeking to draw support from the diverse communities of Chinese people in North America and elsewhere, Kang and Liang founded the Chinese Empire Reform Association (CERA) in July 1899 in Victoria, British Columbia.[8] The foundational goal of the CERA was to depose the Dowager Empress Cixi and return to power the rightful ruler, the Guangxu Emperor, who would continue the reforms needed to modernize China.[9]

The CERA spread rapidly, becoming a global phenomenon with more than 150 branches across North America as well as throughout Australia, Hawaii, Japan, and elsewhere. While it is no surprise that cities with large Chinese populations such as San Francisco, Los Angeles, and New York developed branches of the CERA, its geographic dispersal shows the widespread interest in this movement.[10] Montana's Chinese communities helped lead the early creation of CERA branches. Just five months after the founding of the first branch in British Columbia, founders of the CERA referenced leaders in Montana, noting that "Li Ting Fong in Helena and Guan Guobin in Butte are loyal and righteous."[11] Chinese communities in Montana established twelve branches of the CERA as early as 1901 and both Liang and Kang visited these organizations in 1903 and 1905, respectively. It is easy to assume that the highly educated leaders of such a movement taught the Chinese in Montana the importance of the need for reform. Regarding Montana's Chinese community, however, Kang, Liang, and the CERA did not begin empowerment movements; rather they built upon the pre-existing sense of community pride, nationalism, and empowerment found in Montana's Chinese communities.

As was seen in the fight against the Geary Act, Montana's Chinese people had experience organizing and advocating for their rights. Though the efforts to resist the Geary Act failed, shortly after this struggle the Chinese in Montana won key victories that emboldened the community, predating and fitting perfectly with the efforts of the CERA. Butte, which had one of the largest Chinese communities in the Rocky Mountain region, witnessed a pivotal moment in this use of American jurisprudence for Chinese protection. In 1896 and 1897 several of Butte's labor unions organized a citywide boycott against Chinese-owned businesses. Playing upon fears that the Chinese took jobs from whites and bolstered by racial animosity, the boycott organizers used intimidation against both the Chinese and their white customers. Anti-Chinese agitators lingered outside of Chinese businesses intimidating customers from entering. They also followed Chinese deliverymen on their routes to dissuade whites throughout the city from patronizing Chinese businesses. Banners, floats, and advertisements spread news of the boycott and continued the racist rhetoric against Butte's Chinese community. Chinese businesses felt the impact with lost customers and revenue. Don Len noted "as soon as those walking delegates kept in front of [Hum Fay's restaurant] I believe that his business dropped nine out of ten. That is, hardly anybody there . . . used to be a full house at the noon hour before the boycott."[12] Chinese business leaders Quon Loy, Don Len, and Hum Fay complained to city officials that they paid taxes and deserved protection from such abuse.[13] Quon Loy expressed his frustration at the lack of action by city officials in 1896, reminding him of similar inaction when anti-Chinese forces employed comparable tactics in 1892 and 1893:

> I called on Chief [of Police] Tebo and upon Waters; I told him; I say "our people pay licenses and pay taxes and poor taxes just the same as other people, and the walking delegate prevent them from trading, and I think the City ought to do something." . . . The City do nothing to protect our people. A few years ago . . . at that time that boycott was going on too, and I went and saw [the Mayor]. Nothing done and I had a conversation with Governor Toole . . . He said he couldn't do nothing.[14]

Few options remained for Butte's Chinese residents with city and state officials unwilling to stop the agitators and the general ineffectiveness of Chinese diplomats in America. Not willing to suffer economic disruption and abuse passively, the Chinese in Butte fought back.

Leaders of Butte's Chinese community reached out to the Six Companies in San Francisco requesting advice and support. Reeling from losing the challenge to the Geary Act and concerned that fighting this boycott would cause an outbreak of violence all too common throughout the West over the past decades, the Six Companies advised the Chinese in Butte against taking legal action. Much later, an old Chinese resident of Butte recalled that the Six Companies had told them, "You are crazy to go against labor unions and the American law." Proceeding despite this advice, the Chinese in Butte organized to collect funds for a legal defense: "Each man put up $20, and with a thousand people, we had a big sum to fight with."[15] With the community motivated and well-funded, they brought a suit claiming that their rights had been violated. In *Hum Fay et al. v. Frank Baldwin et al.* the Chinese testified about the intimidation they suffered and the ensuing economic consequences.

Legal representation to fight Butte's powerful, publicly supported labor unions was key, and the Chinese found a strong patron in Wilbur Fisk Sanders. An early settler in Montana Territory, Sanders was an important figure in the vigilante movements of the 1860s, seeking to bring justice and stability to a frontier society that lacked a functioning legal system. Sanders became a respected politician, advocating Radical Republican beliefs in racial equality that may have made him sympathetic to the Chinese in Butte. Certainly, his Democratic opponents in Butte had long taken note of his advocacy for the Chinese, commenting derisively in 1886: "Do the people of Montana wish a man to represent them in Congress who has a pronounced pro-Chinese record, who favors Chinese immigration, Chinese pauper labor and Chinese licentiousness? If so, Wilbur F. Sanders is their man."[16] Throughout the 1880s and 1890s it appears that Sanders advocated for the better treatment of the Chinese in the state. This position stands in contrast to his harsh statements during the debate over the Geary Act when he noted, "It is not desirable that these people shall be multiplied in this country, but that they shall be diminished to extinction."[17] It may be that his stance when addressing a national audience during the debate over the Geary Act had been adapted to suit the mood of his peers in the Senate. Sanders, a Republican who supported the gold standard, had few supporters in Butte, especially during the 1896 election season as the city was largely in the Democratic-Populist camp and backed William Jennings Bryan and the free silver movement. This might have contributed to his decision to take up the case in support of Butte's Chinese population both to live out his Radical Republican beliefs in racial equality and to strike a blow against a hotbed of political opposition. Whatever the circumstance, the fact that Sanders took up the case to argue against the boycott gave legitimacy to the legal claims made by the Chinese of Butte.

With several hundred Chinese people negatively impacted by the boycott, having all of them appear in court to testify was unrealistic. Indicating their solidarity, Butte's Chinese residents signed a petition expressing their desire to seek legal redress against the boycott orga-nizers. Signed by three hundred members of Butte's Chinatown—in

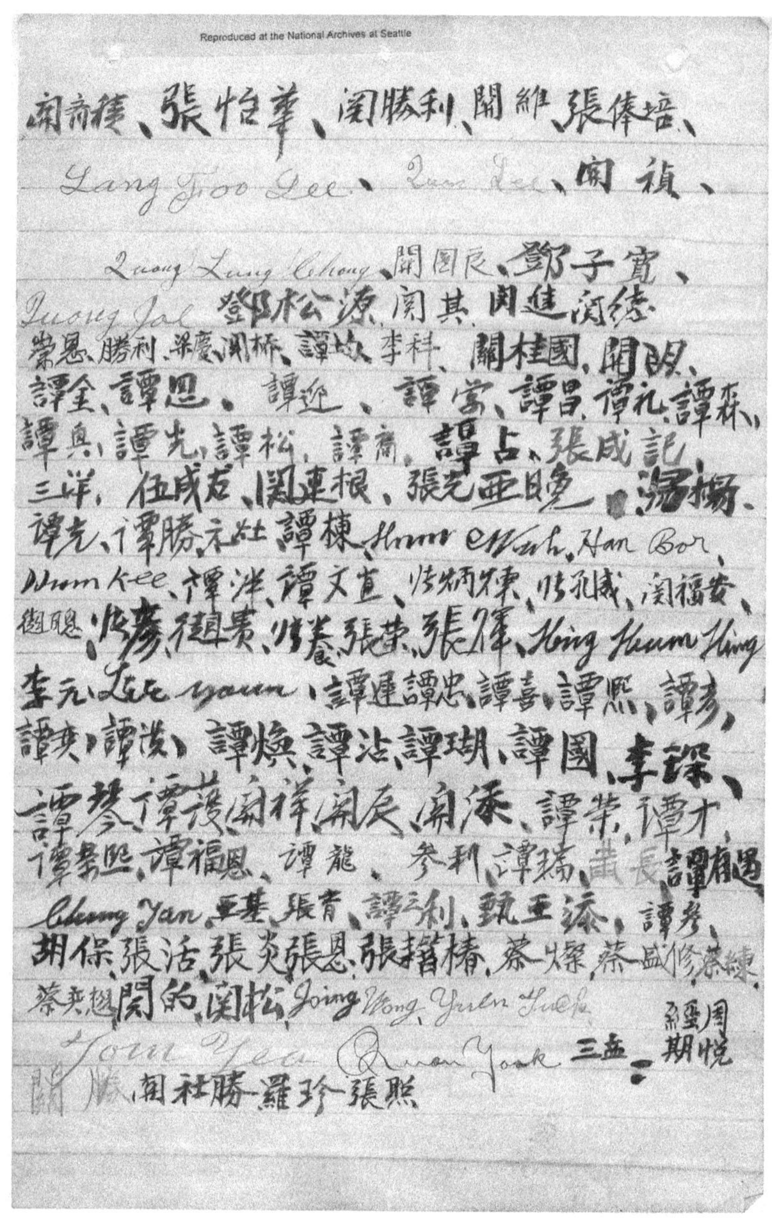

8. One page of petition signed by more than three hundred members of Butte's Chinese community attesting to their support in the legal struggle to end the anti-Chinese boycott of 1897. RG 21, National Archives, Seattle WA.

both English and Chinese—this petition highlights their active fight against discrimination. The legal proceedings unfolded over several years, with hearings throughout 1898, findings announced in 1899, and the final decision reached in 1900. The Chinese won the case, including a financial settlement for legal fees and an injunction against further discriminatory action from labor unions.[18] A Chinese resident of Butte recounted the reaction of the Six Companies, purported to have stated: "The Butte Chinese are the smartest anywhere in the United States."[19] The defendants, however, were unable to pay, and the case was further elevated to the federal level in 1901 with the Chinese consul appealing to the U.S. State Department for financial redress. Secretary of State John Hay saw the case as invalid and had it dismissed. The bold efforts of the Chinese in Butte succeeded locally, but ultimately failed due to China's weakness in advocating on behalf of its citizens.

The local victory in the boycott case is just one example of the Chinese in Montana employing the legal system to fight for their rights.[20] Their sophisticated use of the American legal system was not always successful but provides evidence of adaptations occurring within the Chinese community. Combined with these experiences of empowerment through using western institutions and their frustrations that China was not strong enough to support their efforts, it is no surprise that the CERA thrived among Montana's Chinese communities.

Montana became exceptionally active in the efforts of the CERA, eventually boasting twelve branches. The first formal organization occurred in Helena in June 1901, with Butte's committee forming in August 1901. The *Anaconda Standard* noted the developments under the headline "Chinamen Are Aroused: Those in Butte Have Organized a Reform Society." Readers of the lengthy article learned that Butte's Reform Society "includes about all of the Chinese inhabitants of the county, numbering in the neighborhood of 300." The article featured an interview with the founder of the CERA branches in the United States, Long Ka Tien.[21] Long and his interpreter Gong Hee traveled from Portland to Montana to aid in the establishment of CERA branches. Gong Hee noted:

We are meeting with great success everywhere we go, nine out of ten joining the reform society. We go from here in a day or two to Livingston . . We have been in Helena, where the society claims every Chinese inhabitant. The Chinese in America constitute a very important factor in the regeneration of China from the fact that they have been abroad and are able to judge for themselves whether their posterity is to continue to debase itself in the dust for the maintenance of an obsolete, unsavory form of government, or arise like men and claim recognition from the great family of civilized nations.[22]

Clearly, Gong Hee was enthusiastic about the efforts. Further analysis of his interests gives deeper insight into the organization's practical goals of reform and self-empowerment.

Arriving in America just before the passage of the Chinese Exclusion Act, Gong Hee spent five years in San Francisco before moving to Portland. While in Portland he worked as a bookkeeper and businessman, learning fluent English. He was a man of many interests and was quite busy on his trip across the country. In addition to his job translating for Long Ka Tien and spreading the message of reform he authored a book in Chinese on Yellowstone Park, which he and Long Ka Tien were the first Chinese tourists to visit, during his tour through the West to Minnesota.[23] More to the point of the Chinese's need to acquire practical skills to advance the reform efforts, Gong wrote the first Chinese-language book on electricity. Trade publications noted his efforts, commenting that Gong Hee was a "graduate of the electrical department of a Portland technical school, and has served as an apprentice and operator with an electric appliance manufacturer. His book . . . is an extended translation of American text books, with exhaustive original explanatory addenda, made necessary by the difficulty in translating electrical terms into a language which knows nothing of these."[24]

Gong connected these efforts with the tangible skills needed for the advancement of his countrymen. In 1903 Gong Hee sought to more directly influence Chinese affairs, returning to Guangzhou to "teach my countrymen what they ought to know about electric lighting. . . . I wish to do my part in the awakening of China."[25] Gong offers a perfect example of how the Chinese people who lived in the American West learned modern skills that their counterparts in China lacked. The CERA instilled its members with the high-minded theoretical need to institute reform, as expressed by scholar-reforms Kang Youwei and Liang Qichao, combined with practical skills, as embodied by Gong Hee. In contrast to Kang and Liang, American Chinese people like Gong had much more in common with the mass of the overseas Chinese. He had left China decades earlier due to economic hardship only to suffer oppression and mistreatment while carving out an existence in an inhospitable environment in America. The Chinese across the American West acquired practical skills through their labors in the United States. With the combination of these mechanical skills and their experiences applying the American legal system to their defense, Montana's Chinese possessed the precise knowledge and experiences necessary for China's modernization.

While in Butte in August 1901, Gong and Long were hosted by Quon Loy, a key figure from the anti-boycott struggle, who noted that "We want to let all of our people know just what they are capable of doing when they are given the opportunity. Working and fighting for a good cause . . . our society includes every Chinaman in this county."[26] Long continued this explanation in another interview, noting that "the object of the association is to promote a movement for the opening of China to modern improvements and eventually to rid the empire of the influence of the present administration. We want China to have railroads and telegraph lines and other improvements." The reporter was impressed with the turnout at the event, noting that more than one hundred members of Butte's Chinese community attended the meeting.[27]

Gong Hee spent an extended period in Montana during the summer of 1901, bringing organizational structure to the local efforts and building on the momentum within the state's Chinese communities. Enthusiasm for the reform efforts was indeed high; Chinese communities across the state founded several more branches in quick succession and two became incorporated entities after filing extensive paperwork with the proper state offices. The articles of incorporation for both the Chinese Empire Reform Society of Montana, based in Helena, and for the organization's Butte branch noted that the corporations aimed to accomplish reform by "encouraging general education of the Chinese people in the principles of the Constitution and the laws of the United States of America, in the arts and sciences generally, with the view of ensuring the adoption of the leading improvements, industrial and otherwise . . . to bring about the amelioration of the Chinese people, and to secure for them the advantages of a freer diffusion of useful knowledge."[28]

The organization's bylaws included annual democratic election of leaders, an influence of the American democratic processes they witnessed but from which they were excluded. These statements of goals in the articles of incorporation testify to the hopes of Montana's Chinese community, both regarding their self-empowerment in Montana and their broader desires to empower their homeland.[29]

Montana's newspapers noted the efforts of the Chinese, with reporting ranging from racist mocking of the movement to praiseworthy assessments of the community's organization and reform efforts. The *Anaconda Standard*'s headline of August 22, 1901 announced: "Good-bye to Pigtails: Chinamen who aim to be Americans Desire to Educate Their People Regarding a Few Modern Things." The article reported that the organization's main goal was to: "teach modern ideas among the Chinese and to adopt modern styles and methods, which will mean the abolishment of the queue . . . Articles of incorporation were filed with the county clerk and recorder yesterday, the incorporators and trustees of the society being Quon Loy, Hum Yen, Lu Hing Kin, Dong Lin, Jung Yee Wah, and Quong Hong."[30] It is no surprise that these men also figured prominently in the struggle against the boycott. The strength of the society grew throughout the summer and fall, with the *Anaconda Standard* noting in December 1901: "The Chinese Reform Society is meeting every night in its rooms on West Galena Street and meetings are well attended. The society was originally formed . . . to depose the old dowager empress of China so that in the end the rightful heir of the throne might take his position and give to the Chinaman that brand of government most liked by the common herd."[31]

Not all media coverage was as fact-based and objective. A racially charged statement regarding the efforts of Helena's Chinese community to organize mocked the "strength" of the Chinese in the state capital:

> The Chinese are very strong in Helena. You can detect their presence, blindfolded, at a distance of eight blocks . . . if the wind is in the right direction, and your nose is in full possession of all its faculties, the impression borne in upon you that, instead of being a quarter of a mile from the Chinese colony on West Main street, you are up against the whole Chinese empire with all its 400,000,000 inhabitants, in anything but a good state of preservation. You feel the need of a Chinese Empire Reform society is imperative and you are filled with misgivings lest the world's output of disinfectants be totally inadequate to accomplish the reform.[32]

This derogatory reporting emphasizes the discriminatory sentiments Montana's Chinese community faced. Proud of their accomplishments, emboldened by contacts with other communities seeking change, and eager to be actively engaged in the improvement of their people, Montana's Chinese people focused on self-improvement, unconcerned with the negative sentiments of others in their midst.

Working in concert with the Helena and Butte CERA branches, other Chinese communities across the state organized for self-improvement. The *Billings Gazette* noted in November 1901 that the local branch of the society quickly established a school:

> Almost without exception the members of the Chinese colony of [Billings] are affiliated with the reform party. . . . As evidence of their sincerity to adopt the western ideas of civilization and progress, some of the leaders among the colony have used their influence to establish a Chinese mission school. . . . Tom Quong, [who] acts as interpreter, and is the leader of the school. . . . [stated] "If we succeed in [our reform efforts] China will open her doors to the world and the advantages of education and intercourse with the more enlightened and progressive people of the world will soon work a change. . . . China will have taken the first step in the direction that shall end in making her one of the world's greatest powers."[33]

Quong's call for unity speaks to a key ideological development at this time both driving and aided by efforts like the CERA. Previously, the Chinese in America had self-segregated along regional, clan, and family lines. Fraternal organizations aided immigrants of certain family heritage, and other than sharing general cultural practices and a vague geographical sense of connectedness, the Chinese in America were not bound together by a feeling of political or national unity.[34] To be sure, the dominant American culture saw the Chinese in America as a whole and discriminatory policies did not discriminate. Yet among the Chinese, there was little identification of shared political unity. A growing sense emerged, however, that the vulnerable position of the Chinese in America was due to China's weakness and the only remedy was to strengthen the nation. With this common goal, membership in the CERA transcended social class, clan affiliation, and family heritage. Chinese identity and a desire to see China strengthened were the only prequalifications for participation. As Tom Quong indicated above, this would result in China taking steps to become a world power and allow it to protect its citizens abroad.[35]

Butte's branch built upon the idea of education as key to transforming the community. Interviewed by the *Butte Inter Mountain* in 1903, Quon Loy noted:

A plan now under consideration by the society here is the establishment of a China school, where all Chinese will be educated. It is expected to branch out and grow until we will have a school where we can make statesmen and soldiers. . . . An endeavor will be made to eliminate all dialects from the Chinese language and make one language universal in China. This will enable us to circulate literature more freely, for under present existing circumstances, one cannot travel more than 10 miles before he is confronted with a new dialect.[36]

Montana's Chinese population believed clannish fragmentation contributed to China's weakness. Through concentrated effort for a common cause, enhancing commonalities while overcoming differences, China could gain strength.

Coordination and visits by Montana-based reformers furthered

CERA efforts across the state. For instance, as an article from the *Butte Miner* noted in early 1902: "There is a state lecturer who visits the societies in other cities and has visited and spoken to all of them with the exception of the one in Missoula. His name is How See and is at present in the city of Chicago. He will return in about two weeks and will then visit Missoula."[37]

The newspaper reports and articles of incorporation give insight into the Chinese in Montana as dynamic and empowered rather than passive and powerless. Montana's CERA branches produced photomontages showing the members who had joined. Two of these images still exist. The photomontage of the Marysville branch features thirteen members pictured under a banner with the Guangxu Emperor flanked by four images of modern naval vessels.[38] The Butte photomontage features thirty-three members arranged under an image of the Guangxu Emperor. These photographs differed significantly from the registration photographs mandated under the Geary Act, which presented the subject in strictly regimented poses akin to mug shots. Instead, the CERA photomontages allowed for personal expression, individuality, and choice. Close examination reveals that members have key differences in their dress and hairstyle. Roughly half are clothed in traditional Chinese dress and exhibit the queue, a hairstyle with the hair on the top of the scalp grown long and braided and the front portion of the head shaved. The queue was mandated by the Qing dynasty as a sign of subservience to the ruling Manchu government. Some of those pictured, however, show signs of westernization in dress and forego the queue, indicating that they had crafted a new identity based on their experiences in America. In fact, one man's photograph seems to catch him in the midst of this transformation. The man is the only individual who has western-style dress and the traditional queue. The fact that he had not shaved his head for several days combined with his western dress indicates that he embraced the modern ways of the westernized Chinese in America.[39] His accessories give further evidence of this straddling of two worlds. While all those photographed wear small lapel pins of the emperor, only three wear American flag pins. With such care given to this photograph, it is clear that those pictured intentionally con-

9. Marysville, Montana, a small mining community with a sizeable Chinese population, also established a branch of the Chinese Empire Reform Association. The images of modern naval vessels featured on the photomontage reflect the desire that China would modernize militarily to be taken more seriously in international affairs, affording the nation's citizens abroad increased protection. Committee of the Chinese Empire Reform Association, Marysville MT, 1901. PAC 85–27 M3, Montana Historical Society Research Center Photograph Archives, Helena MT.

10. Member of the Chinese Empire Reform Association of Butte, Montana. Note the western dress, the American flag lapel pin, and the fact that he seems to be in the process of growing out his hair, forgoing the mandatory queue. Detail, Committee of the Chinese Empire Reform Association, Butte MT, 1901. PAC 95–22 MMI, Montana Historical Society Research Center Photograph Archives, Helena MT.

11. Photomontage of the Committee of the Chinese Empire Reform Association, Butte, Montana, 1901. PAC 95–22 MM 1, Montana Historical Society Research Center Photograph Archives, Helena MT.

structed how they wanted to be viewed.[40] These extraordinary documents testify to how the Chinese in Montana viewed themselves, increasingly united by a shared experience and empowered through an understanding and use of the same American systems that sought to oppress them.

It is within this context of an active, homegrown group of Chinese Empire Reform Associations that the leaders of the global reform movement came to visit Montana. Liang Qichao visited North America in 1903, spending two months visiting CERA branches in Canada and five months touring branches in the United States. After his experiences, Liang wrote extensively and quite critically about the Chinese in America. Liang was displeased with the parochialism in many Chinatowns, commenting: "Our character is that of clansmen rather than citizens. . . . We have a village mentality and not a national mentality. . . . When I look at all the societies of the world, none is so disorderly as the Chinese community of San Francisco."[41] Disgusted by the dirty atmosphere of many Chinatowns, Liang's impressions, especially of San Francisco's Chinese community, were not positive.[42] It may be that the highly educated, socially elite Liang was not used to interacting with countrymen from different social classes. While his overall assessment was critical, Liang's visit to Montana left a different impression.

In August 1903 Liang visited Butte, Helena, Livingston, and Billings, as well as smaller Chinese communities. His lectures were very well attended, and he reported afterwards that, "We have met with great success in our work of reform . . . The Chinese of Butte are quite enthusiastic in the work. The reform movements have been started in every city and town which Chinese live and it is our purpose to keep it alive and add fuel to the flame of enthusiasm."[43] Liang's esteem for the efforts of Montana's Chinese population was quite high in contrast to his exasperation with his San Francisco experience. The organization of the Helena and Butte CERA branches and the financial contributions to the organization from throughout the state impressed Liang.[44]

Two years later, Kang Youwei, the founder of CERA and the reformer whose inspiration and connections with the Guangxu

12. Medallion of the Chinese Empire Reform Association featuring the image of the Guangxu Emperor, the Qing dynasty flag, and the flag of the CERA, ca. 1905. Courtesy of Mai Wah Society. Photo by Richard Gibson. (See chap4n45 for more information.)

Emperor had planted the first seeds of reform, also visited Montana.[45] In the interim between Liang's 1903 visit and Kang's 1905 visit, CERA efforts developed a military component. Members drilled at marching, target practice, and the use of battle tactics and strategies with the possible goal of returning to China to force the Dowager Empress from power and reinstate the Guangxu Emperor.[46] While members of Montana's Chinese community began participating in this training, such efforts seemed more about building on the trend of self-empowerment that accompanied the rapid rise of the CERA in Montana than any realistic sense they would march victoriously to reinstate the emperor.

13. Meeting of Chinese Empire Reform Association representatives from across Montana. Location undetermined, ca. 1905. PAC 80–17.70, Bonnie Merrell Collection, Montana Historical Society Research Center Photograph Archives, Helena MT. (See chap4n48 for more information.)

To build upon their shared interests regarding reform and self-improvement, representatives from CERA branches across the state gathered at a banquet in the spring of 1905. A photograph of the event shows representatives from various branches in a meeting hall, likely the headquarters of the Butte CERA. The *Anaconda Standard* described the Butte headquarters in a way that closely mirrored the photograph: "The walls of the association rooms in Butte are covered with photographic groups of different local bodies belonging to the reform guard, there being about 50 in all. The Butte group contains 41 persons, most of whom belong to the military company. In not one of the groups is there the face of an ignorant looking Chinese. Fully 99 per cent of them are well dressed in American costume, showing progressiveness and a desire to attain a height greater than that which the empress of their country would have them attain."[47]

The scroll seen at the top right of the image features calligraphy done by Liang Qichao during his 1903 visit to Montana. As noted by the reporter, the walls of the banquet hall display numerous different photomontages, as many as twenty visible in the half of the room pictured. The large photomontage to the right is of the Helena CERA branch. Several non-Chinese men appear in the back of the photograph. It is possible these are veterans of the Spanish-American War who are training the members of the Butte militia force.[48] These military efforts may have been the primary reason for the gathering of representatives from across the state. As a Chinese newspaper that followed the efforts of the CERA noted, "The Gancheng [Chinese Reform Military School] opened on April 20, 1905, and the colleagues specially prepared a banquet for military teachers and comrades from other cities. Those who came to attend the opening ceremony, where there were more than seventy people, had a grand event."[49] Such productive collaboration between Montana's CERA branches illustrates the energy and enthusiasm for the reform efforts in the state. Kang Youwei would soon see this enthusiasm for himself when he visited Montana in August 1905.

A month before Kang's visit to Montana, local newspapers became intrigued by the militarization of the Chinese community. "Chinese Are Drilling Like Old Hands At It," noted an August 25, 1905 headline in the *Anaconda Standard*. The lengthy article went on to describe how the Butte branch "has a company that can execute the various commands of its officers with almost the same accuracy and precision as a well drilled company of American soldiers. . . . Each member has a Spanish Mauser rifle and uniform consisting of the regulation white hat with a yellow cord, band and crossarms designating the number of the company; yellow canvas blouse and canvas leggings, together with a cartridge belt and bayonet and scabbard attached to the belt. . . . So far they have burned considerable powder and many of them are becoming expert marksmen."[50]

The reality of a large group of Chinese residents in the American West training militarily and possessing and openly working to master modern weaponry may seem surprising, especially as they were often portrayed as passive, submissive victims. It is particularly surprising considering that Butte's anti-Chinese boycott of 1896–1897 was still fresh in the community's mind. Butte's Chinese population seemed to be telling the broader community that they were strong enough to protect themselves from further intimidation. The leader of the global movement, Kang Youwei, stepped into this atmosphere when he visited Montana, stopping in Helena, Billings, Livingston, and Butte, as well as touring Yellowstone Park.[51] The *Anaconda Standard* noted that: "Three members of the Butte branch of the association . . . went to Helena Monday and escorted him to this city. The party was met at the depot by a band of music and many of the prominent Chinese of Butte, among whom were Quon Louie [*sic*], one of the old merchants of the district."[52] Kang toured Butte, taking note of the mining industries and visiting the city's thriving copper mines. Kang sought to gain practical knowledge that could help China capitalize on its natural resources, but his real motivation was to inspire and further urge on China's human resources. Kang "reviewed the soldier boys and paid them a high compliment for efficiency . . . The captain put them through the various movements without a hitch, stopping at one stage to give the president an opportunity to address the soldiers. Among other things, President Wei told them he was proud of the progress they were making."[53]

The CERA's global activity peaked in 1905. As the next chapter describes, Kang Youwei met with President Theodore Roosevelt during his tour of the United States and urged him to reconsider the Chinese Exclusion Act. To try to influence better treatment of the Chinese in America, Kang led a boycott of American goods to use economic pressures to influence American politicians to alter anti-Chinese policies. The boycott mobilized millions of Chinese people around the world and is significant as one of the first mass movements in China's modern history. Building from the networks developed in the fight against the Geary Act and the efforts to spread the CERA, the boycott shook American businesses and showed the power and reach of Kang, Liang, and the organization.[54]

Financial troubles and infighting in the CERA began its decline in the latter half of the decade. With the Qing dynasty still reluctant to accept change, the organization's influence came into question and was challenged by other reformers, notably Sun Yat-sen, who

14. During Kang Youwei's 1905 visit to Butte, he and his party toured the Original Mine. The photo shows Kang with his secretary/interpreter Zhou Guoxian and Tom Leung, an herbalist and student of Kang. Kang is midway up the staircase, next to the inside bannister. Others pictures are part of the production of *Ben Hur*, a major theatrical event in Butte at the time. Tom Leung wrote on the backing of the photo: "[Kang] personally descended 2,000 feet deep into the mine." As Chinese workers were prohibited from laboring in the mines, Kang and his group were likely the first Chinese individuals to descend into the shafts. Collection of Jane Leung Larson.

sought to oust the Qing altogether. Finally, with the 1908 death of the Guangxu Emperor and Dowager Empress Cixi's death one day later, the impetus for reform was gone.

Montana newspapers took note of the organization's misfortune. A headline in the *Anaconda Standard* read: "Reform Army a Dream: The Chinese Wake Up: Kang Yu Wei, The Great Reformer, Admits Failure: Butte Celestials had a flourishing organization and do not yet realize the bottom has fallen out." The author's enjoyment of the demise of the reform effort lessened when the Chinese residents of Butte whom he interviewed seemed unconcerned. The Chinese leaders "claimed to know nothing of the abandonment of the movement. When asked if they were still drilling the company, one of them said 'No, not now, of course; it's too cold. Drill again in summer.' The import of the [news of the CERA's military disbandment] was explained to him, and he showed that that was the first he had heard of it. That it did not affect him deeply, however, he showed when he said, 'Well, the instructions do the young men good, anyway. They learn some things that's fine for them.'"[55]

The Butte members of the CERA and their comrades throughout the state focused on the benefits that the reform movement brought to their local community. For Montana's Chinese community, self-empowerment, the acquisition and application of practical skills, and the use of American legal and democratic principles outweighed the inner workings of the Qing court. While the desire for a stronger China that could more fully advocate for its citizens abroad drove the CERA's larger efforts, the benefits of increased pride and stronger cohesion through the development of a national identity transformed individuals and communities at the local level. That Montana did not witness a major instance of mob violence against the state's Chinese population may be due to the relative strength, unity, and organization of Chinese Montanans.

The efforts of the CERA combined with the Chinese boycott of American goods in 1905 bound the Chinese together through shared experiences in Montana, throughout the American West, and around the globe. Mobilized through these efforts, they developed a Chinese national identity. Far from the nameless "Chinaman" of the census of 1870 through the efforts of CERA, we can now see Montana's Chinese as they saw themselves: as reformers, leaders, soldiers, and comrades actively engaged in a global struggle to strengthen their homeland and themselves through self-empowerment.

FIVE

The Anti-American Boycott of 1905

At the same time that Montana's Chinese communities advanced causes to strengthen China's world standing, changes in the U.S. government's handling of Chinese issues resulted in increased arrests and deportations. Coincidences of Chinese court politics brought Liang Qichao and Kang Youwei into contact with working-class Chinese throughout the American West during this period of increased pressure on these communities. Highly educated elites like Liang and Kang had few opportunities to interact in meaningful ways with lower classes in China. While exiled and working from abroad, however, the reformers experienced the power and possibilities of these communities as well as the mistreatment they faced. Through this close contact with working-class Chinese suffering under the increasingly vigorous enactment of exclusion and expulsion, Liang and Kang built empathy for this group, ultimately elevating their cause to the highest levels of American politics and global economics.

Throughout the 1890s bureaucratic uncertainty and a lack of funding weakened enforcement of restrictions related to Chinese immigrants and alien residents. From the late 1880s to the 1890s, general responsibility for enforcing immigration restrictions shifted between the Treasury Department and the newly created Bureau of Immigration. Enforcement of most laws directed at Chinese immigrants remained under the Bureau of Customs until 1900. However, as the Geary Act dealt not with potential immigrants but with Chinese residents within the country, Geary Act enforcement continued under the Treasury Department and its Internal Revenue Service. Frank Sargent, the commissioner general of immigration during this period, noted the need for centralized control over issues relating to the Chinese: "There was a divided responsibility, due to the disconnected official agencies through which the laws were administered, and it was not possible to effect the organization and systematization for even a reasonably thorough enforcement of the laws."[1] Several changes in agency responsibilities addressed the scattered nature of accountability for enforcement. The Bureau of Immigration, created in 1903, took over issues related to the Chinese people attempting to enter the United States and of those already within the country.[2] Leaders of this bureau included Sargent and Terence Powderly, both prominent labor leaders who brought an aversion to Chinese immigrants that most within organized labor shared. Powderly even led the Knights of Labor during the most violent uprisings against the Chinese in America, including the massacre of Chinese miners in Rock Springs, Wyoming, and their violent expulsion from numerous communities in Washington Territory. In reacting to these violent actions, Powderly noted, "Had the Chinese been as rigidly excluded, as they should have been, the workmen at Rock Springs would not have steeped their hands in the blood of a people whose very presence in this country is contamination, whose influence is wholly bad, and whose effect upon the morals of whatever community they inhabit tends to degrade and brutalize all with whom they come in contact."[3]

With Powderly and Sargent in charge of enforcing anti-Chinese legislation, systematic implementation of the restrictions ensued. The growth of American power abroad—notably the acquisition of Hawaii and the Philippines—also worried exclusionists because these regions had large Chinese communities. Anti-Chinese groups worried that incorporation of these territories would allow free travel of these ethnically Chinese groups to the mainland. Officials sharing these views felt the time was right for the vigorous enforcement of existing laws. With the ten-year life of the Geary Act due to expire in 1902, Congress passed a law reaffirming exclusion and extending it to cover Chinese in Hawaii and the Philippines.

With the U.S. government's power consolidated under the Bureau of Immigration, Sargent developed rigorous tools to test veracity of Chinese claims. First, he created a system of interviews with Chinese immigrants to authenticate or disprove their claims of identity. These interviews created records that followed each Chinese immigrant to be used even decades later to verify the individual's claims and those of alleged family members. Sargent and others harbored deep cultural mistrust of the Chinese, viewing them as "a people who, according to all recognized authorities, are deficient in the sense of the moral obligation of an oath."[4] For this reason, interviews with immigrants were not enough to establish their identity in the minds of government officials. Sargent sought more scientific proof of identity for Chinese individuals, eventually adopting the Bertillon system of identification, originally intended for the identification and tracking of convicted criminals. The Bertillon system consisted of a thorough physical examination with detailed measurements and photographs of all aspects of an individual's body. Much like the resistance to the Geary Act's requirement of mug-shot-style photographs, Chinese reacted strongly against the Bertillon system's invasive examinations.[5] With the newly strengthened, increasingly well-funded Bureau of Immigration empowered to enforce the laws, however, the objections of the Chinese community fell on deaf ears.

These changes systematized enforcement of laws relating to the Chinese in America and empowered agency officials who held deep suspicion of all Chinese people. The results reflected these changes. The number of aliens removed from the United States increased dramatically from 1,630 in 1893 to 13,108 in 1906. While not all deported were Chinese, this spike, which coincided with the more active enforcement of the Geary Act, certainly attributed for the majority of the increase.[6] Specific to Montana, the bureaucratic changes resulted in raids, arrests, and numerous deportations. The state's newspapers carried reports of these actions:

> Wah Quinn and Ham Wah, two Bozeman Chinese, after a hearing before United States Commissioner Russell here today, were ordered deported for not having the proper certificates.[7]

They Must Go Away Back . . . To Be Deported to Chinkdom . . . Chinese Inspector Ebey Arrests Two Hamilton Chinks.[8]

Lee Sing, the Chinaman who was taken into custody last week because he could not produce his residence permit, was taken to Helena today by a deputy United States marshal.

U.S Deputy Marshal Wall of Helena was in Glasgow Thursday and took back with him Sam Sing and Lum Poy, two Chinamen who have been operating a laundry at this place for the past six months.[9]

Increasingly vigorous actions against Montana's Chinese coincided with Liang Qichao's visit to the state in August 1903. Immediately before and during Liang's time in Montana, newspaper headlines carried reports of raids, arrests, and deportations: "Won Way, a Chinese laundryman, was found not to have proper papers today and deported; Inspector Beatty and Chinese inspector Hampton left Kalispell tonight with six Chinamen, whom they charge with being in this country illegally."[10] While Liang intended to gain support for the Chinese Empire Reform Association (CERA) and influence the direction of China, after witnessing the harassment the Chinese in Montana suffered, he empathized with his countrymen and began to fight against their mistreatment. The increased raids, arrests, and deportations caught Liang's attention, as did the indignities of the Bertillon system, which he wrote about at length: "First, the person's picture is taken, full body and from the waist up. Then the face, frontal view; and then from the back of the head, and facing left and right. Afterwards, a machine is used to measure the width of the skull. The distances between the eyes, ears, nose, and mouth are measured as well as one's height and the length of one's hands and feet. . . . All of these measurements are taken while the person is nude. . . . There is nothing that is not recorded in great detail."[11]

Troubled by the hardships the Chinese in America underwent, Liang communicated these difficulties to his countrymen back in China. Kang Youwei also visited Montana to collaborate with branches of the CERA during this time of increasingly forceful action against the state's Chinese residents. He arrived in September 1905, just after the beginning of a major government initiative that reverberated through every Chinese community of Montana.

After a bureaucratic reshuffling of duties, the Chinese Service of the Bureau of Immigration conducted a special census of the Chinese in the Montana and Idaho region in the spring of 1905.[12] The census was part of a planned nationwide effort set to take place in specified regions, the first two being the Montana/Idaho region and the Pennsylvania/New Jersey region. Far different from a normal census, which surveys all residents for the collection of demographic information, the 1905 special census targeted the Chinese as a document check intended to verify who had the certificates that the Geary Act had required eleven years earlier. Chinese inspectors traveled throughout the state recording the details of each Chinese resident, including their occupation, their Geary Act certificate number, and their place of registration from both the 1894 compliance with the act and their location in 1905. With the Chinese population of Montana spread to all corners of the state, the inspectors, while thorough, could not survey every community. To fill in the gaps, the Chinese Service questioned postal workers about their knowledge of where isolated groups of Chinese resided. The census was supported by the full power of the state, including cooperation between immigration officials, revenue collectors, marshals, judges, and postal workers.

Officials conducting the 1905 census rousted not only laborers required to hold a Geary Act certificate but anyone of Chinese ethnicity, even if they had been exempted from carrying the required document. With the census focusing only on the Chinese, it was clear that they were singled out for harassment. Chinese inspector H. D. Ebey acknowledged that the roundups humiliated the Chinese, though his sentiments were expressed not out of sympathy but in a condescending manner, as he noted that a proud nation would not allow such actions to be taken against its citizens.[13]

The results of the special census provided the Bureau of Immigration an updated list of the Chinese residents in the state and intensified action against those found out of compliance with the Geary Act. Raids often exposed Chinese people without the proper documents, either because they failed to register, entered the country illegally, or because their certificate had been lost or destroyed, thus leading to deportation. As the *Western News* of Stevensville reported, "Chinese Inspector, Geo. E. Harris of Helena and City Marshal J.M. Higgins on last Saturday rounded up two chinks who could not show the proper clearance certificates and they were taken to Helena yesterday . . . where they will be tried and perhaps deported to the Flowery Kingdom. One of the chinks, Tom Fong by name, who has been employed in the Hong Kong restaurant here, claims that he was born in Missoula."[14] Similarly, Fort Benton's *River Press* noted, "Judging from the record in the clerk's office the federal court will have plenty to do during the coming year. During the last nine months [there have been] 10 Chinese deportation cases."[15]

Deportation measures proceeded quickly, as indicated by one case in Havre: "Chung Yick was arrested at Havre by Chinese Inspector Harris on Dec. 24, 1905, and was ordered deported by Justice W. B. Pyper on Wednesday, Dec. 27. Mr. Yick will soon start for the land of his nativity."[16] The speed that Chung Yick's case moved from arrest to deportation emphasized the 1893 *Fong Yue Ting v. U.S.* ruling. This case had established deportation as an administrative decision, therefore not requiring the accused be afforded constitutional protections such as due process, access to legal representation, the right to examine evidence, or the ability to summon witnesses on their own behalf.

The Geary Act's redefinition of who qualified to be in the exempt merchant group tightened again in 1902. These changes played out with real consequences. "Billings Chinaman Released at Helena is Arrested Again," announced one newspaper. "Although released on the charges of being illegally in this country, Yuen Chuen Kong, a Billings Chinaman, is still in jail at Helena. . . . At the hearing, he produced a merchant's certificate, but it was proved that he had been engaged in the restaurant business here."[17] During raids on Chinese communities throughout Montana, government inspectors doubted claims of merchant or student status, often going so far as to examine the hands of those detained for evidence of manual labor. For instance, agents arrested fourteen-year-old Missoula resident Tom

Sin, who was registered as a student. Officials doubted his claim of being a student because his hands had sores. When asked, "What caused your hands to be sore on the back?" Tom Sin answered that "It is a disease—it came about a week ago." This answer did not satisfy officials, who thought the sores were evidence of manual labor. On the strength of this evidence, officials deported Tom Sin.[18] Through increased funding, bureaucratic reorganization, and aggressive implementation, exclusionists finally enacted the restrictions initiated by the Geary Act and its subsequent enhancements.

Kang's visit to Montana in the fall of 1905 came as the ramifications of the special census reverberated throughout the communities he visited. Ongoing arrests, deportations, and general harassment challenged each community's standing in the state. The harassment seemed never-ending, with one small Chinese firm being raided by government inspectors nine times in less than two years.[19] As feared by some who opposed the Geary Act at its passing, government inspectors connected being Chinese with being in the nation illegally and made arbitrary arrests based on ethnicity. Montana's Chinese population decreased by more than 30 percent during the decade, with most of this decline occurring during the stringent application of Geary Act restrictions from 1902 to 1906 with Frank Sargent in charge of the Bureau of Immigration.

While resistance to the Geary Act from 1892 to 1894 had mobilized broad support throughout the large Chinese community within the United States, little attention was paid to this fight back in China. In some ways this was due to China dealing with larger issues. For instance, its struggles against the Japanese during the mid–1890s overlapped with the legal battles against the Geary Act. Many viewed the hardships of the Chinese in America as a regional, not national, issue. It must be remembered that the vast majority of the Chinese in America were from Guangdong Province and, more specifically, Taishan County. Residents of Taishan who had a vested interest in events in America like the struggle against the Geary Act paid close attention to American policies. Before a solid national identity had bound Chinese together in a common cause, however, slights against individuals from one region did not capture the attention of Chinese more broadly.

An example of this is the fact that news of the Boxer Rebellion (1899–1901) made little impression within Chinese communities in America. The Boxers were a phenomenon specific to conditions in Shandong province in northern China. The issues facing Shandong differed from the concerns of southern China. Chinese communities in Montana took little note of the actions of the Boxers, feeling no real connection to this group and its movement to oust foreigners from China.[20] To be sure, many American newspapers breathlessly reported on the violence against foreigners perpetrated by the Boxers, but Montana's Chinese expressed little connection with the rebels. As one Montana newspaper noted, "Local Chinamen . . . disclaim any sympathy with the Boxer movement and say that the rebellious Chinamen who have been causing all of the difficulty . . . are inspired by men who know nothing of foreigners and are only following the lead of unprincipled leaders."[21] A unified national identity had not yet emerged to the point that issues facing one region of China captured the attention of all Chinese people.

Despite the lack of global Chinese solidarity in the fight against the Geary Act in the 1890s, the struggle established communication networks and a fundraising apparatus that helped with future efforts. It was this network that the CERA unknowingly tapped into with the travels of Liang and Kang throughout America in 1903 and 1905, respectively. These tours exposed the exiled reformers to the struggles of the Chinese in America, moving what they had known of their harassment and humiliation from the theoretical to the concrete. In a tremendously short period of time, a burgeoning national identity emerged, sparked by the ongoing mistreatment of the Chinese in America combined with the global efforts of the CERA.

In their role as scholars and advisors to the emperor, Kang and Liang experienced little contact with the class of Chinese people who had migrated to North America for work. While visiting communities of Chinese workers, the exiled reformers sought support for the Guangxu Emperor and raised funds for the cause, even hoping that Chinese communities would form militia groups for a triumphant return to China to depose Dowager Empress Cixi. Kang and Liang initially worried little about the hardships facing Chinese laborers, instead focusing on the intricacies of Chinese court politics. When the issues facing Chinese people abroad did gain their attention, they focused on mistreatment of groups exempt from exclusion, such as high-profile cases of students, merchants, and diplomats who had been mistreated by American officials at ports of entry.

Chinese workers across the American West focused on more immediate goals intended to improve their circumstances in the United States by stopping the mistreatment they suffered through increasingly harsh federal laws. Willing to support the CERA because they believed a stronger China could protect its citizens abroad, Montana's Chinese communities proved a leading force in efforts connected to Kang and Liang's larger goals. The exiled reformers' partnerships with Montana's working-class Chinese altered a global movement to fight for better treatment of Chinese of all classes.

The earlier efforts undertaken to combat the Geary Act, including active noncompliance with the law followed by well-funded legal challenges, had not worked. A legal battle based on logical charges of the unconstitutional nature of the Geary Act had failed. Since moral and legal arguments failed to rouse Americans' sentiments, some thought an economic approach would work. Sparked to action by the ongoing harassment, arrests, and deportations, the tightening of the definition of exempted classes, and the invasive procedures of the Bertillon system, Liang, Kang, and others communicated these indignities to Chinese worldwide. These efforts increased popular awareness of the suffering of Chinese in America and sparked a well-coordinated economic boycott that is considered the beginning of modern nationalism in China.

The Gresham-Yang Treaty of 1894 expired in 1904 and the two nations began negotiations to craft a new agreement. Many Chinese people watched with great interest, hoping a new treaty would create more favorable conditions for those moving back and forth between the United States and China. Anti-Chinese forces in American politics used the lapse in the treaty to push for stronger restrictions. Kang, Liang, and others worried that Chinese diplomats were weakening in their resolve to fight for a better treaty. Unofficial Chinese leaders such as Kang and Liang, meanwhile, sought creative ways to influence the negotiations between the nations.[22]

In the spring of 1905, Kang, Liang, and others used their global network of activists and seized on changing conditions within China to launch a boycott of American products intended to influence American lawmakers to soften restrictions on and harassment of Chinese people. In early May 1905, Kang and Liang issued telegrams to Chinese communities around the globe urging that they view the cause of the Chinese in America as the cause of the Chinese people more broadly. Advocating for a shared national spirit and united efforts to fight for their countrymen suffering indignities abroad, these arguments struck a chord. Throughout early May, Chinese groups in the United States, Hawaii, and the Philippines sent more than twenty separate pieces of correspondence urging action against the continued mistreatment of the Chinese and the harsh immigration restrictions.[23] The development of a shared identity and unified spirit to resist harassment against the Chinese in America built upon earlier resistance against the Geary Act and the global network created to advance the CERA.

It is ironic that the CERA, which was illegal in China, was a leading force initiating the boycott of American goods throughout China. While the vast majority of the Chinese seeking relief from humiliation and oppression in America were from southern China, the boycott movement that took up their cause began in outside that region in the city of Shanghai. Several factors led to Shanghai becoming the site where the boycott started. Shanghai was the main economic port of entry to the China market and the foreign population of the city had boomed, bringing western culture, ideas, and modes of communication into contact with a vibrant local culture of protest and demonstration.[24] Foreign goods flowed into Shanghai to then be distributed throughout the nation. Foreign trading firms dominated parts of the city. Striking a blow to U.S. economic interests by direct action against American goods in Shanghai proved a perfect fit between ideology and opportunity.

Numerous foreign powers divided jurisdiction of Shanghai after wresting control of the city from the Qing dynasty following the end of the First Opium War in 1842. Qing officials retained authority in the Chinese portions of the city but not in the vast areas controlled by the French, British, Japanese, Americans and other foreign powers. The city subsequently rose to prominence as the center for trade throughout the region, attracting foreign investors and Chinese laborers in great numbers. This mixture of cultures and the freedom that came through the fragmented nature of control of the city allowed an intellectual flourishing and a vibrant culture of urban activism and protest not seen in other Chinese cities. Though still considered an enemy of the Qing government with a price on his head, Liang Qichao used the confusion of the fragmented nature of Shanghai to his advantage, returning to China to begin his efforts to influence American treatment of Chinese in the United States through economic pressure.[25]

The city's emerging newspaper industry allowed dissemination of the boycott strategy to the literate class of Chinese. Liang Qichao founded the newspaper *Shi Bao* shortly before the official start of the boycott and each edition featured descriptions of the mistreatment of Chinese in America and calls to action from Kang.[26] Shanghai consul general James Rodgers noted the leading role played by the CERA in initiating the boycott: "It is generally admitted that the movement, which is the natural outcome of such an organization as that perfected for the boycott work, is really the expression of allegiance to the reform cause of Kang Yu-wei."[27]

While of a different kind than the harassment faced by overseas Chinese, Chinese residents of Shanghai also felt humiliation at the hands of foreign governments. Since the imposition of unequal treaties after the Opium Wars, foreigners controlled large parts of China, and Shanghai specifically. Furthermore, through the principle of extraterritoriality, they were not held accountable to Chinese laws. The humiliation that Chinese felt about not being fully in control of their nation and not being able to hold foreigners to account seemed analogous to the indignities they heard their countrymen suffering through the reporting of Liang's *Shi Bao*. John Endicott Gardner, a Chinese inspector in San Francisco, obtained key documents on the boycott, noting the methods used by its leaders to spread information and to coordinate boycott efforts. Gardner reported to President Roosevelt that "Kang Yu Wei has a pupil who is at the head of one of the Shanghai dailies, from which position he is directing the thought of the Chinese in and around Shanghai on the matter of the boycott."[28]

In addition to publication of grievances through *Shi Bao*, Liang and his compatriots worked behind the scenes in Shanghai to convince leading merchants of the need for action against American business interests. Through these discussions, the powerful Shanghai Chamber of Commerce agreed that an economic approach might succeed in forcing better treatment of Chinese in America.[29]

Supporting the boycott had economic consequences. Merchants who refused to sell American goods lost out on trade and investments made in previously purchased merchandise. Workers who refused to transport American goods or who quit jobs working for American firms or as domestic help suffered financial consequences. The fact that merchants and workers in Shanghai and throughout China willingly suffered economic hardship to support the Chinese in America speaks to a growing sense of a national spirit, a recognition that mistreatment of any Chinese individual was a slight to all Chinese people. Inspired that action was beginning, Kang sought to stir more support from Chinese communities around the globe, as evidenced by his poem distributed through CERA networks:

> Watch a European with a dog wagging its tail, both landed,
> walking away slowly.
> Chinese should be grieving, lower than a dog.
> Why so despicable, so disgraceful?
> Our own country is too weak . . .
>
> There are 100,000 Chinese in this country.
> We can pool together 100,000,000 dollars.
> Since we have such rich resources and powerful strength, why are
> we afraid?
> We vow to resist the great oppression.
> We vow to work together and cooperate with one another.
> We vow to wipe out our shame and disgrace.

We would risk our lives to fight against exclusion to accomplish
our goal.
My fellow compatriots, do you hear me?[30]

Indeed, Chinese around the world did hear. Reporting on conditions in Shanghai, Liang Qichao echoed the impact of such sentiments: "In the last month, everyone in Shanghai has been thinking about and talking about the Exclusion Treaty. From millionaires to poor workers, millions of people are of one mind, and we must not stop until we win back our rights! . . . All the foreigners in Shanghai have become worried, saying that China, the sleeping lion, has awakened. Since the treaty ports were established, there has never been any activity like this. It shows that we Chinese are not easily bullied."[31]

With the merchants of Shanghai mobilized and the news spreading to all classes of Chinese people, the boycott of American goods went into effect on August 1, 1905. Foreign correspondents in Shanghai took note, with *London Times* reporter George Morrison writing, "The Chinese have awakened to a consciousness of nationality. Outrages on Cantonese who have emigrated to the Pacific coast are no longer resented only by the people of Kwangtung [Guangdong]. They make all Chinese indignant."[32]

Montana's newspapers reported on the boycott and the intended goals of the effort: "The Chinese believed they read in the American the love of the almighty dollar, and are attempting to force retrenchment in the Chinese exclusion law by crippling so far as they are able, our commercial industries in the Orient."[33] As had been the case in the fight against the Geary Act, contributions poured in from Chinese people throughout the nation. Montana newspapers reported that "Chinamen throughout the world have been banded together for the purpose of raising a fund to fight the Chinese exclusion law of the United States."[34] While the Chinese in America could not realistically participate in the boycott of American goods, financial contributions flowed in from Chinese communities in Montana to help support workers in Shanghai and elsewhere who took part in the boycott by refusing to transport American goods or refusing to work for American firms.[35] Montana's press noted the role of newspapers, a recent development in China, in spreading the news of the boycott. As reported in the *Havre Herald*, one American missionary attributed "the spread of the boycott in great part to the power of the new native press. A few years ago there was no such thing as a Chinese press. Now in all of the large cities it is a common sight to see natives reading their own dailies, and these papers have been foremost in promoting the boycott movement and carrying it into the interior."[36]

The boycott effort coincided with a publication boom and the news quickly spread beyond Shanghai, taking hold in port cities and regions across the nation. Virtually every newspaper had columns detailing boycott events and updates, as well as descriptions of ongoing humiliations of Chinese people in America. Essay contests urged students to write their thoughts about the boycott. One trimonthly magazine published in Guangzhou began with the sole purpose of spreading news about the boycott, including schedules of boycott-related events, information on how to identify American goods, and updates on treaty negotiations.[37] With illiteracy rates across China high, boycott leaders realized that spreading news of the effort through newspapers alone was insufficient. Simply winning over literate Chinese people to the cause of their countrymen in need would not be enough to impact American economic interests and prompt change. To spread word of the boycott strategy and build support across all classes, leaders used other means including speeches by street-corner performers, drama troupes, illustrated handbills and posters, and refashioned folk songs featuring boycott-related information. [38]

With multiple means of spreading the message and an emerging sense of national identity, the boycott movement spanned all social classes and reached all regions of China. The *Billings Gazette* noted "that the boycott has assumed surprising proportions, students being especially conspicuous in the demonstrations, but all classes, even the retiring Chinese woman, taking part and creating a sentiment that will be hard to allay."[39]

With the boycott fully underway, Americans worried about the potential economic impact. American trade with China had increased dramatically over the previous decade, from $3.8 million in 1895 to almost $54.4 million in 1905. American products targeted by the boycott included cotton goods, petroleum products, tobacco, and flour. Additionally, soap, candles, cosmetics, and hardware were key imports to the China market.[40] To inform Chinese supporters of the boycott and how to identify American goods, newspapers carried diagrams of seals of American corporations and exhibition rooms displayed American products to educate Chinese consumers what to avoid. Placards appeared in Chinese shops calling on Confucian relationships and a sense of justice to spread the spirit of the boycott: "Fathers must instruct their children, elder brothers must exhort their younger brethren. Let each one tell his neighbor, so that ten may infect one hundred, and one hundred a thousand; thus China's four hundred millions may join their forces; thus strength may come where weakness was, and the start be accomplished. In any affair all that is necessary is a stout heart; by it, mountains are shaken." [41]

American consular officials in Shanghai reported about this activity to the White House, noting the widespread support for the boycott. "Total value of foreign goods likely to feel the effect in Shanghai alone has been estimated at $25,000,000.00 gold," they reported. "Boycott has now spread to all sections. . . . The damage done to American interests in Middle China alone is immense."[42]

Montanans were particularly concerned about the potential impact the boycott would have on the state's agricultural economy, specifically wheat. Montana farmers were increasingly connected with an international market and hoped to maximize profits by engaging in the vast opportunities trade in Asia offered: "There is a widely prevalent opinion that the Oriental trade of the Asiatic millions is the greatest commercial prize of the age, and that it will absorb the entire wheat surplus of the Pacific coast."[43] Coupled with this optimism about tapping into the Chinese market, Montana farmers produced a bumper wheat crop just as the boycott began. "The wheat crop for 1905 will make a new high record. . . . Taken altogether, the prospects undoubtedly are that this will be the most phenomenally abundant of all crop years the United States has ever known."[44] Yet the same headlines that reported record harvests also carried concerns, notably from James J. Hill, president of the Northern Pacific Railway: "President Hill is worried over the probable boycott of American flour by China. It really is something to be worried about, but we are of the opinion that a Chink who has eaten flour flapjacks will never again be satisfied with rice."[45] The reporter's flippant remarks about Chinese dining habits were little relief, as the boycott's effects continued into the fall and winter.

The situation warranted concern. A December article in the *Billings Gazette* reported, "A steamerload of flour recently arrived at one of the Chinese ports . . . but no purchaser was found, although the flour was offered cheap."[46] Reports through Seattle reinforced the seriousness of the situation: "The Chinese boycott has paralyzed the flour trade between Pacific ports and China. No sales have been made since July 15, and all orders for September shipment have been canceled."[47]

The campaign against American flour highlights how various levels of Chinese society mobilized for the cause. To inform the mostly illiterate urban working classes and rural peasants, boycott organizers adapted lyrics from traditional folk songs to advance the cause. For instance, before the Mid-Autumn Festival, when mooncakes are traditionally prepared, a folk song encouraged the people to take up the cause of boycotting American flour:

It is about the time of the Mid-Autumn Festival.
Tens of thousands of families
have their mooncakes ready
to celebrate the bright moon.
But if you use American flour,
the cake will not be clean.
Flour from the Flower Flag [America]
is [made] with Chinese blood. . . .
So, please make a change
and use rice flour to make mooncakes . . .
Let us unite together
with our body and soul;

let us make a resolution to eat our own products,
Thus, the moon and the sun will be bright again.[48]

As the song indicated, many switched to wheat flour substitutes such as rice flour. Other alternatives arose to fill the void created by the boycott. An emerging Chinese flour industry that began around 1900 sought to serve as an alternative for domestic consumers. Aided by the prohibition on purchasing American products, Sun Duosen, an entrepreneur and minor government official, built a series of mills using new technologies and expertise gained earlier from American corporations and consultants. In addition to Sun's mills, other locally owned flour mills emerged in the years before the boycott, six in the Shanghai area from 1900 to 1904 and nine more around the time of the boycott. Though not initially producing enough flour to seriously challenge U.S. imports on the open market, the prohibition on purchasing American goods with the boycott of 1905 was a boon for Chinese companies.[49] Joining the boycott through a combination of righteous indignation against the mistreatment of their countrymen and economic self-interest, the participation of merchants and industrialists in the boycott exemplifies the complex motivations driving the effort.

These Chinese flour mills operated at high capacity during the boycott, helping to meet demand not only in Shanghai but also across the nation.[50] American producers took note, expressing concern about the long-term impact should the embargo continue. As Stevensville, Montana's *Western News* reported in January 1906, "Unless the Chinese boycott on American goods is removed within the next 30 days the plant of the Centennial Milling company, with a capacity of 2400 barrels of flour per day, and that of the Hammond Milling company, with its daily capacity of 2000, will be forced practically to close down."[51] Lewistown's *Fergus County Argus* similarly noted that "American trade with China has fallen off 95 per cent in the past year. . . . the Chinese are going into the Australian market for their flour, paying prices higher than for the American product."[52]

Indeed, the boycott afforded Chinese flour producers with significant opportunities. By 1910, buoyed by the gains made from 1905 to 1906, Chinese flour had seized hold of the domestic market, supplanting American flour in all major cities throughout China.[53] The many means of spreading the boycott message, including newspapers, street performers, drama troupes, and student essay contests, furthered support across China. The boycott expanded throughout all major urban areas in China, into the countryside, and to anywhere that Chinese people had spread through migration.

Though it was not possible for the Chinese in Montana to stop purchasing American goods, they were aware of the ongoing boycott efforts and made financial contributions to the cause. American officials noted the irony that money earned in the United States supported boycotters in China. San Francisco immigration official John Endicott Gardner noted: "It cannot but be regretted that part of the money going toward the defraying of expenses incidental to the maintaining of the boycott on American goods, and towards the spread of inflammatory literature detrimental to the interests of the United States, and possibly the lives and property of American citizens in China, should be money made by Chinese in the United States."[54]

As Gardner's comments indicate, many Americans thought the boycott would eventually turn violent. To Gardner's point about the funding of "inflammatory literature," the extent of boycott propaganda was so thorough that Montana newspapers even featured some images and placards meant to spread the calls for the boycott throughout China. For instance, the *River Press* of Fort Benton, a town of just over one thousand inhabitants and fewer than forty Chinese residents, reprinted a pro-boycott image along with an explanation of the pressures put on the Chinese to refuse American goods. The article claimed that the text "threatened with death those who refuse to obey instructions" and that those working for American firms "must give up their employment unless they wish to be shot or have their throats cut, their houses burned down and their families destroyed."[55] In fact, the image and text, while informing the public of the upcoming boycott and stressing the need for solidarity, did not mention threats of death or destruction. Turtle imagery was common throughout boycott propaganda. The characters

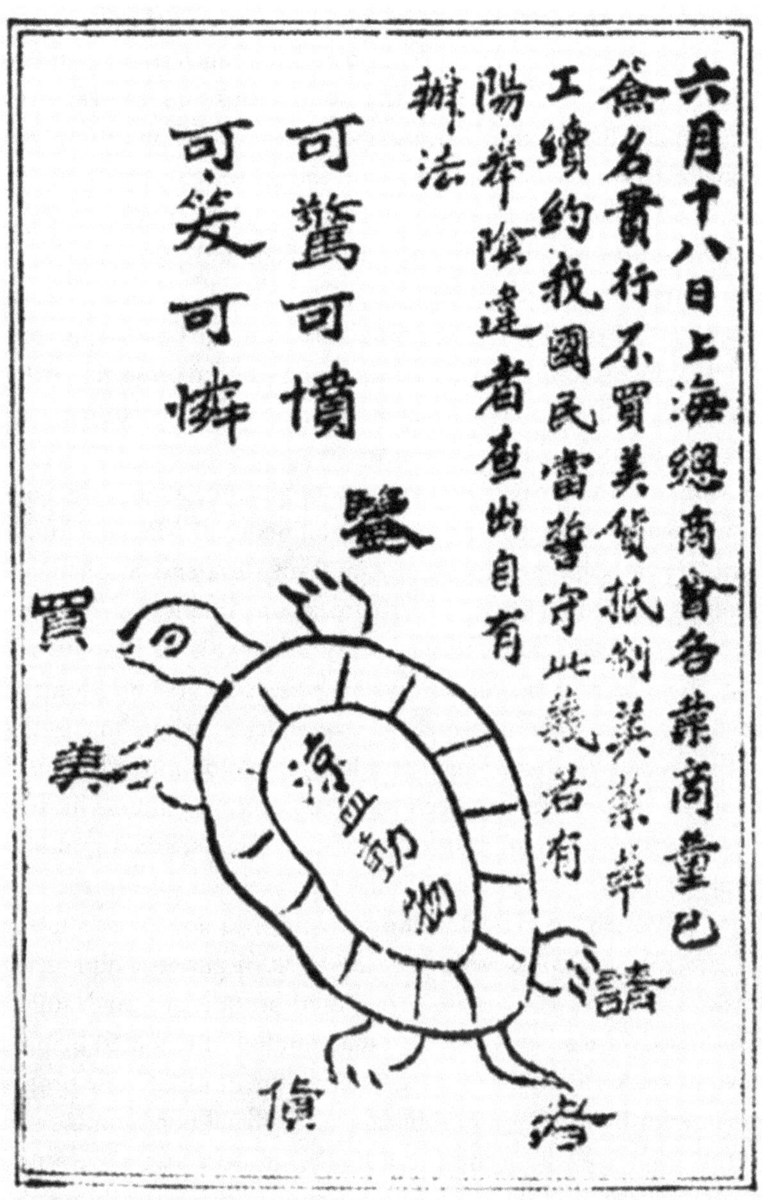

15. Turtle imagery, commonly used by pro-boycott groups in 1905, was used to indicate that any Chinese person who did not support the boycott was a cold-blooded animal. "That Chinese Boycott," *River Press* (Fort Benton MT), February 14, 1906.

around the turtle and the writing on the shell suggests that anyone who buys American goods is a cold-blooded animal, unsympathetic to the cause of fighting against the hated exclusion laws. That this image made its way into a newspaper in rural Montana shows the global reach of the boycott effort and the growing interconnectedness of Chinese communities around the world. The tendency of the American press to insert salacious accounts of death threats exposes a common thread in the reporting of Chinese-related topics. When Montana's newspapers covered issues related to the Chinese, reporters often focused with fascination and exaggeration on secret societies, blood feuds, and Tong Wars, exoticizing Chinese culture to sell newspapers to a public eager for mystery.

Montana's newspapers stoked fears of violence among the boycotters against foreigners in China. Headlines read "Massacre Imminent," "Fear Chinese Uprising: American Residents at Shanghai Looking for Trouble," and "Fear Attacks on Americans." [56] Given the violence against foreigners five years earlier with the Boxer Rebellion, these fears of violent outbursts were not surprising. Montana newspapers played on this threat of mass violence, reminding readers of that earlier bloodshed and spreading reports of impending antiforeign outbursts. As had been the case in recent Chinese history, threats against foreign nationals in China often sparked multinational military incursions that purportedly aimed to stop the violence, but often led to further efforts by the invading forces to carve up control of Chinese territory. The threat of gunboat diplomacy was ever present. For instance, an American official near Nanjing sent President Roosevelt a confiscated handbill distributed by pro-boycott students depicting the brutal treatment of Chinese people in America by immigration officials. The official noted ominously in the letter, "We have the *U.S.S. Quiros* in port here at present," reminding the president that force could be exerted to break the boycott when needed.[57]

The leaders of the boycott continually emphasized that their efforts should remain peaceful. Organizers advocated "civilized boycott" actions, "That is, to use peaceful means without much fanfare yet powerfully enough to paralyze American commerce."[58] Any violent

16. A placard, in Chinese, detailing the treatment of Chinese immigrants by American officials, meant to encourage support for the 1905 boycott. Chinkiang, China, August 7, 1905. 58/12264, Chinese General Correspondence, 1898–1908, RG 85, National Archives, Washington DC.

outburst against foreigners in China would undercut the morality of the boycott as a righteous stance against unjust treatment of the Chinese in America. An event in October 1905, however, tested the resolve of the protestors to remain peaceful. An American military official and his son were involved an incident near Nanjing, roughly 180 miles west of Shanghai. According to several news reports, the reason for this attack was clear: "The assault upon Rear-Admiral Charles J. Train, commander-in-chief of the American Asiatic squadron, and his son Lieut. Charles R. Train, by a mob of Chinese peasants displaying unmistakable signs of race prejudice." Reporters believed that "it is plain that the anti-American feeling, which has been assiduously cultivated in China, was what moved the ignorant and ugly natives. It has threatened other Americans over there. Admiral Train is one of the most genial and good-natured men to be found . . . [the attack] was for some larger reason than anything personal."[59] Buried in these stories was the inciting incident that caused the action against Train and his group. While pheasant hunting, Admiral Train's son accidentally shot a Chinese woman. Locals surrounded and disarmed the hunting party. Eventually a contingent of forty marines from the USS *Quiros* landed and rescued the Admiral's party. American forces shot and wounded two Chinese men during the altercation. While many reports were quick to blame the attack on the "race prejudice" of the "ignorant and ugly natives," Montana's *Anaconda Standard* reported the details more directly, and, given the sentiments expressed in the article, quite tellingly: "Shooting of Chinese is Nothing Unusual: Common Occurrence with Hunters in the Orient: Woman Becomes Hysterical: This rouses the people, who mob Admiral Train."[60] The American press expressed surprise and disappointment that Chinese officials seemed sympathetic with the "mob," reporting that "an alarming feature of the reports from Nanjing is the attitude of the Chinese authorities, who are represented as having upheld the mob's action in attacking Admiral Train and capturing his son."[61] This incident with Admiral Train and the overall issue of the boycott highlights the difficult position of the Chinese government during the events of 1905.

Many Chinese officials hoped the economic pressure of the boycott would force the U.S. government to agree to a treaty with more favorable terms than the Gresham-Yang Treaty of 1894. Additionally, many government officials, moved by the stories of Chinese students and diplomats harassed while traveling to the United States, agreed with the sentiment of the boycott. These views could not be stated publicly, however, for fear of angering American diplomats. Newly appointed U.S. minister to China William Rockhill sought to intimidate the Chinese government into ending the boycott. Rockhill continually informed the Chinese government "that the United States would hold it directly responsible for all losses our trade or other interests may have incurred, or may hereafter incur, on account of its failure to protect us in the rights guaranteed us under Article XV of our Treaty of 1858." Rockhill also informed Chinese officials that ongoing discussions to determine a new treaty in replacement of the Gresham-Yang Treaty of 1894 would not proceed until the boycott had ended. Finally, Rockhill identified a key boycott leader, a local government official, and demanded that he "be deprived of his rank and otherwise punished."[62] As the boycott spread throughout China, taking hold across class lines, it became largely a leaderless movement, making the elimination of one or two charismatic leaders meaningless amid the wave of nationalist unity sweeping the country. Rockhill's mounting frustration with Chinese officials and his inability to affect definitive action are evident throughout his communications with Secretary of State Hay and President Roosevelt.

At the same time, President Roosevelt received numerous requests from American business leaders to resolve the situation in order to stem economic losses and prevent their exclusion from the precious Chinese market. Communications reached the president from the Washington State Millers Association, wholesale furnishers from San Francisco, the Northern Pacific Railway Company, the Cotton Goods Export Association of New York, and the Trans-Mississippi Commercial Congress. The chambers of commerce of Portland and Tacoma requested that Roosevelt soften the government's stance on Chinese immigration to protect American business relationships with China. Interestingly, especially considering that Tacoma had violently expelled its Chinese residents in 1885, these calls also included requests to loosen restrictions on laborers as "the states west of the Rockies need workers."[63]

While some white westerners worried that increased deportations would reduce the availability of Chinese workers, boycott leaders began their efforts by intentionally omitting calls to allow the increased admission of workers. Instead, they focused on securing better treatment for exempt classes. Kang Youwei, for instance, expressed his views on who should be allowed to enter the United States: "America is making a great mistake in adopting such stringent laws to exclude the Chinese. Of course, these laws are passed to keep out our lower class of cheap labor. However, their rigid enforcement is excluding a desirable class of Chinese." He continued, "Upper class people, businessmen, travelers, and students ought to be treated with leniency."[64] Kang and most boycott advocates ignored the mistreatment of working-class Chinese already in the United States. Other high-ranking Chinese officials expressed the sentiment with more callousness toward Chinese working classes. Wong Kai Kah, former Chinese minister to England, noted that:

> the coolies who come to [America] are from Canton [Guangzhou] and vicinity and are the most despised people in the empire. We do not care whether you exclude them . . . But we do object to the inhuman treatment to which our merchants, professional men and travelers are subjected. . . . They are met at the wharf by a none too polite inspector, who drives them, with curses, if not with blows, into a filthy pen. There they are herded with filthy coolies . . . If they protest mildly, they are cursed afresh and even subjected to blows, are called "chinks" and told to "shut up."[65]

Wong's unsympathetic position toward the Chinese workers was due to the class divisions, regional differences, and the fact that he had few opportunities to interact with working-class Chinese. Similarly, throughout his time in North America, Kang Youwei generally interacted with Chinese elites and sympathetic Americans who admired his intellect, cultured ways, and the romantic notion of his challenge to the dowager empress. Through his connections in the highest levels of society, Kang gained access to President Roosevelt. During two meetings in June 1905, on the eve of the start of the boycott, Kang advocated for better treatment not of Chinese laborers coming to or already within the United States but of Chinese exempt from the exclusion laws.[66]

Roosevelt agreed with Kang's message both because he understood that immigration officials had treated Chinese migrants with exceeding harshness and because he hoped to protect American business interests by bringing a quick end to the boycott. Following his meetings with Kang and a consultation with his cabinet members, Roosevelt issued new guidelines for immigration officials that required more courteous treatment of Chinese travelers entering the United States.[67] The new standards held that "officers charged with the enforcement of the laws are cautioned to act with discretion. While laborers must be strictly excluded, the law must be enforced without harshness, and unnecessary inconvenience or annoyance must not be caused such persons as are entitled to enter the United States. Chinese persons whose appearance or situation clearly indicates that they do not belong to the class of laborers must be treated with the same consideration extended to members of any other nationality."[68]

These concessions pleased Chinese leaders like Wong Kai Kah who resented being lumped in with Chinese workers, a group for which he had few sympathies. Boycott advocates also welcomed the changes, excited to see their efforts have results. They continued the economic pressure throughout summer and fall hoping for even more concessions.

Regarding issues relating to working-class Chinese, in his December address to Congress, Roosevelt reaffirmed his view, shared by Kang and other boycott leaders, that softening treatment of Chinese elites at the ports of entry did not mean throwing the door open to Chinese workers: "Chinese students, business and professional men of all kinds—not only merchants, but bankers, doctors, manufacturers, professors, travelers, and the like—should be encouraged to come here . . . Much trouble has come during the past Summer from the organized boycott against American goods which has been started in China. The main factor in producing this boycott has been the resentment . . . against the harshness of our law toward educated Chinamen of the professional and business classes."[69]

Certainly, this statement to Congress and President Roosevelt's actions earlier in June were significant concessions to boycott advocates protesting the harsh treatment of exempted Chinese travelers. These proclamations, however, did little to alleviate the harassment experienced by Chinese laborers already within the United States.

By January 1906 Kang's focus shifted dramatically. Kang took up the cause of the working-class Chinese, broadening the goals of the boycott for the first time to include their concerns. What had changed? Between his June meetings with Roosevelt and his January letter to the president, Kang spent extensive time in Montana touring Chinese communities to build support for the CERA. Kang met Chinese workers who had fought the hated Geary Act through strategic noncompliance, waged successful legal battle against a Butte boycott that had been designed to force their expulsion, and built twelve CERA branches, including one with an active militia that trained with live ammunition.[70] When Kang visited in September 1905, however, this empowered, active, engaged community of Chinese workers was reeling from the impact of the special census, raids, arrests, and deportations. Had he visited when Liang Qichao came through two years earlier, he would have seen a much larger Chinese community. Deportations had reduced the Chinese population in Montana by 23 percent in just three years.[71]

Through his visits to large Chinese communities in Butte, Helena, and Billings and to smaller Chinese communities across the state, Kang came into extended contact with laundry and restaurant workers, gardeners, peddlers, miners, wood cutters, and railroad section hands. Chinese who were deported often connected their plight with the ongoing boycott, which they viewed as key to advocating for their protection. Chen Bow, a Chinese resident of Billings deported for violating the Geary Act, vowed, as reported in pidgin English in the *Billings Gazette*: "The Melican man make Chinese boy go back home when he gotta right to stay here, but Chinee boy all same boycott Melican goods and tell people of his country how he was treated here."[72]

Exposure to the hardships of Montana's working-class Chinese population stirred Kang's sympathy for this group. Many had been in Montana since before the passage of the Chinese Exclusion Act in 1882. They built the infrastructure of the state and had technological knowledge, not to mention experience with the American legal system that could prove useful to modernizing China. Kang's interactions with the Chinese laborers in Montana who faced these harsh realities and who wholeheartedly supported the anti-American boycott, changed his perspective on the demands of the boycott. Following his time in Montana, Kang again appealed to President Roosevelt. In a twenty-six-page letter authored from Mexico City in January 1906, Kang continued his calls for better treatment of Chinese but focused more intently on the policies as they affected Chinese workers. Kang indicated an awareness of the previous circumstances that

17. Billings, Montana, resident Chen Bow while arrested and awaiting deportation. Chinese Exclusion Case Files, 1895–1943, file 4/282, RG 85, National Archives, Seattle WA.

welcomed Chinese workers, notably the Burlingame Treaty, which provided essential workers in the process of constructing the Central Pacific railroad: "45 years ago . . . [Chinese] were urged to emigrate to America for the purpose of building railroads, by means of which the great Western country could be opened for settlement [which] increased enormously the wealth of this Republic. But the Chinese laborers in the work of tunneling through mountains, clearing forests and filling hollows . . . suffered from exposure to the inclemencies of the weather . . . so that thousands of them perished."

Reminding President Roosevelt of the contributions made by Chinese workers, Kang emphasized how the intensification of legal action against them dishonored these contributions and violated the spirit of American law "since those laws see a guilty laborer and illegal resident in every Chinese person . . . [they] reverse that maxim of common law, which ways that a man is innocent until he is proven guilty, thus placing the burden of proof on the Chinese suspect himself." Kang lingered on the humiliations caused by the Bertillon system, which he claimed, "is only used by other nations for the identification of criminals." Noting that even those Chinese "with requisite certification are . . . transferred to a detention pen, where they are measured and their naked bodies are fumigated and where they are packed and confined in dirty quarters like tramps and fed on a prison diet." Broadening his complaints beyond concerns for diplomats, students, and other exempt classes, Kang began to advocate for common workers harassed by the Geary Act and the special census. Kang noted the indignation of the Chinese people

> when they are hunted down as illegally residing in this country . . . [due to exclusion laws,] each harsher and more drastic than its predecessor; resulting in the employment of an army of officials to enforce their provisions. . . . The Geary Law . . . established the system of identification, rigid inspection, sudden arrest, imprisonment and deportation of all whose only crime was a desire to earn a living like other people. . . . The Chinese inspectors are invested with full power to break into houses and stores of Chinese suspects and to make arrests at all hours of the day and night.

Kang's letter continued to emphasize the plight of Chinese workers by noting, "So it seems that no matter who they are, so long as they are Chinese persons, they must suffer these indignities. The result is that the whole Chinese population whether of high or low degree, whether educated or ignorant, is disaffected towards Americans. This disaffection is now manifested in the boycott."[73]

Again, Kang's connection to Roosevelt produced results. In February 1906 Roosevelt took further action to reduce the harsh treatment of Chinese seeking to enter America and those already in the United States. The federal government ended the humiliating Bertillon System of identification, stopped the ongoing special census, agreed to allow Chinese to present witnesses on their behalf, lengthened the period for appeals, and transferred the most intransigent immigration officials away from positions relating to Chinese travelers.[74] A 1906 report to Congress from the Bureau of Immigration speaks to the influence of the boycott and general resistance from the Chinese in the West: "Since the institution of the boycott no arrests have been made in the interior." Regarding the special census, which the bureau had planned to conduct nationwide, "The Chinese persistently resisted and obstructed the efforts of the officers . . . finally, such a storm of protest arose that the Department ordered officers to desist from any further efforts." The report noted the leadership of Kang in these efforts, citing a letter from him that connected exclusionary policies with the boycott: "Two decades' rigid enforcement of the exclusion laws has brought about the ill will of 400 million people. The exclusion of Chinese labor on the one side is now met by the boycott of American products on the other."[75]

The boycott persisted, spreading from its base in Shanghai across most of China and into the consciousness of Chinese communities around the world. Kang's time with the working-class Chinese community in Montana made him attuned to the struggles this group faced. Using the ongoing boycott and their global reform network, Kang and Liang made the conditions facing Chinese workers in the United States known to and a concern of Chinese elsewhere who previously felt little connection with this group. Plans for the boycott's continuation into another year fell apart, however, partially due to the San Francisco earthquake in April 1906, as the needs of the city's large Chinese community took precedence. Some Americans thought the destruction of records in the earthquake and fire presented an opportunity to take decisive action against the Chinese. As reported in the *Fergus County Argus*, "The San Francisco Chinamen are up against it . . . twenty thousand of them have lost their certificates of residence in the quake and fire and are in danger of deportation. . . . It may be the means of getting rid of many of the undesirable 'chinks.'"[76] The destruction of records instead opened a path for thousands more Chinese to enter the United States by claiming that they were native born and that evidence of their birth in America and resulting citizenship had been destroyed in the fire.

Though the boycott ultimately failed to end the Geary Act or to force a treaty favorable to China's interests, Chinese communities in America gained key concessions. Overall harassment of Chinese people at the borders and in the interior declined. For instance, the rejection rate for Chinese seeking entry to the United States went from 29.4 percent in 1904 to 7.0 precent in 1906.[77] Additionally, arrests and deportations of those already in America declined by two-thirds after 1905.[78]

In a larger sense, the boycott provided the shared experience of advocating for the just treatment of Chinese people of all classes, established communication and advocacy networks around the world, and built a foundation of shared national identity that grew through the first decades of the twentieth century. Traveling through the American West put these exiled Chinese intellectuals in touch with a class of their countrymen that they otherwise would never have encountered. The borderlands atmosphere of Shanghai allowed these reformers the opportunity to launch a global protest movement, sparking the first manifestation of unified Chinese nationalism. This movement had its unlikely roots in the experience of the Chinese in the American West.

SIX

Chinese Religious and Burial Practices

While the enforcement of the Geary Act and the implementation of the 1905 special census caused disruptions throughout Montana's Chinese communities—contributing to the decline of the population by more than 50 percent from 1890 to 1910—natural life processes added to this population decline. Due to the gender imbalance, the often-dangerous nature of their work, and the increasing age of the population, Chinese communities had far more funerals to witness than births to celebrate. Montana's newspapers include frequent accounts of Chinese funerals from the early days of the territory through the 1940s. A funeral for Lung Yoo, a Chinese woman who died in Virginia City in May 1867, caused a serious spectacle: "Intensely interested, with wide distended eyes and a most ludicrous desire to see who could get nearest the grave without falling in, were several hundred people of every nationality represented in Montana . . . all in one conglomerate mass, mounted on horses, wagons . . . while a portion stood on the earth, but none on their dignity."[1] The author's limited interactions with the Chinese celebrants due to the language and cultural barriers clouded their ability to understand these rituals. Accounts written by Montanans who viewed the Chinese as unwelcome and to be excluded lingered on the oddity of their practices and labeled their expressions of spirituality heathen superstitions. Often, however, newspaper articles, even while emphasizing the exotic and foreign nature of Chinese ceremonies, reported with respect and genuine interest in the practices.

To a predominantly Christian population, the spiritual beliefs and expressions of the Chinese seemed exotic and curious at best, heathen and silly at worst. One report in 1918 noted that a Chinese funeral took place "with all the mystic rites of the Orient."[2] Some Montana newspapers sought a more specific categorization, describing Chinese beliefs as Confucian and observing that a funeral was for the "death of a disciple of Confucius" or claiming that offerings at a temple were to satisfy "the wants, whims and caprices of the graven image of Confucius."[3] At other times, journalists described the spiritual beliefs of the Chinese as Buddhism: "At the grave the coffin was placed on the ground and a Chinaman in blue jumper and overalls began the Buddhist burial rites. Kneeling on the ground and uttering this unintelligible jargon."[4] A report on a funeral conducted in 1928 showed more honesty about not truly understanding the exact spiritual systems practiced, noting that the burial was conducted by "Chinese who understood how to conduct a Chinese funeral, whether under the Buddhistic or Taoist [*sic*] religion is unknown."[5] This last expression approximates the truth more than the author could have known.

The spiritual beliefs of Chinese migrants combined elements from Confucianism, Buddhism, and Daoism. Folk traditions that developed regionally over thousands of years added to the eclectic spiritual synthesis.[6] Confucian elements infused Chinese practices with an emphasis on order, filial piety, and respect and reverence for ancestors demonstrated through the performance of rituals. Daoist beliefs are evidenced through the emphasis on harmony with nature and the balance of forces—*yin* and *yang*—that flow through the universe. Daoist and Buddhist beliefs in supernatural forces that exert influence on the living are clearly seen in funeral practices, seasonal religious celebrations, and formal temples, sites of prayer where attendees also left offerings in hopes of influencing the spirit world to look with graciousness on the living.[7]

In a strange land far from home, Montana's Chinese residents gained comfort from the continuation of their spiritual practices. Many communities had temples—referred to as Joss houses by the non-Chinese community—where believers observed yearly religious holidays.[8] Depending on the size and wealth of the population, these temples were either standalone structures or located in corners of local homes or businesses. For instance, in Anaconda, where the Chinese community had declined in the face of boycotts in 1885 and again in 1893, the temple was in a local laundry: "In this establishment the god of love, war, prosperity and peace makes his home in one corner of the laundry department. The Anaconda joss is not a very pretentious god, yet he receives much reverence . . . In Anaconda he is merely a gaudy colored picture of an almond-eyed heathen."[9] With a much larger Chinese community than Anaconda, Butte had several temples during the late nineteenth and early twentieth centuries.

In 1899 Wong Ken Chung, keeper for the Butte Chinese temple, gave a lengthy interview to a reporter from the *Anaconda Standard*. Claiming to be 107 years old, Wong had served as the temple keeper for several decades, noting that the "joss house location has been moved three times since the first time we worshipped in Butte . . . At first we had a little joss, just the head made of a piece of log. Next we made a larger one with arms and no legs. Ten years ago we made this fine big joss with outstretched arms, beautiful face and legs."[10] The statue of the temple god continued to evolve and improve. The statue of Guan Di arrived in Butte from China around 1905 and was the center of worship ceremonies in the temple for several decades.[11]

A combination of Chinese migration patterns and American immigration laws limited the number of religious leaders available to conduct observances. While the 1880 census lists two Chinese Montanans as priests, few men of this occupation came to the American West, as the common motivation to migrate was financial enrichment. American immigration policies further complicated the proper celebration of religious customs. The Geary Act reclassified priests as being in the laboring class and excluded entry for this group after 1892.[12] American legislators broadened prohibitions to keep out religious leaders to lessen the likelihood that Chinese communities would take root in America. To aid in religious observance, some temples throughout Montana employed "temple keepers" such as Wong Ken Chung, mentioned above. Wong seems to have passed on shortly after the 1899 interview in which he claimed to be 107 years

18. The altar of Butte's Chinese Temple. Note at the center the image of Guan Di, imported from China, ca. 1905. "Chinese Temple, Photo 02.002.06." C. Owen Smithers Photo Collection, acc. 2014.204. Courtesy Butte–Silver Bow Public Archives, Butte MT.

old as he does not appear on the 1905 special census which noted that Missoula, Bozeman, and Livingston all had individuals serving as "Temple Keeper."[13] In her 1947 sociological study of Butte's Chinese community, Rose Hum Lee noted that the temple keeper "assists the supplicant with religious offerings (burning joss sticks, lighting candles, pouring wine before Kwan Ti's [Guan Di's] altar, and burning spirit papers)" and helps observers interpret signs and the oracle's response to prayers. Community members paid fees for the institution's upkeep and operations, with these offerings adjusted based on the "weight of the supplication and the economic status of the supplicant." Additional collections funded yearly festivals and supported the temple keeper. As the population declined, however, the temple keeper's income from community "offerings [was] insufficient to maintain the guardian's salary, he [was] forced to accept other employment. He has waited on table and washed dishes in restaurants, is an assistant to the owner of a merchandise store, is the only herb doctor for Chinatown, is secretary to the only Tong in Butte, and is the Chinese teacher for the few young Chinese in the community."[14]

Anti-Chinese actors often targeted Chinese temples. Chinese communities reported numerous attempts to burn down the houses of worship, rob temples, vandalize statues, and harass worshippers. In one instance that occurred in Butte, "Three gods were permanently retired from business when a man whose brain was filled with devils broke into the Chinese joss house at an early hour this morning [leaving] broken gods and the prayer rugs thrown over chairs."[15] This 1902 attack necessitated that a new figure be ordered from China. It finally arrived in Butte in 1905. Similarly, in 1909 in Billings, two rowdies "very rudely and forcibly broke up the services to the gods of China which were being held in a joss house on the south side. Hampton and Dennis entered the holy of holies without proper credentials and warning and proceeded to defy the deities of the orient by rough housing the worshippers and overturning the idols."[16] While the temples did attract violence and vandalism from non-Chinese Montanans, Chinese residents from across the state continued to visit larger population centers to take part in religious celebrations with their fellow countrymen: "The Chinamen of Neihart, in order to change their luck, did obeisance to Joss and observed celestial new year at Helena this year. Tom Gong and Lee Gee got back Monday, and chattered the delights of the occasion," having traveled close to 250 miles to take part in the observances.[17]

Beyond maintaining cultural connections through shared worship, Chinese Montanans believed proper adherence to religious rituals soothed spirits and pleased the gods who provided good fortune to those who paid appropriate respect. If not properly honored after death, spirits of the departed wander as hungry ghosts, bringing misfortune to individuals and the community. Conducting a proper funeral in the southern Chinese tradition required key personnel, including a priest, musicians, and corpse handlers. As the authors of an anthropological study of funeral traditions of southern China described, "To bury a person without proper attention to ritual details is to create a hungry ghost who will return to plague the living. . . . Anyone who attempts to bury a family member without the services of these . . . specialists would be risking serious consequences."[18] In a new land far from the formal structures needed to carry out every rite with proper precision, adaptations emerged. Few priests or personnel required for religious rituals came to Montana, necessitating that the rites be performed by those who had witnessed these proceedings in China but who had not received formal training. Through a close reading of the many descriptions of Chinese funerals in Montana's newspapers seen through the lens of the spiritual practices of southern China and the adaptations made to their new atmosphere, a full sense of the importance of these religious beliefs to the Chinese of the state emerges.

Montana's newspapers show a fascination with Chinese spiritual beliefs about death, burial, and funeral rites as well as a frustration with not knowing more about these practices. In 1881 the Fort Benton newspaper lamented, "It would be interesting to know the significance of the various rites and we have made several efforts to obtain the information; but the Chinese are very reticent and are not all willing to communicate what we are anxious to find out."[19] While the newspapers reported in great depth on common aspects at funerals, the meaning behind each element remained mysterious. Montana's Chinese population brought cultural traditions unique to their home region with them and, specifically regarding practices involving death and burial, felt strongly about following these prescriptions to honor the dead and to avoid spiritual contamination.

The Chinese color of mourning and death is white. Newspapers noted that corpses were often "covered with a white cotton cloth" and that mourners wore white pieces of clothing to burials.[20] In a larger sense, Chinese people refer to the intricate cultural principles governing rituals related to death and burial as "white affairs." Death brought the possibility of spiritual pollution due to exposure to the corpse. Anyone who benefited financially from "white affairs" or who touched the corpse risked contamination.[21] In the absence of individuals who would normally undertake exposure to contamination, Montana's Chinese people adapted. Western undertakers

19. This rare photograph of a Chinese funeral procession in Missoula may have been from the ceremony described in the 1891 article "The Dead Mongol: Impressive Ceremonies Held Yesterday Over a Celestial's Grave": "The Chinese funeral held Sunday was a gorgeous affair . . . witnessed by nearly the entire population of Missoula. The Mascot band was engaged for the purpose which with the assistance of the unearthly tom-toms of the Celestial musicians succeeded in making all the noise desired. . . . The usual supply of pig and other mysterious edibles was on hand . . . lamentations were numerous . . . the personal effects of the deceased were burned, thereby obviating any possibility of their being wrangled over by the many heirs present." *Missoula Weekly Gazette*, March 25, 1891. Photograph from private collection.

replaced Chinese corpse handlers, German American marching bands replaced traditional Chinese musicians, and community members did their best to adjust to the realities of life and death in Montana.

Mourners from southern China avoided handling corpses, believing they emitted polluting forces that caused illness and misfortune. The role of corpse handler, while necessary and important, was considered lowly, making the person an outcast in society and unlikely to be part of the group that migrated to America. The corpse handlers ritually bathed, prepared, and dressed the body, dug the grave, and placed the coffin in the grave. These steps exposed corpse handlers to pollution and contamination that all others sought to avoid. In the Daoist worldview, yin and yang are balancing forces that infuse all aspects of life. Yin is viewed as a feminine characteristic and, for the purposes of death rituals, is associated with death. Men possess yang forces and handling a corpse infused with yin would be more polluting to men than to women.[22] Therefore, in the absence of official corpse handlers, women often prepared the body. For instance, Chinese women solely presided over the funeral of a Chinese woman who died by suicide in Helena in 1873. As a newspaper article about the event reported, "The chief mourners and conductors of the ceremony being the female portion, the men looked coolly on and took no part whatever."[23] The men's refusal to participate was likely due to the contaminating nature of the funeral itself but may also have been influenced by the fact that the woman died by suicide. In a source from several decades later, another hint emerges as to the role women played in death rituals. In an interview conducted during World War II, a resident of Butte's Chinatown indicated that the man who served as the guardian of Butte's temple was instructed in matters related to death by his assistant, "the oldest Chinese woman in Chinatown." Additionally, this woman was "expected to remind the men when [religious] festivals occur . . . and to aid sojourners in times of deaths."[24]

Because of the dramatic gender imbalance in Montana's Chinese communities, most simply did not have enough women to serve the roles in funeral rites to protect men from contamination.[25] When necessary, Chinese men served in the funerary rituals, adapting to conditions in the American West. Even this service had limits, however, as it was believed that "after a man touches seven corpses, he can no longer be made clean again."[26] Of the many descriptions of Chinese burials reported in Montana's newspapers, one gives especially strong insight into the reluctance of Chinese men to suffer contamination by handling the corpse. "At the Chinese section in Mount Moriah, the leader lined up the mourners in two rows, the pallbearers carried the coffin down the center and laid it beside the grave. [He] scattered more paper into the grave at the same time singing and chanting. Suddenly, he changed the key, stamped furiously and seemed to give vent to a tirade of abuse. No sooner had he ceased than a yell went up from the assembled Chinamen, and the pallbearers springing forward, almost dumped the coffin into the grave . . . leaving the undertaker's men to fill the grave."[27] This reporter viewed the abrupt deposit of the coffin and the passing of responsibilities to the undertaker's men as disrespectful, not understanding the concepts that governed Chinese participation in funeral rites and the pollution these men exposed themselves to in performing the service.

Montana's Chinese residents adapted to the lack of formal corpse handlers by partnering with non-Chinese funeral homes. They were happy to have undertakers prepare the body so they could remain free from contamination.[28] In Billings, which served as a regional collection point for Chinese remains from five states, the Chinese community worked with undertaker Herman Smith.[29] The Chinese in Helena contracted with Herrmann and Company not only to purchase coffins and dig the graves but also to handle and prepare the corpse.[30] As the *Billings Gazette* reported, the "undertakers who bury Chinamen say they are the best of pay and will provide anything that a Chinaman needs in the way of funeral, casket, etc."[31] Thus, the Chinese community adapted to demographic realities, transferring the contamination that came through the burial process to white Montanans who were happy to have the business and unaware that profiting from "white affairs" carried certain contamination.

Similar adaptations regarding the use of music emerged in Montana's Chinese communities. In traditional southern Chinese funeral rites, music was deemed an essential element for its ability to attract and soothe the spirit of the recently departed, ensuring that it does not become confused and separated from the body before burial. Because musicians were closely associated with death and profited from the role they performed, many believed that they took on a degree of contamination. While the stigma they faced was not as severe as what corpse handlers experienced, it affected their social status.[32] Similar to corpse handlers, musicians serving in this role were rarely among the Chinese who migrated. The specific type of music was not important, however, merely the presence of music to soothe and guide the spirit. As a result, Montana's Chinese communities used non-Chinese bands to perform this key service. This adaptation protected the Chinese from undue exposure to pollution.[33] An 1873 account from Helena noted that "the silver Cornet Band discoursed the Dead March."[34] Another account describing the funeral procession of a prosperous member of Butte's Chinese community observed: "First came Orton's band in a large wagon drawn by four black horses; then the dead body in a hearse."[35] Similarly, one account from 1885 explained, "The remains, already coffined in two coffins, were placed in a hearse and a wagon, headed by the Turnverein band."[36] Using this German American band met the requirement for music to guide the process. While some have viewed the incorporation of western music and musicians as evidence of the Chinese integrating into American society, when understood through the lens of the belief systems of southern China, the practice can be seen as a necessary adaptation to conditions in America that allowed for proper care of the spirit while avoiding contamination for the mourners.[37]

Montana newspapers often described other key roles in the funeral process, including ritual wailing and the distribution of ceremonial items. These roles were socially expected of mourners, as performing these rituals carried minimal risk of contamination. Mourners expressed grief through ritual wailing to announce the death of a community member. This wailing, accompanied by singing and praying, was also prominent along the funeral path and at the gravesite. Usually, this role was conducted by the women of the community, as described in this account from Virginia City from 1867: "Arrived at the grave-yard, the mourners alighted and the most demonstrative cast herself headlong on the earth, singing, praying and bewailing by turns, while the coffin was lowered into the shallow grave." Other mourners carried on this "hideous wailing," as the reporter described it, at key parts of the ceremony. [38]

The most frequently reported element of Chinese funeral processions was the distribution of pieces of paper with holes in the center. Whether a large funeral for a community leader or a lonely affair with one mourner, the same ritual caught the attention of several

Montana journalists. For the funeral of Wong Quong, who died in a mining accident in Boulder in 1905, reports noted that Chinese funeralgoers took "precautionary measures to protect the deceased from being reached or captured by the devil. On the march to the cemetery and at the grave many bits of paper were scattered, each having holes punched, and it is supposed that in order to reach Wong, the devil would have to pass through all of the holes in all of the papers scattered to the winds."[39] This tradition reflected the belief in southern Chinese folk traditions that ghosts could be distracted in such a way, preventing interference from unhappy spirits in the orderly enactment of the burial. Although often overlaid with the Christian notion of Satan as the spirit the mourners sought to distract, the frequent reporting on this practice indicates both consistency in Chinese funeral practices and some degree of interaction between Chinese and non-Chinese Montanans. For instance, when describing the funeral of a Chinese woman in May 1867, a reporter noted that many of the rituals are done to "to drive away the evil spirits 'Gwe.'"[40] The term "gwe" very closely approximates the Cantonese word for ghost or spirit, indicating some degree of communication between Chinese and non-Chinese Montanans on the topic of funeral traditions.

Once at the gravesite, a consistent element of Chinese burial practices that Montana's newspapers noted was the ritual burning of items from the deceased. The reasons given to readers to explain this tradition varied. Some believed the goods were burned "to prevent wrangling by the heirs."[41] Others claimed that "belongings . . . were piled up at the grave and burned to keep away the evil spirits."[42] Many reports, however, captured the true religious intent of this practice, which was to transform the goods from the earthly world to the spiritual world to be of use to the recently departed. Often, personal items were burned on the ground next to the grave: "The personal property of the deceased, candle-sticks, calicos, plates, platters, pictures, peppergrains and pomatum; shoes, chemizettes, 'ol' clos,' etc., *ad libitum*, were meanwhile heaped up near the grave, fired with sacred paper and sent up sweet incense to the 'empyrean vault.'"[43] Yet having an open fire next to the grave, given the dry climate and high winds in most parts of Montana, was not advisable. In areas with larger Chinese populations, a fact that increased the likelihood of frequent burials, the community constructed traditional funeral burners. A section in the far southwestern corner of Mount Moriah cemetery in Butte was set aside for Chinese burials. The large Chinese community of Butte built a funerary burner to be used both for burning the personal items of the recently departed and during seasonal holidays dedicated to honoring ancestors through burnt offerings.[44] Philipsburg's considerable Chinese community also had a cemetery section and a funeral burner.[45] Helena's China Row cemetery once featured a funeral altar that Bob Morgan, a noted Montana artist, remembered seeing in use when he was a boy in the 1940s. Morgan recalled that the ceremonies featured offerings of food and drink that he and his friends sampled after the rites concluded. Morgan recreated his memory of the altar in a small watercolor painting that gives a sense of how the alter, now merely a pile of bricks, appeared during its years of usage by Helena's Chinese community.[46]

Montana newspapers frequently featured specific descriptions of the food served at funeral ceremonies. What the newspaper reporters did not know, due to their lack of understanding of southern Chinese spiritual beliefs, was that the types of food and the presentation of the utensils had a specific purpose. The type of food, how it was prepared, and how it was presented gave clues as to which supernatural spirits were being "fed."[47] An 1881 account presented a common description of offerings that "contained pork and mutton, roasted and raw; fruits, confectionary and other delicacies . . . beside a number of mysterious dishes, the names of which it was impossible to learn." It was believed that the food offered to the recently departed and the spirits was consumed as essences. Therefore, the account, which noted "if the dead men derived any benefit from the feast it must have been by sniffing in the delicious odors," almost captured the beliefs practiced by the mourners.[48] Ritual practice dictated that recently departed family members and the spirits of ancestors be served cooked meat and vegetables with chopsticks inserted vertically into a bowl of rice, approximating a tombstone. Offerings for gods included wine or another alcohol and cooked meat.

20. Robert F. Morgan painting *Chinese Altar* of funeral altar at China Row Cemetery, Helena, Montana. Watercolor, 1993, 1995.78.01. Courtesy Montana Historical Society Collection, Helena MT.

Raw food served with no utensils was intended for ghosts.[49] Thus, through the types of food served and their different preparations, the celebrants had different intentions. According to one account these varied offerings included "one tin pail full of rice, one plate full of pork . . . one cup full of rice, with a spoon, and a brace of chop-sticks, symbolically inserted, in an upright position, a bunch of pastilles burning, two bunches of grapes, a quantity candy, some quartered apples, a bottle of brandy, a tin-cup with some in the bottom, a cup of tea, a paper of Chinese tea, and a paper of rice."[50] Even though non-Chinese observers could recount what was served with such specificity, these outsiders to the ceremony could not have known the power of each offering, the significance of its arrangement and preparation, or its spiritual intent.

The carefully prescribed steps from the death of an individual to the person's interment only began the ritual requirements. Twice a year, important religious observances took place in Chinese cemeteries. In the spring the Qingming Festival or Tomb Sweeping Day necessitated community members tend the graves of the departed, clearing tombs of physical debris and repelling evil spirits. As noted in an April 1869 edition of the *Helena Weekly Herald*: "Today is the Mongolian's annual Josh Day, on which occasion their custom is to visit the burial places [and] burn incense and innumerable small wax candles about the head stones or boards of the graves, . . . recite propitiatory prayers to the Savior, (Josh), and otherwise show themselves sacredly mindful of the welfare of their dead."[51] Similar observances took place across Montana each April, wherever Chinese were buried and residents remained in sufficient numbers to conduct proper observances. In April 1901 Havre residents noted the ceremony and expressed surprise that the rituals were not more somber.

> A strange ceremony took place the other day at the burial ground, when a wagonload of Chinamen went out to the cemetery to say a Chinese mass for the soul of a departed Celestial . . . [T]hey proceeded to carve oranges and slice ham, which they placed upon the grave. Chinese brandy was likewise wasted upon the cold earth. No solemnity accompanied the ceremonies; all was gay yet serene. A smile was upon every Chinese countenance, but the rites were evidently something necessary to the repose of the dead Chinaman's soul, a duty which all Chinamen owe to their dead.[52]

Later in the year, the Hungry Ghost Festival, known as Yulanpen in Buddhism and Zhongyuan in Daoism, required community members to visit graves and feed the spirits of the recently departed.[53] The *Helena Daily Independent* described the observance in 1883: "Several wagon loads of roast pork, fowl, sweetmeats and other edibles were scattered upon the grave of defunct Mongolians at the cemetery, and Chinese candles, colored sticks, papers, etc., were burned at the grave, while hired mourners rent the air with weird lamentations. The ceremony is observed once a year and is supposed by the heathens to be a potent factor in securing happiness for the departed in the other world."[54]

As important as Qingming and Yulanpen were to Montana's Chinese communities, population decline through the mid-twentieth century meant that fewer community members remained to aid in the religious observances. As Rose Hum Lee noted in 1943: "When the community was large, there were sufficient individuals, relatives to the deceased kinsmen, to accompany the guardian of the Temple . . . to the Chinese cemetery twice a year, as these were two of the important sacred events of the community. . . . Now the guardian performs these rites unaided. . . . [He] addresses the dead souls and begs their pardon for not being able to bring their kinsmen."[55]

Most Chinese in Montana and throughout the American West did not intend to relocate permanently to America whether living or dead. Chinese beliefs emphasized that one's bones must reside in Chinese soil, honored and tended to by respectful descendants, for the spirit to be happy and for the connection between the living and those who had gone before to be maintained. Reports in Montana's newspapers indicated a familiarity with the practice of exhuming bones to be returned to China, but coverage of the actual process was rare. As one article claimed, "It has been long generally known that all Chinamen had this superstitious regard for their bones to be laid in their last rest in the sacred soil of China . . . We have no doubt that it is done here in Helena, but when, how, or by whom we have had no curiosity to know. So long as it is done in such a way as not to offend or injure any one, we certainly would not interpose an objection or an obstacle."[56]

To some Montanans, already unhappy with the Chinese presence in the region, the practice of sending remains back to China further fueled resentment of the Chinese Montanans. An 1871 article in the Missoula *Pioneer* criticized "the Chinaman" because "he clings to his idolatry and heathenism with the tenacity of life" and is a "superstitious barbarian, whose hatred of our institutions and country is so deeply implanted that they will not so much as make our soil the receptacle for their dead."[57] The vitriol of this sentiment was echoed, in a more joking manner, through an attempt at humorous poetry in 1879:

> John Chinaman, my Joe John,
> Spend money at the bar;
> Chew Christian weed, not opium feed,
> Nor send your money far. . . .
> And when you get so old, John,
> You cannot work or play,
> B. Butler shall a pension get,
> To smooth your downward way.
> Then send not home your bones, John
> For Chinese guano,
> But keep them to enrich our soil,
> John Chinaman, my Joe.[58]

The "poet" went on to assert that he, and all like him, would rather their spirits reside forever in hell than to share heaven if the Chinese were present. Years later the Butte *Bystander* repeated these criticisms, focusing on the religious practices of the Chinese as being the key factor distancing them from becoming truly accepted in the state: "The Chinaman's life is not our life; his religion is not our religion. His one object in life is to make all the money he can and return again to his native land, dead or alive. His religion, superstition and low mode of life are so ingrained into his anatomy that all the waters of Jordan can never wash them out."[59] Montana attorney general Henri Haskell commented on his perception of Chinese residents' unwillingness to allow their dead to remain in America, noting this practice as evidence of their opposition to assimilation: "The Chinese are not bona fide residents in any sense of the word; they will not even permit their bones to have sepulture in our soil."[60] For many who harbored anti-Chinese sentiments, this cultural practice served as further evidence to justify the ongoing prohibition against the Chinese becoming citizens.[61] Answering this criticism, Quon Loy of Butte compared the desire to have remains returned to China as similar to Montanans who shipped their dead back east to rest closer to family members. Quon noted that "the bodies of his countrymen are shipped back to China for the same reason that the bodies of eastern people, who die here, are sent back East, that they can be laid beside relatives."[62] Put in that way, the custom of returning remains seemed less foreign. This practice had, however, become far more ingrained into Chinese belief systems than Quon Loy's apt though dismissive comment suggests.

From an understanding of southern Chinese spiritual beliefs, the practice known as "second burial" was common. This custom dictated that the recently departed individual be buried with proper rituals, allowing enough time for the flesh to decompose. After five to ten years the bones were exhumed, cleaned, and buried again. Key aspects of Confucian traditions are evident in the practice, specifically the reverence for ancestors and the importance of ritual. Spiritually, Daoist principles guide the reasoning behind second burial. In Daoism, the yin-infused flesh is given time to decompose. Bones, which are believed to contain yang and to be where the soul of the individual resides, are exhumed, cleaned, and buried a second time. Additionally, Daoist principles of *feng shui* were used to select the proper placement of remains, with preferred second-burial sites being on a rise with a high mountain to the right, lower mountains to the left, and water below.[63] The practice of second burial was expected for those residing in southern China. In terms of the Chinese who had traveled outside their home country, it was common only for wealthy, powerful individuals to expect their remains to be repatriated for burial in family tombs.[64]

With migration trends intensifying due to the Gold Rush and opportunities building the railroads of the American West, calls for second burial increased for more than just the rich and powerful. For the Chinese who came to America, work in dangerous occupations and the threat of racially motivated violence made death on Gold Mountain a possibility. Anxieties about one's spirit wandering as a lonely ghost far from home and untended by descendants increased the call for repatriation of remains. With Chinese workers spread across North America, however, finding, exhuming, and returning remains was complicated and costly. Working with community and business leaders in Hong Kong, Chinese people in America developed extensive systems to extend the tradition to serve the needs of countrymen far from home. Regional aid organizations developed charitable branches focusing specifically on death observances. Aided by the fact that earning opportunities in America helped fund the location and repatriation of remains, a tradition common to southern China and the Chinese elite evolved to apply to Chinese people in America and worldwide.[65]

For Chinese arrivals in the United States, "It was always part of every contract under which the Six Companies brought out emigrants, that in case of death their bones should be returned to their relatives in China."[66] District associations, including the Chinese Six Companies and other organizations, provided a type of death insurance. The cost of such insurance was divided to support general efforts of the organization as well as the process of finding and returning remains. Some scholars have asserted that the fee changed in relation to economic conditions in America. Furthermore, wealthy merchants were expected to pay more, with the extra fee being distributed to those in need.[67] For instance, the charitable branch of the organizations took note of those without means. Yanghe Association records note that: "For the injured or sick who cannot labor and the kinless poor, their travel expenses for home return will be provided by the company. . . . For those who died in poverty, the company is responsible for their coffins."[68] Wealthy merchants had multiple motivations to take part in such charity. First, caring for those in need through such generosity was significant through the Buddhist understanding of karma. Second, as merchants were not considered of high status in Chinese culture, taking on such societally important roles as caring for those in need can be seen as Chinese merchants advocating for upward social mobility in the American West by taking on obligations usually shouldered by the gentry.[69] Third, merchants who succeeded at serving the community's needs in this way signaled their efficacy, thus enhancing the trust afforded them by the community and increasing business opportunities.

Chinese diplomats and intellectuals traveling through communities of countrymen in America expressed fascination with this adaptation and the application of both charity and traditional spiritual

practices to working-class communities. During his visits throughout North America to build support for the Chinese Empire Reform
Association, exiled reformer Liang Qichao conveyed surprise at the
systematic evolution of the tradition to apply to classes of Chinese
society not normally part of this process. Liang detailed the various
native-place societies, or huigan, that had created systems to serve
needs of their members in life and in death. Chinese diplomats
took note as well, with Huang Zunxian, Chinese consul general in
San Francisco in the 1880s, noting to his superiors that "the huigan
arranged for the transport of their bones after exhuming and the re-
interment at hometowns."[70] The needs of overseas Chinese people
combined with the accumulation of wealth made possible through
work in North America changed the traditional practice of second
burial, extending it to new groups who developed complex systems
to navigate the movement of people and goods between two conti-
nents. While acknowledging these cultural adaptations, it is important to note that these considerations did not extend to all within the
Chinese communities of the West. A journalist describing a funeral
for a murdered Chinese prostitute in Helena in 1867 noted "that
the bodies of women are seldom removed, especially those of such
women as the one whose funeral we are describing."[71]

The organizations conducted ritualized ceremonies and facilitated
the collection and return for second burial of association members.
Bone pickers employed by the associations traveled throughout the
West serving the needs of their deceased countrymen. Often this
meant following the physical path of the railroad as many Chinese workers died during its construction and were buried close
to its tracks. Joe Boyer, who worked alongside Chinese laborers on
the Northern Pacific Railroad from 1879 to 1893, noted that "there
was truth to the claim that the track was laid on dead Chinaman."
Boyer recounted an incident in which debris from blasting operations killed Chinese workers, with countrymen burying them where
they fell. The construction of the railroad cost many Chinese lives,
with some estimates tallying more than one thousand dead in building the section from Spokane, Washington, through the mountains
of northern Idaho and western Montana.[72] Buried in shallow graves

alongside the tracks, it was hoped that huiguan representatives could find, exhume, and return remains for reburial.[73]

Due to the distances traveled by huiguan representatives and their relatively infrequent stops at Chinese communities spread across the West, bone pickers often collected remains of many individuals at one time, sending all back in one shipment. A 1913 article from a Bozeman newspaper noted: "The bones of nine Chinese taken from the graveyard are now on the way to China for their last rest with their ancestors. The cost of this work is borne by the dead man's relatives or societies . . . The bones are now on their way to San Francisco and will be a part of the shipment that leaves in September."[74]

To assist in the exhumation and repatriation of remains, proper identification of who was buried where was key. The identifying markers were not meant to be permanent, in contrast to Euro-American burials marked with engraved stones. Instead, for Chinese burials, the person interred was identified on a simple wooden headboard with black ink noting their name, date of birth, date of death, and home village location. Observers noted that "a board was placed at the foot of the grave instead of at the head; it was covered with hieroglyphics and one half of it was buried."[75] The expected timeframe for removal of remains was five to ten years, meaning a wooden headboard would last long enough to aid in this process. Another form of identification was a burial brick placed inside the coffin. While this method was common throughout California and Nevada, only one known instance of a burial brick in Montana exists. A construction crew doing road work in Missoula in 1937 uncovered a burial brick in an empty grave. Buried with other ritual items that mourners had left in the grave, the identifying details on the brick indicated, "Lee Foo Lim is buried here." Since the remains were not in the coffin with the brick or the offerings, it appears that Lee Foo Lim successfully returned to China for final resting.[76]

Chinese graves were often shallower than non-Chinese burials both to speed the decomposition of the flesh and to make the exhumation process easier.[77] In 1901 a non-Chinese undertaker in Butte reported that "a Chinese grave was not to be dug so deep as the grave in which the body of a Caucasian is interred. In a couple of years now, the Chinese undertaker will come to Butte and remove the decayed remains of all Chinamen buried in our cemetery."[78] A report on the process in German Gulch in 1874 described the process by which "the dead are disinterred, the flesh scraped from the bones and these are placed in a crucible and reduced to ashes, which, in this instance are to be packed in tin boxes, each box of ashes separate, and sent to the Flowery Kingdom for a final interment."[79] This mention of cremation is unusual as it was not the common practice. It is possible that the reporter mistook burning of offerings, common during the performance of the rituals, for cremation. A description more in keeping with the tradition explains the exhumation process and importance of accounting for each bone:

> The Celestials were preparing to send ten of their defunct country-men back to the Flowery Kingdom . . . Their dry bones are enclosed in unpretending canvas bags and in charge of guards provided by the Chinese companies . . . The bones . . . are those of Celestials who have been buried here for ten years of more. In such cases the coffins or boxes in which they have been interred are generally rotted away and it is not the easiest task in the world to gather the bones together. But the ingenious Chinese have adopted a plan by which they are absolutely certain of finding all the bones of their dead countrymen. They pan them out. They turn loose a lot of Chinese placer miners in the graves, and these fellows go to work as if mining for gold, and by digging up the earth and panning it, every bone even the carpus, metacarpus and tarsus bones, which are very small, are found. They are then washed and spread out to dry, after which they are sacked for shipment.[80]

The process described above illustrates the fulfilment of the death insurance arranged through fraternal and village associations as well as the systematic manner that these groups accounted for all bones and respectfully returned them to China. Forty years after the above account, the process continued. One story recounting the return of the remains of a Chinese man from Anaconda even included a specific citation of the district association overseeing the process: "Encased in a box 14 inches square and two feet in length, the bones of Lem

Chung . . . have been sent to San Francisco where the box . . . will be added to the cargo of a ship chartered by the Yan Wo [Yanghe] society of San Francisco."[81]

In areas with a sufficient Chinese population to have numerous deaths, a leading figure in the community organized the process, keeping records of who was buried where and coordinating the exhumation and return of remains. Often this individual was a successful merchant, which indeed was the case in Helena. In the 1870s Tong Hing, described as "the big chief of the Chinese in this city," coordinated return of remains. Apparently, Tong had been shipping remains for some time, which was legal according to freight regulations if the contents were labeled clearly and an appropriate fee was paid. Yet Tong attempted to avoid this fee by shipping remains in barrels labeled as "All the Same Pickles." Officials discovered this attempt to circumvent the shipping regulations and fees. Tong then contracted with local "hardware merchants [paying] $1,000 for zinc coffins in which to ship the remains of his dead countrymen to the sacred soil of China."[82] The outlay of $1,000 in 1875 for zinc coffins indicates Tong Hing's commitment to his role in this process as well as his expectation that he would complete this service for numerous countrymen. It is likely that Tong Hing was motivated to serve his community's needs and by other factors, including a desire to increase his standing as a successful businessman and to elevate his status among his countrymen by taking on a role normally held by Chinese society's elites.

In regions with Chinese spread across vast areas, sometimes with only one or two Chinese in each town, larger communities served as a central collection point to make the job of repatriation easier for all involved. In 1907 the *Billings Gazette* noted: "The Chinamen in North and South Dakota, western Nebraska, eastern Montana, and northern Wyoming [intend] to ship all their dead to Billings and have them intered [*sic*] in the local cemetery under the auspices of the local colony of Chinamen. Eventually it is expected that even the Chinamen buried here will be taken to the orient for interment."[83] Newspapers noted burials for Chinese throughout the region and commented on the process of shipping the remains back to Hong Kong.

When the process went smoothly, it provided for the deceased spirit's peaceful rest and assured the living that their spirits would be tended to through the mutual aid association's handling of such matters. However, due to local discrimination, violence, and the threat of violence, the process broke down at times. As noted previously, residents of the city of Great Falls were hostile to the Chinese from the city's founding. Various stories describe how Chinese entrepreneurs who tried to establish businesses in Great Falls were escorted to the city limits or dumped in the Missouri River. These stories persist throughout the 1880s and 1890s with slight alterations, giving them a somewhat apocryphal air, though it certainly is true that Chinese people were not welcome in Great Falls. Similarly, a story has long persisted in Great Falls of a box with the skeleton of a Chinese man inside surfacing at various points in the city's history. Allegedly, a box containing bones identified with Chinese characters was periodically rediscovered in the basement of the shipping company of Murphy, Maclay, & Co. in the Bach-Cory block of businesses. It seems that every decade the box resurfaced, caused a stir, and was housed in another basement to be found years later. The first mention of these remains occurs in August 1892 when they were said to have been present in the city for at least three years. Over the decades, various layers accumulated onto the story of this box and its contents. Most noted that the remains were labeled to be shipped back to China via San Francisco, though forgetfulness, indiscretion, and lack of funds impeded this planned return. Yet one version of the story speaks to both the Chinese cultural imperative to have remains returned to China for reburial and the fear that the Chinese in Montana had of Great Falls.

An October 1892 article purports to solve the mystery; notably, it is the only version of events that tells the story from a Chinese perspective, albeit through a non-Chinese recounting. A Great Falls man related that during a trip to Helena he met Wang Hong, the brother of a Chinese man who was killed in Great Falls in the early days of the city. According to Wang Hong, in 1885 a group of Great Falls rowdies accosted several Chinese residents walking next to the river and threatened to throw them in the water:

They took my brother into a boat. There were some logs in the river. One of these was made fast to the boat, which was then rowed out to mid stream. They told my brother to get out on the log. He did so and it was sent adrift and my brother went over the falls on the log. Next day in company of a countryman, a search began for the body. After two days it was found. It was partially decomposed and we removed the flesh from the bones and had them sealed in a tin can and then enclosed this can in a wooden case. . . . Then we hid the box in a cellar on Central avenue. . . . That evening we crossed the river in a skiff and walked to Sun River. We then came to Helena and have lived here since. . . . We never got my brother's bones from Great Falls, and they will never be shipped from that place if I have to go after them. I do not think that it is a healthy place for Chinamen. We tell all our countrymen not to go there.[84]

Newspapers recount similar stories of treatment of Chinese who tried to settle in Great Falls during the city's early days, with narrative elements varying possibly due to the passage of time or because several similar incidents took place. Notably, the above account is the only version in which a Chinese man that was treated so roughly died and may have been embellished. The above account rings true for several reasons, however, and it comes the closest of any recorded document to recounting the incident from the perspective of the Chinese victims. The alleged name of the man who gave this testimony was Wang Hong. The 1905 special census of the Chinese in Montana recorded a man named Wong Hong living in Helena and working in laundries. The special census checked Geary Act certificates obtained in the mid–1890s and show that this man had lived in Helena since at least spring of 1894. Additionally, the oft-repeated story in Great Falls that Chinese were intimidated in these ways dates to an article from the summer of 1885 that recounted the events thusly: "Declining to leave the town, a number of boys treated them to a boat ride on 'Old Muddy.' The boat unexpectedly upset and the almond-eyed martyrs received a bath, probably the first since their birth. The lesson proved a salutary one, and no Chinese have shown up since."[85] The connection between Wang Hong's account and the bones left behind in Great Falls may tie together two mysteries of the city's history. Over the decades, stories of the box with a Chinese man's bones resurfaced often. At one point the inscription on the box was published in local newspapers to try to facilitate the shipment of remains to those who could tend to them as intended. The *Great Falls Leader* claimed that the box was addressed to "Nine Young, No. 742 Commercial street, San Francisco," but was held in Great Falls as no one had guaranteed payment on the shipment.[86] As detailed in chapter 2, the Ning Yeung huiguan was the largest of the native-place associations serving Chinese from Taishan county. It appears that the box was intended for this organization so it could fulfill the death insurance that came with membership and repatriate the remains to China for reburial. Newspapers across the West reprinted the article, catching the attention of the Ning Yeung huiguan in San Francisco. Ma Chuck, a representative of the huiguan, wrote to the *Leader* hoping to facilitate the transport of the remains: "Dear Friend: I heard your storehouse had some Chinaman skeleton ghastly burden has remain, that it belongs Ning Young company the advertisement said; I wish you would please find the right address and so tell any one of our Chinese and have it sent for my company . . . Yours sincerely friend, Agent of Ning Young and Co., Ma Chuck."[87] Ma asked that other Chinese in the region be consulted to aid the process of returning the remains, not realizing that Great Falls took pride in having expelled all of the Chinese people who sought to settle in the city. The newspaper reported that every effort would be made to deliver the box if payment was received in advance. It appears, however, that the process broke down either due to the difficulty of communication or disorganization in Great Falls. City residents reported rediscovering the box periodically over the next two decades. While the story remained in the city's lore, the box and its contents disappeared.[88]

Remains collected from across the American West were first taken to San Francisco for eventual shipment to Hong Kong. Just as Hong Kong served as the point of departure for migrants coming to the United States, the city's geographic proximity to the migrants' home counties and the services that evolved to aid in migration and remittances also assisted families receiving the remains of their loved ones. Upon the arrival of steamships in Hong Kong, newspapers published lists of the names of the departed for family members or representatives from local Gold Mountain firms to claim the remains. When the process went smoothly, remains traveled back to the home village where a burial site was selected through reflection on feng shui principles and the spirit rested well, fed by respectful descendants. At times, however, the remains went unclaimed, awaiting family members who never came. In these cases, the remains were kept at the Tung Wah Coffin Home for a time before being buried in one of several charitable cemeteries throughout Hong Kong. Evolving from the 1850s through the middle of the twentieth century, these adaptations of the traditional second burial to apply to a new class of Chinese workers served the needs of migrants and their family members in southern China well into the twentieth century.[89]

Several cemeteries in Montana—notably burial grounds in Billings, Butte, Bozeman, and Helena—have stone tombstones cataloging the details of those interred there and indicate changes in burial practice for some of the state's Chinese residents. A few of these markers, especially in Helena's China Row, clearly show that the body was exhumed and that the stone tablet is likely all that remains. In Billings, Butte, and Bozeman, though records indicate that exhumation did happen, the remaining tombstones and the ground around them give no indication that the specific persons indicated were removed and returned to China for reburial. The transition from temporary wooden headboards or funeral bricks to more permanent stone markers indicates that burial practices shifted and that some chose to remain in Montana after death. Many of the markers are for Chinese women, whose remains rarely would have been exhumed and returned to China for reburial. In other cases, it appears that many of the deceased had lived in Montana for several decades. The trend toward more permanent stone markers, then, may indicate both a permanency of interment and that many of the state's Chinese residents had a transitioned to viewing Montana as their true home. Most of these markers show that the individuals passed away well into the twentieth century, with many indicated deaths occurring in the 1910s and 1920s. It is possible that these Chinese Montanans had families in the state who they felt confident would perform the proper rituals and venerate their remains as expected, exemplifying how Chinese cultural traditions adapted to transnational networks and continued in America.

For those still desiring to have their remains returned to China, exhumations continued in Montana into the 1940s. Records show that more than two hundred Chinese were buried in Helena's China Row from 1892 to 1955. At least twelve clear depressions and iron remnants of fasteners for coffins strewn throughout the area indicate that exhumation of remains took place.[90] An eyewitness account by Elfreda Paulson—the wife of the caretaker of Forestvale Cemetery, which abuts China Row—described this process. Paulson remembered that in the early 1940s, "A member of a Chinese Society came to Mr. Paulson, presented his credentials, and asked for permission to open graves of certain Chinese. This was done at the bearers' expense. The remains were packed in designated boxes . . . to be taken to San Francisco and there transported to their native China."[91] Given the date of the account, it is likely that these remains were among the last to be exhumed and returned to China. The disruption caused by World War II interrupted the process, even causing some remains to be stranded in Hong Kong indefinitely. Finally, when the Chinese civil war concluded with the Communist victory in 1949 and the establishment of the People's Republic of China, Cold War tensions led to an American embargo on trade with China that halted the return of remains. These changing political realities complicated relations between the United States and China, as political tensions disrupted freedom of movement between the two countries, as Cold War tensions heightened the long-existing suspicions of Chinese Montanans.

SEVEN

The Changing Status of Chinese Women, 1860s–1950s

One of the difficulties of writing the history of Chinese communities throughout the American West is finding sources that describe the experiences and contributions of Chinese women. The region's relative lack of Chinese women—caused both by Chinese migration patterns and restrictive American laws that kept their numbers intentionally low—has made the documentary record for this group even more sparse than for Chinese men. In this absence of source material, the story of Chinese women in Montana has fallen victim to generalization, assumption, and exoticization. By examining the origins and development of these overgeneralizations, a more accurate picture of Chinese women in Montana is possible. Through close investigation of the experiences of several exceptional women who transcended these stereotypes, Chinese and Chinese American women in Montana emerge as courageous, empowered, and resilient.

From the beginning of the Chinese presence in Montana, anti-Chinese agitators directed vitriol at Chinese women. Thomas Dimsdale, editor of Montana's first newspaper, exclaimed in 1865: "The yellow looking bipeds called China-*women*, God save the mark! debauch our citizens and degrade the community."[1] Such claims stemmed from the view that all or nearly all Chinese women who came to America were prostitutes.[2] Building from these views, American legislators passed the Page Act of 1875 to ban Chinese women suspected of seeking entry to the nation for "lewd and immoral purposes."[3] The act empowered immigration officials to bar applicants thought to be prostitutes. With the common view at the time that all Chinese women were so employed, enforcement of the act took the form of excluding Chinese women more broadly. After 1875 the number of Chinese women working as prostitutes declined nationwide. In San Francisco the percentage of Chinese women working as prostitutes dropped from 71 to 50 percent from 1870 to 1880, while the percentage of married Chinese women increased from 8 to 49 percent. These changes were due to the impact of the Page Act, the migration of more wives of workers to America, and the likelihood that some women left work as prostitutes and married Chinese men.[4] In Montana, however, the numbers did not follow the same trend. In 1870 census enumerators counted 128 Chinese women in Montana and recorded that 53 of them, or just over 40 percent, worked as prostitutes. By 1880 the number of Chinese women in Montana dropped to 82 but the number of reported prostitutes rose to 61, or more than 74 percent.[5] The question arises as to why the trend seen in California was not mirrored in Montana. While it is certain that many Chinese women in Montana did work as prostitutes, other factors influenced the possible overestimation of how many of them had this role.

The 1870 territorial census provides few details about most of Montana's Chinese residents beyond their age and the total number of them in the territory. The 1880 census seems to give more information, as it offers an increased depth and breadth of questions about each individual surveyed and includes their physical address, marital status, familial relationships, and number of months employed in their current occupation. Yet census enumerators that year brought certain assumptions into their interactions with Chinese Montanans that were based on cultural stereotypes and worsened by the language barrier. It is instructive to look at their interactions with Chinese women in Helena. Of the twenty-six women who appear on the records, twenty-four are noted to be prostitutes. For the two others, the occupation is left blank. In the column that asked the "number of months the person had been employed within the census year," the census enumerator recorded a check mark for each Chinese man, a choice that ignored the intent of the question and likely stemmed from difficulty communicating. For each Chinese woman, however, this column was left blank. The marital status of all Chinese women in Helena was left blank, though the men were also asked this question and had their results recorded. The evidence suggests that the census enumerators, at least in Helena, did not actually interact with the women who appear on the census and left key portions of the record blank for them but not for Chinese men. If these conversations did not happen, then how did the enumerators determine the occupation of the twenty-four supposed Chinese prostitutes in Helena? The official instructions for census takers in 1880 gave leeway that facilitated broad assumptions: "The enumerator is not required to accept answers which he knows, or has reason to believe, are false. . . . Should any person persist in making statements which are obviously erroneous, the enumerator should enter upon the schedule facts as nearly as he can ascertain them by his own observation."[6] When encountering a Chinese woman, it seems census enumerators automatically viewed her as a prostitute and assumed they did not need to question her about her employment or marital status. These overgeneralizations were from the same census takers who ascribed the name "Ah" to more than 44 percent of the Chinese residents of the city. That number that does not accord with records taken by those possessing Chinese language abilities, who identified less than 5 percent of the state's Chinese residents as "Ah." The census enumerators saw what they had been culturally prepared to see through biased newspaper reporting and overall racist impressions of Chinese women. Tellingly, the records did not identity white women who were known to work as prostitutes as such.[7] Beyond merely the stereotypical assumptions of individuals, these census records became official documents. Supposedly a neutral recording of raw data, they presented a flawed record derived through cultural stereotypes and racist impressions. To be sure, many Chinese women in Montana did work as prostitutes; however, the exceedingly high estimates in Montana's official count overstated the reality.[8]

Restrictions such as the Page Act and the subsequent Chinese Exclusion Act made the entry of Chinese women as workers or wives unlikely. The result was a severe gender imbalance within Chinese immigrant communities. Many scholars attribute the skewed gender ratio to Chinese cultural traditions that dictated that men migrate for work while women stay home to work in the village, raise children, and care for aging relatives. This view held that by leaving a wife behind, a male migrant tied his efforts back to the village, helping to ensure responsibility and loyalty. While this certainly was an element of how traditional southern Chinese culture viewed gender roles, these factors alone do not explain the extremely low number of women in America's Chinatowns. As noted by George Anthony Peffer in his study of Chinese migration to other regions—including Singapore, Penang, and Malacca—during the same time period, these communities had a more balanced gender ratio than the United States, indicating that Chinese culture and family traditions did allow female migration. Peffer and others argue that the severely skewed gender ratio in Chinese communities in the United States was caused less by Chinese cultural dictates and more by the treatment of Chinese women at American ports of entry and before the law.[9] Because of this gender imbalance and the restrictions placed on marriage, it was difficult for Montana's Chinese population to increase naturally. Indeed, for those who sought to minimize the chance that the Chinese community would take root in America, these laws helped accomplish the goal that Montana senator Wilbur Sanders outlined when he stated, "It is not desirable that these people shall be multiplied in this country, but that they shall be diminished to extinction."[10] Chinese cultural practices combined with American immigration restrictions severely limited the possibility of family formation within Chinese communities.

Following restrictions on the entry of Chinese women established by the 1875 Page Act and efforts to bar laborers or their families from migrating such as the 1882 Chinese Exclusion Act and the 1892 Geary Act, the most likely route for Chinese women to enter the United States was as the wives of merchants, who were exempt under the exclusion dictates. Immigration officials nonetheless often sought reasons to exclude these women, continuing to assume that all Chinese women were prostitutes. Officials suspected Chinese marriages to be shams intended to gain entry for women who would further degrade the American populace through illicit behavior. One official summarized this view and revealed the extent of this cultural divide when he stated, "The Chinaman would have to demonstrate to me that woman is his wife according to our ideas of marriage." [11] The distance caused by the Chinese diaspora and Chinese cultural traditions created marriage scenarios that did not look to American officials like their "ideas of marriage." Most Chinese marriages were arranged by a matchmaker, with the bride and groom separate until the ceremonies had concluded. As one woman from Butte's Chinese community recounted: "I was married by proxy. A live rooster symbolized the bride-groom . . . A month after the marriage, I sailed for America with my husband's relative . . . On the day the boat docked at Port Townsend . . . he pointed to a figure walking up and down the wharf. He said, 'See that man smoking a big cigar? He is your husband.'"[12] American officials suspected such marriages were fraudulent means of gaining entry for women who would then work as prostitutes. As such, entry interrogations even for merchants' wives, who should have been exempt, were intense and included questions not asked of other groups of immigrants that many applicants found inappropriate and embarrassing.[13] Despite these difficulties, merchants' wives began to arrive in the 1890s, allowing for the development of a second generation born in America, making them American citizens through one of only two paths open to people of Chinese ethnicity.

For merchants' wives, cultural assumptions from the broader non-Chinese community that viewed all Chinese women as prostitutes meant arrest and deportation loomed if they were not able to prove otherwise. The case of Mrs. Wo Hop of Butte illustrates these anxieties. As a merchant's wife she was not required to register under the Geary Act, but nevertheless sought documentation to guard against misunderstanding. She carried a statement bearing her photograph and attested to by four white witnesses that she was the wife of Wo Hop, who "habitually makes his living as a merchant" and "is not a day laborer, nor does he earn his living or any part thereof, as a laborer."[14] She hoped that this document would protect against possible government action to deport her if inspectors assumed she was

BUTTE, Montana, October 22nd, 1892.

We, the undersigned, residents of Butte City, Silver Bow
County, Montana, do hereby certify and declare: that we are well
acquainted with MRS WO HOP, a chinaman, resident of Butte City,
Montana, and ___ Mrs. Wo Hop ___ his ___ wife ___, whose photograph is
hereto attached and made a part of this certificate, to-wit:

That the said Wo Hop is one of the firm of "Wo Hop & Company"
chinese merchants, doing business in general merchandising and
chinese goods, in Butte City, Montana; and that we believe the said
Mrs. Wo Hop is the Wife of the said Wo Hop; that the said
Wo Hop habitually makes his living as a merchant as aforesaid, and
is not a day laborer, nor does he earn his living or any part thereof, as a laborer; and that from his said merchandising business
said Wo Hop supports and maintains the said ___ Mrs. Wo Hop ___
and his family.

WITNESS our hands and seals this 22nd day of October, 1892.

+ N a m e +
Business or official position.

+ N a m e +
Business or Official Position.

21. Documentation for Mrs. Wo Hop, Butte, Montana, to attest to her right to be in the United States as the wife of a merchant, 1892. DIG 036, 1999.103, Hum Family Collection, Butte–Silver Bow Public Archives, Butte MT.

a prostitute. Her repeated statements of her husband's occupation show the anxieties that merchants faced as well.

Within the Chinese community, cultural practices guarded against assumptions that a "family woman" was a prostitute. In an extensive interview with one of the first women to arrive in Butte as a merchant's wife, Rose Hum Lee documented the precautions that this patriarchal culture took to guard against assumptions from the broader community:

> When I came to America as a bride, I never knew I would be coming to a prison. Until the [Chinese] Revolution [of 1911], I was allowed out of the house but once a year. That was during New Year's when families exchanged New Year calls . . . The father of my children hired a closed carriage to take me and the children out calling. Of course, he did not go with us, as this was against the custom practiced in China. The carriage would take us even if we went around the corner, for no family women walked. Before we went out of the house, we sent the children to see if the streets were clear of men. It was considered impolite to meet them. . . . The women were always glad to see each other; we exchanged news of our families and friends in China. We admired each other's clothes and jewels. As we ate separately from the men, we talked about things that concerned women. When the New Year festivities were over, we would put away our clothes and take them out when another feast was held. Sometimes, we went to a feast when a baby born into a family association was a month old. Otherwise, we seldom visited each other; it was considered immodest to be seen too many times during the year.[15]

One goal of these highly restrictive practices was to protect against assumptions of impropriety held by many against Chinese women.

As restrictive as life was for the wives of merchants in Montana's Chinatowns, conditions could be worse in southern China. Women suffered disproportionately from the tragic economic conditions in Taishan County during the mid-nineteenth century. Facing the Chinese cultural preference for sons in addition to food shortages and a lack of resources, some families chose drastic options: "The able-bodied go abroad. The fields are clogged with weeds. . . . Daughters are often drowned rather than raised."[16] An alternative for families was to lessen the burden by selling daughters through a system known as *mui tsai*, Cantonese for "little sister." In the Chinese culture of the time, this practice "was generally regarded as a form of charity for impoverished girls."[17] A family struggling against crushing poverty could choose to sell a daughter into domestic service, stipulating that the girl would be freed at the age of eighteen and married to a suitable husband. During their years of service, mui tsai received no wages, experienced severe limitations in movement and freedom, and worked under difficult conditions. In the best scenarios, the family to which the mui tsai was attached treated her well and released her after she turned eighteen. In many circumstances, however, mui tsai were mistreated, abused, and often sold into prostitution. Aware of these abuses, American social reformers viewed this system as a form of slavery and fought to free Chinese girls from these arrangements. The most prominent force fighting this system was the Presbyterian Mission Home based in San Francisco, which had branches throughout California.[18] These social reformers had a long reach, even becoming involved in family issues in Montana. The cases of four Chinese women in Montana illustrate the complexities of family formation in a region with such a skewed gender ratio. These conditions led to instances of high drama that garnered extensive newspaper coverage, including stories of rescue, redemption, kidnapping, and murder. Sometimes these stories of mui tsai freed by the reformers had happy endings, such as with the family of Dr. Wah Jean Lamb; sometimes, as in the case of Tom Sing and Na Loy, tragedy followed tragedy.

In the first case, Chinese physician Wah Jean Lamb came to Butte in the early twentieth century with a new bride found through the Mission Home system. Lamb had entered America as a student in the late 1880s. It is likely that he was educated and possibly raised by Christian missionaries in southern China. Lamb studied for his medical degree at the University of Southern California, becoming the first Chinese graduate of the university's medical school. As one report from the occasion described: "Among the graduates was . . . one Chinaman, Wah Jean Lamb of Canton [Guangzhou], China.

There were several of the latter's countrymen among the audience. The graduate had discarded his queue and was in American dress."[19] Lamb was Americanized not only in dress and hair but also in religion, as he was a Christian following his experiences with missionaries in China.

As a student in Los Angeles, Lamb boarded with the Saddlers, a white family connected to Christian missionary work. Edith Saddler, the youngest daughter, struggled with ill health. Lamb and Edith fell in love and married. It appears they went to Nevada to marry, possibly to circumvent California laws against such a union. Shortly after having a daughter, Edith passed away. Relocating to Montana to practice medicine, Lamb sought a new wife and reached out to the Presbyterian Mission Home in San Francisco to inquire about a suitable bride.[20] The Mission Home rescued Chinese women from prostitution and from the worst abuses of the mui tsai system. Girls lived at the Mission Home, studied English, conducted twice-daily Bible study, and learned domestic skills such as the "organization of a home on Christian principles . . . the first step upwards from heathenism to civilization."[21] Imbued with Victorian Protestant sensibilities, the Mission Home philosophy sought Christian conversion for its Chinese charges, hoping to match the women with Christian Chinese men.

Marriages arranged through the Mission Home were generally of two kinds. The first were unions between women working as prostitutes and their male clients. In these cases, the couple sought assistance from the Mission Home to extricate the woman from prostitution and to facilitate the marriage. Couples agreed to submit to intense acculturation to the Mission Home's ideologies, promising to live as Christians and maintain a virtuous home. Additionally, the woman agreed to live in the Mission Home for six months to a year, a mandate enforced by Mission Home reformers to ensure her preparedness to lead a virtuous life. It was not a simple affair for a woman to leave prostitution, as she was usually controlled by *tongs*, Chinese secret societies specializing in vice. Losing out on their investment and the future earnings they may have accrued from the woman made tongs and brothel owners harsh opponents of Mission Home reformers. Recapture through kidnapping and retribution against women or those who aided their escape were real dangers.

Though Mission Home organizers did facilitate marriages between recently extricated prostitutes and their former clients, they did not publicize these unions as widely as the second type of marriage—that of a long-term resident of the Mission Home matched with a Chinese Christian husband. As the Mission Home took in young girls rescued from brothels or from slave-like circumstances, more young women came up through the system and stood, in the eyes of the reformers, as perfect examples of the positive effects of a Protestant Christian upbringing and Victorian-era domestic sensibilities. When products of the Mission Home system found matches with husbands viewed as respectable members of American society, the organization highlighted these marriages to supporters who financed the Mission Home's efforts.[22] This was the case for the marriage between Lamb and Mission Home resident Ah Oie. Accounts are vague, but it is likely that Ah Oie was rescued from prostitution or an abusive mui tsai contract and lived as a resident at the Mission Home.[23] Familiar with the work of the Mission Home from his time in California and his interactions with fellow Christians, Lamb reached out following the death of his first wife and "requested the ladies of the Mission to furnish him with a wife, and Miss L. Ah Oie, a comely Chinese girl, was chosen. She was quite willing to become a bride. The bridal couple were both dressed in conventional American fashion."[24] With such a notable suitor, the Mission Home featured the wedding as the centerpiece of the organization's annual conference in 1901, displaying to supporters the success of the Mission's purpose. "In the presence of a large assembly" the attendees enjoyed the wedding between "Miss L. Ah Oie, a bright young girl who has been making her home at the Mission house where she has been trained, and the groom Dr. W.J. Lamb, a Chinese graduate of the Los Angeles Medical College."[25] By featuring this arrangement, the reformers celebrated the highest achievement of their work—extricating a Chinese girl from the evils of the brothels, converting her to Christianity, and arranging a marriage to a successful member of society, in this case a fully Americanized Christian doctor trained in west-

22. Alice (Ah Oie) Lamb and children, 1914. Courtesy of Mai Wah Society, Butte MT, donated by Winnie Nishimine.

ern medicine. From 1874 to 1901, the time of the union between Ah Oie and Lamb, Mission Home leaders had arranged 160 such marriages, an impressive number considering the few Chinese women in the region.[26]

After relocating to Butte, Lamb and Ah Oie, who went by the name Alice, continued to perform Christian missionary work. The Lamb family grew quickly in Butte. Lamb worked as a physician while Alice taught at the Chinese Baptist Mission. It is likely that Ah Oie's experience of rescue by the Presbyterian Mission Home influenced other Chinese women in Butte, allowing for some to escape the abuses of the mui tsai system.

The experiences of the family of Quong Tuck Wing illustrate the issues brought about by the scarcity of Chinese women in the West, the far-reaching efforts of the Mission Home, and the tensions when the mui tsai system came into conflict with American reformers. Quong, a prominent member of Butte's Chinese community and successful merchant, used his position to secure entry for his wife, Choy Gay, and also to gain entry for a young woman whose status seems to indicate that she was a mui tsai. At times referred to as his "niece" and at times as a "daughter," Quong brought Wong Lon Ying into the United States in 1895. Her exact age is difficult to determine; she may have been around ten years old or younger upon entry, as the census of 1900 lists her as twelve. Details of the experiences of Choy Gay and Wong Lon Ying are also difficult to determine, though not for lack of evidence. Rather, conflicting accounts from Choy and Wong's perspective, supported by Mission Home activists, compared to the testimony of Quong Tuck Wing portray events in drastically different ways. This drama played out in newspapers in Montana and California due to these differences and the dramatic events that saw the two women escape from Butte.[27]

According to Choy Gay, life with Quong Tuck Wing was oppressive and violent. She claimed that Quong beat her and Wong and confined them to a "miserable, foul-smelling hole where the two had to live without a single breath of outside air."[28] Furthermore, Choy asserted that Quong threatened sexual advances toward Wong. It seems that Quong and Choy had failed to conceive a child and Quong may have been considering taking Wong as a wife. Choy had bonded with the girl and objected to the threat of Quong's advances. Seeking a solution, the two women found salvation from the same Presbyterian Mission Home that had raised Ah Oie, who had arrived in Butte that year. It is possible that Ah Oie informed Choy Gay of the services of the Mission Home and that Choy put a plan in place to save herself and Wong. Mrs. A. A. Browne of the Mission Home reported that the organization received a letter from Choy Gay in 1901 in which, "She asked the mission people to rescue her, as [her husband] intended to sell her and marry his slave servant girl, Lon Ying." As the Mission Home staff worked for a solution, Choy Gay wrote again, noting "that if she was not rescued she would kill herself." In September 1902 Browne traveled from California to Butte, secured the help of the chief of police, and removed both Choy Gay and Wong Lon Ying from Quong Tuck Wing's residence while he was out.[29]

Upon realizing the women were gone, Quong assumed that rival tongs had kidnapped the women. When the circumstances of the women's departure became clear, Quong reported the disappearance to the police, claiming the women had not only been taken but that valuables also were missing. Because the chief of police assisted in the women's departure, however, local authorities did little to aid Quong. Butte's newspapers covered the situation with great attention, excited by the drama and the competing claims of kidnapping or escape from abuse. Quong claimed he treated the women well: "I always gave them everything they wanted, and no home was happier than ours until this happiness was wrecked by a woman from San Francisco with the help of the police here."[30] After coming to understand the role of the Mission Home in the women's departure, Quong remarked, "The white woman who was seen at the house last night was an agent of a San Francisco society which has for its purpose the rescue of fallen Chinese women."[31] Quong believed the Mission Home was a front to obtain Chinese women as wives for powerful Chinese men.[32] Given the scarcity of Chinese women in the American West, it was a common complaint that the Mission Home procured Chinese women for marriage to powerful Chinese men.

Though many Chinese women were not allowed out, fathers and husbands did permit missionary women to instruct their daughters and wives during home visits.[33] As a representative of Butte's Chinese Baptist Mission, "Mrs. Whitmore visits the homes of the few Chinese women here, and teaches the women and children, of whom there are fourteen, English and Christianity." Commenting on the strife within Quong Tuck Wing's home, a reporter from the *Butte Miner* noted that, according to Mrs. Whitmore: "The Chinese women in Butte seem to be well taken care of by their husbands, and have no complaints to make, the only case that has come to the knowledge of the mission of alleged mistreatment in the twelve years was that of the two who were recently taken to San Francisco by Mrs. A. F. Brown [*sic*]. In this case Mrs. Whitmore says that the girls talked with her often of their condition, and that while they did complain, she never saw the husband abuse either of them."[34] This view contrasted with information that prompted the rescue of Choy and Wong. San Francisco newspapers attributed the women's knowledge of the Mission Home's services to instruction from Whitmore, noting, "It was through her that the Chinese girl learned of the Mission Home in this city. [Choy] had mastered enough English to write letters here imploring the mission workers to come and save her before her master carried out his threat of placing her and Lin [Lon] Ying in a den."[35] It is possible that Whitmore later downplayed her role given the uproar that followed in Butte's Chinese community.

Quong Tuck Wing pressed for the women's return, with others vouching for his good name, attesting to the women being treated well in Butte, and demanding their release. It became clear, however, that the Mission Home would not relent, and Quong's legal and moral claims to release the women abated. The women acclimated quickly to life at the Mission Home. Choy Gay was noted for her "beautiful character—polite and lovable in her manner. . . . She desires to be received into the church."[36] She aided Mission Home efforts as a "native helper," assisting in rescues much like her own. During one of these trips accompanying a woman to meet her waiting groom, Choy met a man in Chicago whom she later married. After staying at the Mission Home for two years, Wong Lon Ying married Jin Fong, a Chinese Christian who lived at the Mission Home in Santa Barbara. As a noncitizen and a laborer, Jin could not bring a wife into the United States. For Chinese men like him, finding a bride through the Mission Home presented an opportunity to marry and start a family.[37] Restricting pairings to Christian men, Mission Home directors carefully questioned potential suitors, inquiring about their past relationships, religious beliefs, and ability to support a family, believing "he who would win a member of the Mission Home family for his wife must present the very best credentials."[38] For Chinese women rescued by the Mission Home, marriage was a way to move forward free from difficulties they suffered through the mui tsai system and forced prostitution. Jin and Wong had eight children and made a life farming near Santa Barbara, happy to have left the dramatic events of Butte in the past.[39]

A similar story from Bozeman's Chinese community does not end with such contentment.

The story of Bozeman couple Tom Sing and Na Loy also shows the Mission Home system at work but reveals how complicated histories followed those seeking a new life. Tom Sing, a laundry worker in Bozeman, studied English with Christian missionary Julia H. Emery. As a laborer with no prospect to bring in a wife, Tom sought a bride through the Mission Home. Na Loy claimed to have been brought to America at age seven, likely in the mui tsai system.[40] At some point, Na Loy escaped or was rescued, possibly by Mission Home activists. She lived at various Mission Homes throughout California from 1891 to 1895.[41] Her path from California to Montana may have included marriage to a Chinese man in 1895 and a time living in Portland, Oregon. Finally, in 1897 Na Loy wed Tom Sing in Bozeman. Officials noted the rarity of the event, commenting: "This was the first license ever issued in this county to a Chinaman to wed."[42] With Emery signing the marriage certificate as a witness and hosting a luncheon for the couple, all seemed to be in order. Yet circumstances turned over the next few years, prompting Emery to write a long exposé about the events before and after the wedding. Appearing as early as October 1903 and running throughout 1904 in newspapers in Utah, Maryland, Kansas, Pennsylvania, South Carolina, Emery's article recounted how Tom Sing, referred to as Wong Wa Foy in an apparent attempt to hide his identity, met Na Loy, but also foretold with surprising accuracy Tom's murder for interfering with a woman claimed by another Chinese man.

Emery recounted how Tom told her of his interest in marrying. Her reply indicates the social prohibitions present in the West: "But how can you marry? Not a white girl, surely? Yet you don't know any China woman. There are no Chinese girls here. . . . Have you bought a Chinese girl—paid six or eight hundred dollars for her?" Tom assured her the match was legitimate, explaining that he contacted Na Loy through the Presbyterian Mission Home in San Francisco, that she was Christian, and the two were in love. Emery approved, observing that when Na Loy arrived in Bozeman, Tom "brought his heathen sweetheart and placed her in my care. She was bright and

23. Na Loy, Bozeman, Montana, ca. 1900. Defendant's Exhibit B. U.S. Commissioner. Alamy stock photo.

attractive, spoke and read English fairly well, and seemed perfectly at home in her new surroundings. . . . Close questioning convinced me that this was a true love match—no bargain and sale, as I had feared, such as is common on the Pacific Coast. All they asked was American protection and freedom from molestation."

Unfortunately for the couple "protection and freedom from molestation" were not to be found. Later in the article, Emery tells of her need to travel for work. Before leaving, she ensured that Tom and Na Loy were acquainted with the church folks and knew who to call on if they needed help. Upon her return, both Tom and Na Loy were gone. Emery inquired with Chinese residents in Bozeman who told of Na Loy's past and how Tom had interfered in complicated affairs, claiming that Tom had stolen Na Loy as his wife. Some believed that Na Loy belonged to a powerful Chinese Free Mason (Zhigongtang) and that Chinese newspapers called for Tom to be held accountable for his interference. Chinese men in Bozeman told Emery that a notice went out indicating: "'One thousand dollars for some one stick a knife in [Tom].' . . . No one kill for one thousand, paper say, 'Two thousand, three thousand.' Some night [Tom] die. No one know, Flee Mason pay, Six Company pay. [Tom] Flee Mason. Na Loy b'long to Flee Mason. [Tom] steal him wife; tell much big lie. Velly bad." Emery's account appeared as early as October 1903.[43] By October 1905 Tom Sing was dead. A month earlier, Lu Sing came from Butte, working odd jobs and apparently conducting surveillance before carrying out the assassination. Lu killed Tom with a hatchet and was apprehended at the scene. "When Lu was asked why he did the deed, he would give no direct reply, but stated that if Tom was dead he was glad and happy, and that if he was not dead, he was sorry and not a good Chinaman."[44] Montana newspapers claimed, "It is certain that he was the agent of some society of highbinders that he was enraged at Tom Sing for marrying the pretty little Mongolian woman, and thereby depriving them of their female slave and the profit she brought to them."[45] Emery's strangely prophetic article foretold Tom's murder, giving a glimpse into the complexities of attempts at family formation when so few women lived in the American West and the few who did were often claimed by powerful men or contracted into a life of prostitution.[46]

The now widowed Na Loy's situation went from bad to worse. As Emery stated, "All they asked was American protection and freedom from molestation." The couple's status as laborers in America, issues with registration under the 1892 Geary Act, and possible attempts to gain illicit entry for a "paper son," however, subjected Na Loy to investigation, arrest, and possible deportation just as her husband's murder tore her family apart. In fact, her arrest placed her in direct proximity to her husband's assassin: "In the county jail not thirty feet from the cage in which Lu Sing is awaiting execution for the murder of her husband, Mrs. Tom Sing, or Na Lay [*sic*], a pretty Chinese woman, [awaits] deportation to China on the ground that she is illegally in this country, not having been registered."[47] In the summer of 1904 Tom Sing and Na Loy had petitioned to bring a person they asserted was their son into America. They claimed that Ham Hung Wah had been born on American soil, returned to China, and sought reentry as a native-born citizen. Montana Chinese inspector Howard Ebey investigated Ham Hung Wah's application for entry, which was rejected, and checked Tom and Na Loy to see if their paperwork was in order. Notations in the file indicate that immigration officials "suspected perjury [due to] discrepancies in testimony."[48] While Tom Sing had registered as required under the Geary Act, Na Loy had not. She testified "that she did not register [believing] she did not need a certificate, as her husband's would serve for both." With uncertainty as to when and how she initially entered the United States, Na Loy's status had been undocumented during her many years in the country. Upon marrying Tom Sing, she took on his status as a laborer, requiring compliance with the Geary Act. Unable to prove her right to reside in the United States, Ebey arrested Na Loy in August 1904. After a trial in July 1905, the court ordered Na Loy to be deported.[49]

Her case elicited sympathy from supporters from across the state. Billings newspapers picked up the story, complaining: "Just what is to be gained by the deportation is not quite clear, except that the letter of the law is to be followed. . . . The woman does not speak a word of her native language or write Chinese, according to dispatches from Bozeman. She is educated in English, however, and is a member of the Presbyterian church and lives an exemplary Christian life . . . despite all this, she is to be sent back to China, a strange country to her, and where she will probably meet death or torture."[50]

Supporters in Bozeman circulated petitions, urged legal appeals, and elevated Na Loy's cause to President Roosevelt. Montana senator Thomas H. Carter criticized Ebey, complaining that he overstepped his authority, callously persecuted Na Loy, and tore apart a Christian marriage.[51] Lodged by a sitting U.S. senator, these claims prompted a full response from the government agency that enforced laws pertaining to entry and residence of Chinese people. It was clear that Na Loy had not registered in accordance with the Geary Act and thus, by law, should be deported. Supporters sympathized with her due to her fluency in English, Christian conversion, the tragedy of her husband's death, and the traumas she had suffered. Yet the agents in charge of enforcing the laws saw no room for sympathy and took offense at claims that they overstepped their authority. The final report, which included surprisingly candid character judgements, commended Ebey for his actions and condemned Na Loy, indicating that she was "herself to blame for the predicament in which she now is. Not only did she defy the Chinese exclusion laws in her own case, but by perjury she endeavored to violate it in the case of another whom she claimed as her son by a man whom she had never met at the time of the birth of such son. She is, therefore, an evil doer, both in the light of civil and moral law, and yet has been overtaken by no retribution other than her probable return to her country of birth."[52]

With all avenues of appeal exhausted, officials deported Na Loy in 1908. Likely brought over as a mui tsai as a child and serving as a prostitute until being rescued by the Mission Home, her marriage briefly offered her the prospect of starting a new life. The circumstances faced by Na Loy, though extreme, illustrate the difficulties that many Chinese women in the American West faced.

Despite these difficulties and the relative scarcity of Chinese women in the region, family formation did occur. Whether through marriages arranged through the Mission Home system or with merchants bringing wives directly from China, a second generation soon followed. These Chinese American families had the same experience as many immigrant communities; the second generation integrated into American society and then assisted the first generation in navigating the culture and institutions of their adopted home. The same woman who detailed the restrictions on the lives of merchants' wives in the 1890s noted distinct changes brought about by events in China and cultural integration of her children: "After the Revolution in China, I heard that women were free to go out. . . . I discarded my Chinese clothes and began to wear American clothes. By that time my children were going to American schools, could speak English, and they helped me buy what I needed. Gradually the other women followed my example."[53] No longer limited to a life of confinement, Chinese women in Montana began to venture out. The children born in the late nineteenth century aided this process, serving as a bridge between traditional Chinese culture and American society, which was changing rapidly during the Progressive Era.

In Helena the family of Lee Sam Fong exemplifies Chinese American families taking root and exercising rights as American citizens, even though many saw them as forever foreign due to their ethnicity. As described in chapter 3, Lee obtained extensive documentation, with testimony from twenty-two prominent members of Montana society, to visit China and reenter the United States. With this documentation in order, Lee travelled to China in 1890, married, and brought his wife to Montana. In 1893 the Lees welcomed a daughter. Helena newspapers reported it was "the first Chinese baby born in lawful wedlock in Helena." Lee sought the help of local firemen to summon the doctor and to assist in delivering the baby. The article joked that the firemen "fear[ed] that the United States marshal will be after them for having assisted in bringing a Chinaman into this country." Yet the article acknowledged that birth in America equaled citizenship, which was not available in any way to the parents: "She can go to China and return as she pleases, being an American citizen."[54] American citizenship conferred far more rights than being able to travel back and forth to China. Lee and his wife went on to have three more daughters. When they exercised their rights as American citizens, Montana newspapers took note.

As the nation changed during the Progressive Era of the early twentieth century, social and cultural trends impacted the Lee family as well, though their ethnicity was always emphasized more than their status as citizens. Montana newspapers took pride in the accomplishments of the Lee sisters. Countering an assertion that Cincinnati "claim[ed] to have the only Chinese typist in the United States," an article proudly announced that the Lee sisters of Helena were remarkable for their role in the workforce. The article noted with pride that Helena had "two Chinese girls who are typists and stenographers. They are sisters, the Misses Ruby Lee and Jennie Lee, daughters of Lee Sam Fong, a merchant, who died there 12 years ago. There are two other Lee girls, Miss Lilly Lee, a photographer, and Miss Mamie Lee, a bookkeeper."[55] Montana women earned the right to vote in 1914, making the state an earlier adopter of women's suffrage. In 1916 the Lee women gained attention by exercising this right, but not without questions about the legality of their doing so. Upon applying to register to vote, the clerk at the county office "was not sure that they were entitled to registration," due not to their gender, but their ethnicity. After the issue had been raised to the county attorney, it was finally determined that they were "qualified under the law to have all the rights of other women in the state." Asked for whom they would vote, "each sister said she was going to vote for the best man."[56] In fact, they had the opportunity to vote for a woman in the election of 1916. Montana's Jeannette Rankin had worked to gain the right for women to vote and was elected to the U.S. House of Representatives that year.[57]

During the early twentieth century, Montana's newspapers celebrated Chinese American women who they viewed as modern and empowered. One such woman was Billings resident Annie Lewis, also known as Annie Luie or Art Tin, though newspapers often confused this last name for that of the husband she sought to divorce. Her request for a divorce in 1901 garnered frequent coverage, with Billings newspapers observing, "What is undoubtedly the first petition for divorce ever filed in the state in which both the plaintiff and defendant are Chinese."[58] As with the daughters of Lee Sam Fong, this reporting ignored the fact that Lewis was an American citizen owing to her birth in the United States.[59] In addition to her advocating for a divorce, Montana's newspapers took interest in Lewis's modern views on Chinese workers. Yet even in an extensive feature praising Lewis for her modern ideas, cultural stereotypes persisted, with the writer describing her as "Dainty, petite and 21 years of age, she is remarkably handsome—for a Chinese woman." The article portrayed her appearance as quite modern before transitioning to the point of the commentary—her views on labor organization across racial lines. Lewis believed that

> instead of competing with American workingmen, Chinamen will occupy their niche in the world and all will work to a common end, the betterment of the condition of mankind. Such is the dream of little Annie Luie [who] with American notions, has some very broad ideas of reform. She believes that her Mongolian brethren would make valuable and worthy members of labor unions—were they only taught what it means. She purposes doing that. . . . Her plan is simple enough. She would join a labor organization herself . . . and teach the doctrines in every city in the United States where there is a Chinese laundry or tea store. A very laudable ambition, is it not? . . . [She] cherishes the plan to redeem her countrymen from the race prejudice which exists. She secured employment in a Billings restaurant, where she is still working [and studying] for the time when she will start out upon her evangelical work.[60]

It is interesting that the article celebrating Lewis as a "A Chinese Girl who thinks the American Way is the Right Way" originally appeared in the *Anaconda Standard*, a city whose residents had expelled the Chinese from their midst. Other papers across the nation took note of the reform-minded Lewis, with versions of the article appearing as far away as Mississippi.[61]

While some women from Montana's Chinese communities who entered jobs emerged with new technological skills—such as the Lees, who worked as stenographers and typists—others sought a return to the work that first brought Chinese migrants to the region. Ah Hee

Yong, often referred to by her stage name Soo Yong, gained attention in Montana in the 1930s for her efforts to restart the state's gold mining industry. She took a circuitous route to Montana. Born in Hawaii in 1903, she graduated from the University of Hawaii with a bachelor's degree in education and drama. In 1927 she sought to attend graduate school at Columbia University. Though an American citizen through her birth in the Territory of Hawaii, Yong had to undergo an extensive interview process to travel from Hawaii to New York. Suspected of impropriety because of her gender and ethnicity, she was finally allowed transit, though her file carried the qualified status of "Chinese in America."[62] Yong completed her master's degree in education, having been one of only fifty women of Chinese descent studying in an American institution of higher education at the time. While in New York, her interest in acting resulted in numerous opportunities on Broadway. With her elegant presence on stage and bilingual abilities, Yong earned a role that launched her acting career and, in unlikely ways, prompted a reinvigorated Chinese presence in Montana's goldfields.

In 1930 famed Peking Opera performer Mei Lanfang began an American tour. An adaptation of traditional Peking opera, the program featured selections from classic Chinese operas. Advertisements noted: "Mr. Mei is supported by his own company of actors, dancers and musicians, in four short plays and dances, the meaning of which is fully explained before each scene by the charming mistress of ceremonies Miss Soo Yong."[63] New York audiences adored the presentation, causing the theater to extend the performance by three weeks to meet demand. Crowds clamored for tickets, willing to pay six times their face value. Diners reportedly paid $500 per table and $1,000 for balcony seats at banquets for Mei that five thousand guests attended, a surprising amount given the context of the economic depression.[64] Following the run in New York, Mei's tour travelled to Chicago, San Francisco, and Los Angeles, introduced and interpreted along the way by Soo Yong. San Francisco newspapers noted the impact of Mei's tour, stating that he "has done more to give America some sympathetic understanding of his race than reams of diplomatic correspondence could do."[65] While spectators responded to the performance itself, much of the enjoyment was due to Soo Yong's interpretation and connection with English-speaking audiences.

During these travels Soo Yong met powerful people across the nation both from Chinese communities and the broader American elite. They included R. A. Brett, who had connections in Montana's mining industries. Yong convinced Chinese investors to back Brett and the revival of gold mining in Montana. In 1931, based on connections made during her travels, Soo Yong (referred to as Ah Hee Yong while in Montana) joined a group working to revive gold mining in the state. The efforts attracted attention of the state's press: "The famous Wanetka [*sic*] gold quartz property has been taken over by a group of Chinese headed by Miss Ah Hee Yong."[66] Serving as secretary for the Winnetka mine outside Virginia City, Yong advised on financial matters and facilitated an infusion of capital from Chinese investors. Articles noted her frequent visits to the area and her desire to become more knowledgeable about mining practices. Some reports claimed that she was "the only Chinese woman mining engineer in the world."[67] While this overstates her formal training, her desire to gain expertise was sincere: "Since her arrival in Butte four months ago, she has acquired an intense enthusiasm for mining prospects there. She intends to devote her life to mining engineering, and is at present studying under R.A. Brett, president of the Winnetka company. Later she expects to seek a formal engineering education." Considering her rising star in the acting world, that she devoted so much time to these initiatives in Montana is noteworthy.

Beyond her desire to learn modern engineering techniques, Yong brought a deep understanding of the contribution that Chinese miners had made to Montana's development. In an extensive interview, Yong noted that thousands of: "Chinese once mined in the placers of Alder Gulch, and it is altogether fitting that one of the race should aid in bringing a renaissance to the famous camp. . . . I feel that mining engineering is not only a natural but a worthy ambition for a Chinese girl. Only, I shall have to be a good miner to live up to the traditions of the race."[68] The Winnetka mine produced good results throughout the 1930s.[69] Despite her interest in mining, her stage career drew her away, though it had allowed her to spread a view of Chinese American women as strong, capable, and modern.

After arriving in Hollywood, Soo Yong acted alongside Greta Garbo in *The Painted Veil* (1934), Mae West in *Klondike Annie* (1936), Clark Gable and Jean Harlow in *China Seas* (1936), and Gary Cooper in *The Adventures of Marco Polo* (1938). Building upon these successes, Soo Yong sought a role in the screen adaptation of Pearl Buck's novel *The Good Earth*. She expressed her desire to play a leading role, noting that she was "eager to play O-Lan, who has been made the central character of the film. I want to play her as an intelligent, respectful Chinese wife, not a stupid woman who takes her husband's blows without complaint. I want to make her the great kind woman I knew in my own village—the Chinese woman unknown to the American screen."[70] Hollywood, however, was not yet ready to cast an Asian actress in a leading role; the role of O-Lan was played by German-born Luise Rainer. Soo Yong did have two roles in the film and her status in Chinese American and Chinese cultural circles grew with her success.

While Yong's professional career accelerated during the decade, she remained connected to Montana and her business partners from the Winnetka mining endeavor. She visited the state often, hosting gatherings to talk about Chinese culture and her time in Hollywood. During her climb to stardom, her views on the role of Chinese women remained consistent with the thoughts that she expressed in 1931 during the efforts to restart mining in Montana. "Chinese women," she argued, "are quite as modern as American women. They have representatives in almost every profession."[71] She even combined her talents at public performance with her views on Chinese women to develop an original monologue "depict[ing] the changing status of the Chinese women during the last 25 years."[72] The performance, titled "Out from the Inner Apartment," interested audience members and spoke to the transition noted earlier with merchants' wives in Butte progressing from being restricted to the home to becoming modern, contributing, equal members of American society.

Perhaps no woman from Montana's Chinese community embodies

the "Out from the Inner Apartment" transition more than Rose Hum Lee. The extensive interviews cited above about arranged marriage and the habits of Chinese women in Butte are from Lee's study of the city's Chinese residents in her role as a sociologist. Her life embodies the complicated trends of Chinese American women becoming more assimilated into American society, serving as a bridge between the two cultures, yet seen as forever foreign in the eyes of many non-Chinese and, in some ways, before the law. Born in 1904 to a successful merchant—making her an American citizen from birth—Lee was troubled by the separation of Butte's Chinatown from the non-Chinese community. In her scholarly work, Lee encouraged the Chinese in America to assimilate and do away with traditional culture to become fully American.[73] Circumstances, however, complicated Rose Hum Lee's claim to the Americanness that she advocated.

In 1921 Lee married Ku Young Lee, a student at the University of Pennsylvania. Since her husband was not an American citizen, the marriage changed Rose Hum Lee's official status. The Expatriation Act of 1907 defined a woman's status based on that of her husband. Since Ku Young Lee was not and could not become an American citizen, Rose Hum Lee forfeited her American citizenship upon marriage.[74] While the Expatriation Act applied to more residents than just Chinese American women, it disproportionately impacted this group due to the longstanding legal definition of Chinese people as "ineligible for citizenship." Marriage prospects for American-born Chinese women who sought to keep their citizenship were few due to anti-miscegenation laws aimed at preventing marriage outside one's ethnicity and the small number of Chinese men who were American citizens. As women across the nation advocated for equality during the early twentieth century, however, increasing access to rights allowed them to challenge to such restrictions. One of the first causes that Jeanette Rankin took up while representing Montana in Congress was to work for the repeal of the Expatriation Act. Rankin argued in 1917 that "an American man has the right to citizenship regardless of his marriage, and that the woman has the same right."[75] Despite her efforts, the disruption caused by American entry into World War I and the complications of split citizenship during wartime delayed action on this subject. The 1922 Cable Act erased much of the intent of the Expatriation Act, enabling an American wife of a noncitizen to retain her citizenship as long as she had not resided in her husband's home country for more than two years or spent five years in any foreign nation. If she had been abroad longer than the terms indicated, she could regain American citizenship by going through the naturalization process. For women of Chinese ethnicity, this remained impossible. While the Cable Act was a step toward independent citizenship for most women, Chinese American women remained distanced from their citizenship, gained at birth, lost through marriage, and impossible to regain.[76]

Lee and her husband lived in Guangzhou (Canton) during the 1920s and 1930s.[77] It seems she fought with her in-laws, possibly due to the lack of children the marriage produced and the cultural clash between her Americanness and their Chineseness. When war broke out between China and Japan, Lee worked with Madame Chiang Kai-Shek's "Chinese Women National War Relief Society" caring for thousands of "warphans," children left parentless due to the fighting.[78] With the fighting expanding and her marriage deteriorating, Lee left China just before Guangzhou fell to the Japanese. Amendments to the Cable Act throughout the 1930s finally corrected the situation that caused American-born Chinese women to lose their citizenship after marrying a noncitizen. While Lee reentered the country with her citizenship restored, her loss of citizenship remained a painful reminder of the perpetual foreignness that Chinese women in America experienced. In letters to her adopted daughter, Lee expressed frustration that the government had no right to revoke her "birthright as a citizen."[79] Especially for Lee, who argued that the Chinese in America could be accepted as fully American if they abandoned outdated traditions, the federal government view that her ethnicity and the foreignness of her husband superseded her citizenship reinforced anti-Chinese sentiment both in law and society.

Upon her return to America, Lee lectured across the nation about the war in China, noting the benefits of wartime unity: "The war has [unified] us because Chinese people are determined that they shall not be dominated . . . The war has given all Chinese a common purpose and the new unity will carry the country to greater heights."[80] After the attack on Pearl Harbor and the entry of the United States into World War II, China and America forged an alliance against Japan. With this bond, continued restrictions on Chinese immigration and citizenship were seen as embarrassing remnants of past racist policies. As the next chapter will describe in more detail, the 1943 Magnuson Act ended Chinese exclusion and the prohibition on Chinese becoming naturalized citizens.

This wartime unity dissolved after World War II when the Chinese Communists prevailed against the Nationalists in the Chinese Civil War. By that time Lee had divorced her first husband and had completed her academic training to become a sociologist. By 1947, Lee had earned her doctorate in Sociology from the University of Chicago, having studied with some of the most renowned individuals in the field. In 1956 Lee became the chair of the sociology department at Chicago's Roosevelt University, the first woman and first Chinese American to lead an academic department at an American university. A well-respected teacher and scholar, Lee's studies focused on Chinese communities throughout the nation, especially her home community in Butte, Montana.[81]

In 1952 Lee married Glenn Ginn, a lawyer and leader of Tucson, Arizona's Chinese community. As the tensions of the Cold War and Red Scare gripped America, Lee felt increasingly anxious about Chinese Communist plots she thought were aimed at her and her husband. She believed her academic study of America's Chinatowns angered some in these communities and that they sought retribution. With Lee living and teaching in Chicago, she and Ginn stayed in touch by mail, but she suspected their "enemies" intercepted these letters. Lee believed that she and Ginn were the victims of a plot that combined tactics from Chinese secret societies with new Communist schemes that sought to intimidate, slander, and threaten them. She informed various government agencies of her suspicions and promised information that would reveal vast Communist schemes in Chinese communities in America. It appears, however, that her paranoia was not grounded in fact.[82] Throughout the late–1950s she became increasingly distant from Chinese culture and communities, continuing to stress the need for assimilation. She nonetheless remained troubled by her past experiences, which showed her that citizenship did not always mean inclusion into American society. She chafed at being part of two cultures but somewhat outside both. She advised her adopted daughter to be wary of Chinese communities to avoid "all the mean pressures and blackmailing that goes on." Yet her daughter also experienced racist treatment in non-Chinese circles. Lee, perhaps reflecting back on the time when her ethnicity and the foreignness of her first husband resulted in the loss of her American citizenship, advised her daughter "the fact that you can't lose your physical identity is something beyond my control." [83] Trapped between two cultures, Rose Hum Lee's experience, though considerably more modern than her Chinese American predecessors, shows how the feeling of being seen as forever foreign lingered well into the twentieth century.

From the earliest days of Montana's development, when many assumed that every Chinese woman must be a prostitute, to the tentative status of citizenship they gained but could easily be stripped away, Chinese and Chinese American women in Montana struggled to overcome many obstacles. Some of these barriers came from within Chinese culture, with its patriarchal practices that confined women. Many of the hurdles were from assumptions, stereotypes, and laws projected onto Chinese women from non-Chinese Montanans. Unfortunately, most of individual struggles can be known only in the most general way due to the paucity of sources. Yet several extraordinary women appear in the documents, such as Annie Lewis, Rose Hum Lee, Ah Hee Yong and others who illustrate the ability to persevere and emerge "Out from the Inner Apartment."

EIGHT

Cold War Fears and Chinese Communities, 1930s–1950s

The 1930s and 1940s brought new dangers to China and new challenges to Chinese American communities. The Chinese Civil War, with fighting between the Nationalists and the Communists, gripped the nation. These forces only paused their conflict when the Japanese invaded China, causing incredible destruction from the late 1930s through 1945. The civil war resumed following the end of the Japanese occupation, ultimately resulting in the victory of Mao Zedong and the Communists in 1949. China's turn to Communism caused suspicion of Chinese communities in the United States and of Chinese people seeking to enter the country. Over the course of three decades America's Chinese residents went from excluded, to allies, to suspects, reflecting the geopolitics of the time. One family's saga reveals the ongoing difficulties of traveling between the nations, providing for family members back in southern China, and striving to be accepted in Montana. The story of the Hom family illustrates how they experienced change, adaptation, and acculturation while also highlighting how Chinese individuals faced continued suspicion based on their assumed illegality and the sentiment that they were unassimilable into American society.

Wing Hong Hom, though born in China in 1919, was recognized as an American citizen upon entry to the United States in 1933.[1] Despite this status, Wing Hong Hom found his rights limited during his almost three decades of residence in Montana. Laws restricted his movement, choice of occupation, and even marital opportunities. Most significantly, though Wing Hong Hom gained entry to the United States through his status as an American citizen, his brother Wing Goon Hom found his claim, based on identical circumstances, questioned to the point of being barred from joining his brother in Montana. The brothers' story spans many eras important to the Chinese experience in the West, notably the Exclusion Era (1882–1943), the war years (1941–1945), and the Cold War, when the Communist victory in the Chinese Civil War cast new suspicions on the Chinese community in America.

Separated by hardships due to war, global depression, and revolution, in 1949 the brothers sought to reunite in Montana where Wing Hong Hom had lived since 1933. At first the brothers were optimistic that the process of getting Wing Goon out of China and into the United States would be simple. After all, Wing Hong had gained admittance to the United States. He had also visited China recently and successfully reentered America. Race-based immigration restrictions long in place due to the Chinese Exclusion Act of 1882 ended in 1943 as America and China allied to fight Japan. With exclusion over and knowing relatives who had successfully been recognized as citizens, Wing Goon Hom was optimistic as he traveled from the family's home village in Taishan County to Hong Kong in July 1949. Writing to Wing Hong Hom in Butte, Wing Goon expressed his optimism: "I am now in Hong Kong going through the process of applying to go to the U.S. All the formalities should be completed within a short period of time. . . . When you see this letter, please go quickly to arrange a passport so that I can start working on it in Hong Kong. Best wishes, Younger Brother Wing Goon."[2] Wing Goon wrote again four months later: "I would like to know the status of my immigration application. Is it proceeding? Please be honest with me and let me know if I have done anything wrong."[3] His desperation mounted as geopolitical tensions rose. Nine months after starting the process, Wing Goon wrote: "If the passport application is successful, please send it to me immediately so that I may proceed. Right now, the U.S.-Soviet standoff is at a deadlock. At any provocation, a real war might begin. Please, brother, send it quickly so that obstacles can be avoided."[4]

Despite the efforts of both brothers, who submitted every document, photograph, payment, and affidavit requested by the government, the rules kept fluctuating. America's post–World War II immigration policies changed so frequently that sometimes documents submitted in accordance with the letter of the law were negated due to changes in policy between submission of the forms and their evaluation. Immigration officials and diplomatic personnel in charge of enforcing Chinese exclusion for so long found new energy for exclusion through growing fears of Communism. Bureaucratic red tape and ever-increasing levels of proof frustrated would-be migrants. As one letter regarding the family's case read, "Dear Sir: I am sorry that it is necessary to return your petition for the issuance of a visa. . . . It is necessary, however, that you answer all the questions under item #7. I know that this is contrary to the instructions contained in the form but this is necessary in the case of Chinese petitioners for the reason that there are no vital statistics."[5]

What this actually meant was that government officials did not trust evidence provided by Chinese applicants due to suspicions of fraud. The denial of the visa request continued, "We also have new instructions in regard to this type of case under which it is necessary that all Chinese petitioners have a blood test by a certified physician and submit to this Service a certified statement from that physician as to the type of blood."[6]

With these ever-changing rules and the constant suspicion about the validity of claims of family relation, Wing Goon Hom remained trapped in uncertainty. In contrast to his earlier optimism, after being stranded in Hong Kong for years Wing Goon wrote despairingly to his brother in 1953: "I beg you to find a powerful westerner and ask him to be the guarantor of my documents. Please ask the westerner with his reputation and authority to write a request to the Department of State to accept my application to go to America . . . Brother, I beg you, I am in a dire situation in Hong Kong . . . my present chance is slim."[7] Wing Hong Hom, diligently working on his brother's behalf since 1949, reached out to a "powerful and renowned westerner." Yet even the help of Montana senator Mike Mansfield proved insufficient. Wing Hong began working with Glenn Ginn, a lawyer with experience in similar cases. After repeatedly submitting all

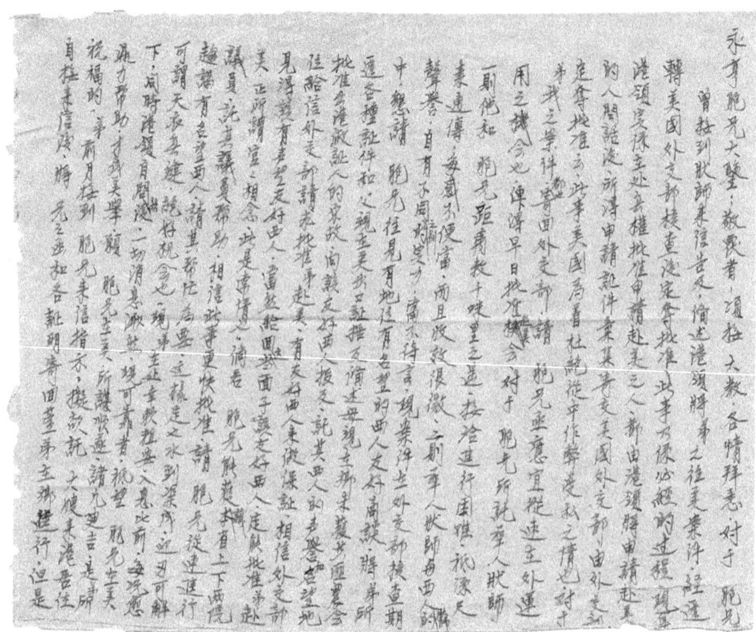

24. Letter from Wing Goon Hom to Wing Hong Hom, August 11, 1953. Wing Hong Hum Papers, 89–30.194, UPMC 87:2–4, Montana Historical Society Research Center Archives, Helena MT.

the required documents, Ginn too began to lose hope. Four years to the day of Wing Goon's optimistic assessment, Ginn despaired to supporters interested in the brothers' affairs: "Hom Wing Hung has been trying for several years to bring his brother Hom Wing Goon to the United States to which he is entitled to enter as an American citizen by virtue of the father's American citizenship. The application for entry was filed at the American Consulate at Hong Kong and the strongest evidence conceivable was presented in support of the application. For reason or reasons unknown to all interested parties, the Consul was not satisfied."[8]

Unfortunately for the Hom family and thousands of others in similar situations, staunch anti-Communists who held deep suspicions of all potential Chinese migrants had ascended to control the American consulate in Hong Kong. Many of these officials held deep-seated hostility against the Chinese for racial reasons, feeling that the population was racially unassimilable and inclined to fraud and perjury. By raising the fear of Communist infiltration through the systems that some Chinese had used to subvert exclusion, these officials succeeded in reasserting Chinese Exclusion in all but name.

Wing Goon and more than 117,000 others stuck in Hong Kong in 1950 faced dizzying bureaucratic red tape allegedly designed to vet potential migrants but truly intended to exclude.[9] Officials required ever more evidence, including lengthy interrogations, extensive photographic proof of family relations, blood tests, x-rays, and the testimony of white witnesses.[10] American officials in Hong Kong assumed deceit in every interaction. With this level of suspicion, it is no surprise that Wing Goon became frustrated. The more interesting question is why he had been so optimistic in 1949, when he believed that "all the formalities should be completed within a short period of time."

During the Exclusion Era, Chinese people seeking to come to America faced increasingly restrictive laws first designed to exclude certain classes of immigrants and eventually Chinese people altogether. Those who had gained entry legally were restricted in leaving and reentering the country, prohibited from becoming naturalized citizens, forced to register and obtain character references from white witnesses, and required to carry identification at all times or face deportation. Chinese residents of the American West faced hostility, legal discrimination, violence, complaints that they failed to assimilate into American life, and general suspicions that their presence was based on devious circumvention of the law. Indeed, some sentiments of the questionable nature of Chinese migration were merited. Since the passage of the Chinese Exclusion Act in 1882, many Chinese people exploited loopholes to gain entry to the United States. Sometimes this included posing as merchants or students, groups that were allowed entry even during exclusion. By far the more common practice was through the "paper son" system. Chinese who had gained entry to the United States would return to China for family visits. Upon reentry they would indicate the birth of a child, almost always a son. Whether or not an actual child had been born, the indication of this birth to American officials created a paper trail called a "slot" that could be used for anyone matching the description to enter the United States as the professed offspring of a legal migrant. These paper sons, as they were known, gained entry in large numbers even during the period of exclusion designed to bar Chinese admission.

Many Chinese felt morally justified in circumventing exclusion due to the racially motivated nature of the law. Having been welcomed as workers previously through agreements such as the 1868 Burlingame Treaty, for many Chinese employment abroad meant survival for family members back home. This was especially true for the residents of Taishan County in southern China, a region that had been ravaged by flood, famine, rebellion, drought, and economic instability from the mid-nineteenth century on. Until 1960 more than half of the Chinese who came to America came from Taishan.[11] As one migrant stated: "The reason we Chinese come to the United States is because of . . . extremity at home, we have no other method by which we can keep our bodies and souls together. Should we be blocked in this . . . will our calamity not be inexpressible?"[12] If survival meant perpetrating fraud against a government that passed racially motivated laws to discriminate against an entire ethnicity, so be it. "We didn't want to come in illegally, but we were forced to because of the immigration laws. They particularly picked on the Chinese. If we told the truth, it didn't work. So we had to take the crooked path."[13]

To discover if the person attempting to enter the United States was indeed the blood relative of a legal migrant, immigration officials developed extensive interrogation techniques. With hundreds of questions designed to trip up pretenders, Chinese migrants used coaching books to memorize family specifics. The interrogations were so minutely detailed that even true relatives relied on coaching books, as families had often been separated for years and memories could not keep up with the level of detail required during the interrogation.[14] As interrogations proved ever less effective at detecting lies, officials required submission of more evidence to prove relationships.

Many Chinese entered under false circumstances, pretending to be the son of a citizen or to have been born in America. Undoubtedly, however, many were who they claimed to be. Given the secretive nature of how the Chinese approached the issue and the paranoid viewpoints of the immigration officials, the number of true versus fraudulent cases can never be known. For the case of the brothers Wing Hong and Wing Goon Hom, through close reading of correspondence over several decades, it is clear that a family affinity was present.[15] At times the U.S. government acknowledged this familial connection; yet at other times the government called it into question.

In early 1956, as Wing Goon Hom remained stranded in Hong Kong, his paperwork having been submitted numerous times with additional documentation provided as requested, the man in charge of his fate was Everett F. Drumright who viewed Chinese people as "culturally inclined to fraud and perjury."[16] Serving as the U.S. Consul in Hong Kong from 1954 to 1958, Drumright epitomized the combination of Cold Warrior seeking to prevent Communist infiltration and old-fashioned exclusionist seeking to keep out Chinese due to the view that they were racially unassimilable. In late 1955 Drumright reported that his office had succeeded in proving fraud in 85 percent of cases investigated and suspected fraud in the rest.[17] With men like Drumright in charge of entry, chances were indeed slim.

Wing Goon Hom's chance to be granted entry rested on his claim to derivative citizenship. The Hom family's claim to entry was based on the assertion that the patriarch, Hom Fook, was born in San Francisco in 1878. Shortly after his birth he was taken back to China, where he remained until seeking reentry to the United States in 1898. Port officials initially denied his admittance. Advocating for his rights, he secured legal counsel and a district court judge affirmed his status as a citizen. Before returning to America, Hom Fook married and fathered three sons. Due to his status as an American citizen, though they had been born in China, his sons could claim American citizenship through derivative citizenship as long as they traveled to the United States before they reached a certain age (either sixteen or twenty-three depending on the ever-changing American laws) to establish their citizenship. Two of these sons, Hom Kee and Hom Fong, came to America, arriving with their father in June 1916 and gaining admittance as U.S. citizens. Hom Kee settled in Butte where he worked in a laundry. He returned to China several times, marrying and fathering Wing Hong (1919) and Wing Goon (1920). Thus, the status of citizen that passed from Hom Fook to Hom Kee also passed to Wing Hong and Wing Goon. The U.S. government nonetheless looked with suspicion on these claims of citizenship and family ties not only for the Hom family but all Chinese attempting to gain entry as derivative citizens.

Hom Fook returned to America in 1916 accompanied by two of his sons. Immigration officials questioned them to assess the validity of their claims. These interrogations produced records that stayed in the family's file to be cross-referenced against future applicants for entry.[18] Similar to the Hom family, between 1920 and 1940 71,040 Chinese gained entrance to the United States as derivative citizens.[19]

The Hom family fell on hard times during the worldwide depression in the late 1920s. Early in 1933 Hom Fook initiated the process to bring his son, Hom Hong, and his grandson, Wing Hong Hom, to the United States. Hom Kee, Wing Hong Hom's father, had died in China in 1929. The economic disruption of the Great Depression, coupled with the loss of Hom Kee's earning power, necessitated that Wing Hong Hom take on increased responsibilities. Additionally, Hom Hong, who was eighteen, and Wing Hong Hom, who was fourteen, intended to establish residence in the United States and secure American citizenship as derivative citizens. Hom Fook undertook the lengthy process to bring his son and grandson to America by submitting an affidavit with detailed descriptions of his family members and their home village. This document, along with considerable fees, started the process. Immigration officials detained Hom Hong and Wing Hong Hom upon landing in Seattle in March 1933 to evaluate their alleged status as U.S. citizens.

Immigration officials accessed files detailing the family's history to use during the interrogation of supposed relatives with the intent of catching fraudulent "paper sons." Officers assiduously recorded these answers and compared them against Hom Fook's details as recorded during his reentry to the United States in 1916. Officials separated the boys for interrogation, with Hom Hong answering 124 questions on April 4 and Wing Hong Hom fielding 120 questions the following day. Immigration officials noted that: "Applicants

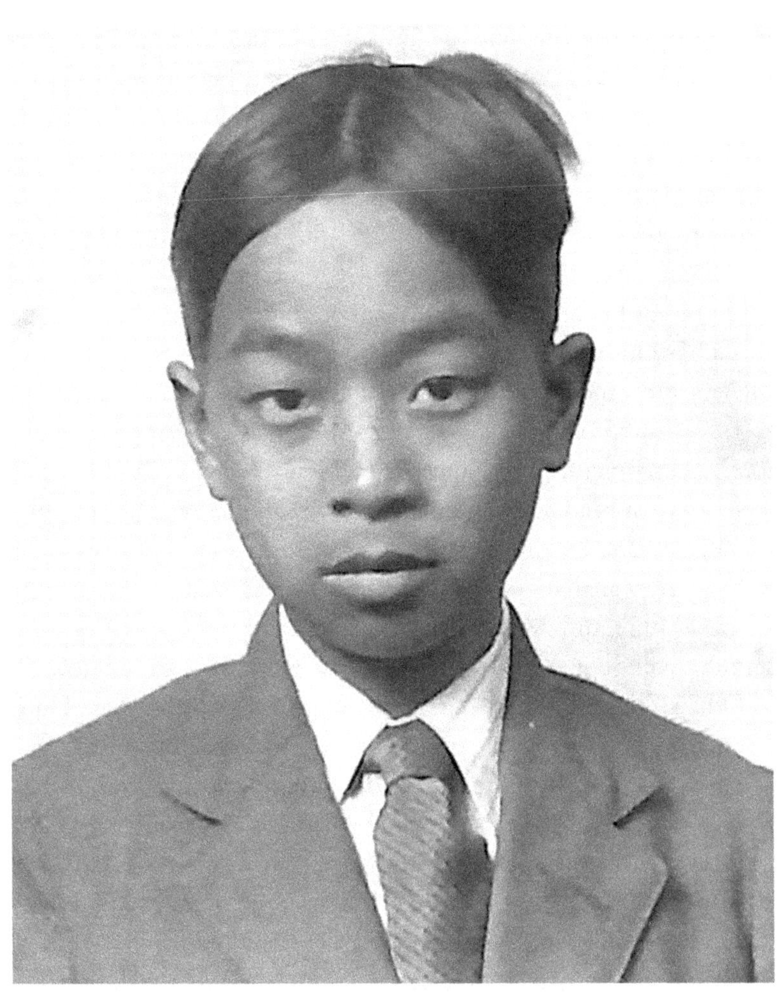

25. Wing Hong Hom, 1933. Immigration file for Hom Wing Hung. Chinese Exclusion Act case files, file 7030/5252, RG 85, National Archives at Seattle WA.

have been examined along the lines of testimony taken at San Francisco in 1916 from Hom Fook's two oldest sons, Hom Kee and Hom Fong, and no differences have been noted. Applicants' testimony is also in entire agreement with each other."[20] However, this was not enough proof of their alleged status as sons of citizens. To further corroborate their identity, copies of these interrogations were sent to immigration officials in Denver where Hom Fook traveled from his home in Laramie, Wyoming, answering more than three hundred questions with a level of detail designed to ferret out fraud. The interrogation included exchanges such as these: "Q. Are there any pictures or photographs in your house. A. Yes. Q. What pictures are there? A. My picture and Hom Kee and Hom Fong. Q. Are they full length or just head and shoulders? A. Just half pictures. Q. Are they framed? A. Yes. Q. Are they sitting on a table or hanging against a wall? A. They are hanging on the wall. Q. What room are they in? A. In the sitting room. When I was home about 17 years ago they were on the small door side. Maybe they have changed them by now."[21]

Officials in Kansas City questioned Hom Fook's second son, Hom Fong. These officials were somewhat less rigorous, only posing one hundred questions to Hom Fong to test his purported relationship with his alleged brother and nephew detained in Seattle. Bureaucrats returned records of these interrogations to Seattle where officials identified discrepancies, requiring the reexamination of Hom Hong and Wing Hong Hom. On May 3 both young men were "recalled and questioned further, after being admonished to tell the truth." Questions included: "To Hom Hong: Q. Can you explain why your alleged father should state that Hom Hoy Wah and his wife are living? A. They may have been living when my father returned to the U.S. the last time, but that was when I was 4 or 5 yrs. Old." They also asked Wing Hong Hom, "Q. Can you explain why your grandfather reverses the locations of Hom Tai's house and Hom Gong's house? A. I think he is mistaken; he hasn't been home for a long time."[22]

This reexamination satisfied immigration officials that Hom Hong and Wing Hong Hom were indeed who they claimed to be. Officials admitted the Homs to America after six weeks in detention, with their status as U.S. citizens acknowledged on May 4, 1933.

With opportunities for Chinese Americans limited in general and worsened by the Great Depression, the Hom family took work in roles traditionally open to Chinese throughout the nation. Both Hom Fook and Hom Fong returned to restaurant work in Laramie and Kansas City, respectively. Hom Hong traveled to New York City to work in a laundry. These occupations had developed as key economic opportunities given restrictions from other job sectors. As "Mr. Low, who grew up in New York City's Chinatown, recalled before World War II, the vast majority of Chinese earned a living in only three types of work: 'In those days, it's the laundry, the restaurant business, or a store helper. That's it.'"[23]

Wing Hong Hom came directly to Montana and joined Butte's Chinatown, formerly the Rocky Mountain region's largest Chinese community. Yet opportunities in Butte had dwindled. Throughout the first half of the twentieth century, major population shifts in the Chinese American community caused Chinatowns in the mountain and western regions to decline. Historian Ronald Takaki quantified this move to urban areas, noting: "By 1940, 91 percent of the Chinese population, compared to only 55 percent of the Japanese (and 57 percent of the total U.S. population), was classified by the Census bureau as 'urban.'"[24] With this shift in population came decreased job opportunities in Montana. For instance, in 1905 in Butte Chinese businessmen operated thirty-one different laundries. By 1940 the number had decreased to six, with only three remaining in business in 1945.[25] Even with these limited opportunities, Wing Hong Hom found employment in the Tong Sing Laundry and the Quong Sun Laundry working throughout the 1930s and into the 1940s. Wing Hong Hom regularly sent remittances back to Taishan to aid relatives and fulfill his familial obligations.

While life in Butte during the depression was not easy, circumstances in southern China were even more difficult. For sixty years, flood, famine, rebellion, drought, and economic instability ravaged Taishan. During the 1930s and 1940s a new disruption threatened the region and China as a whole. As a Wing Hong Hom's brother wrote in 1941: "In the 30th year of the Republic of China, the Japanese army occupied Hong Kong. . . . Third brother and I finish breakfast everyday at 6 o'clock and go to Taicheng to sell old clothes every day until 6 o'clock at night. The business is hard, and profits are thin."[26] With the region's stability disrupted by war, money sent from Wing Hong Hom and other relatives working in America was increasingly vital to support the family. Letters thank him for sending money and encourage him to send more. Being confined to work only in the laundry business, however, limited Wing Hong Hom's earning power.

For Chinese residents of Montana, these occupations were not only the traditional roles filled by Chinese workers, but legislative restrictions limited non-citizens from numerous other occupations including "attorney, auctioneer, dentist, guide, liquor, mine, optometrist, pharmacist, physician, teacher."[27] Chinese Montanans had been key to early placer mining in the territory but with the onset of underground mining, law and local custom systematically excluded the Chinese. While this restriction technically should not have applied to a citizen like Wing Hong Hom, it appears that the intent of the law was to limit those of Chinese ethnicity regardless of status. Yet opportunities emerged with the onset of World War II, which caused an increased need for Butte's copper. Wing Hong Hom became the first Chinese miner to work in Butte's underground mines in more than six decades.[28] Wing Hong Hom later commented on his work as a motorman in the Mountain Con Mine:

> I knew a friend who worked in the mines; I became acquainted with him as he is a customer of ours at the laundry. He took me to the [Anaconda Copper Mining Company] employment office and helped me fill out the blanks. After that I was handed a card and told to go to work in any mine I wanted to. I went to the one in Meaderville, but didn't like it. The work was new to me, and the foreman told me to go to the "students" slope to learn operations. I did not like to do that, but finally did so when I was told the same thing by the foreman in the next shaft. The work was not hard; I did this for three whole months; measuring the ground to be dug. I wanted repair work later on; I was immediately given a job. Then I learned how to do other work. That paid $10 a day. I contracted directly with

the company for it, but it was dangerous work. I never knew what diggings I would be assigned to. Finally I gave it up and went to a supply job. This was safer than handling dynamite at the diggings job—several times the earth caved in and I almost got into accidents.[29]

Increased industrial needs were not the only impact of the threat of war. The U.S. government instituted a peacetime draft to increase military preparedness as American involvement in the war became likely. Because Chinese American men so often were without dependents due to limited marriage opportunities in America, they were drafted at a rate higher than the non-Chinese population.[30] Wing Hong Hom received notification to appear before the local draft board in January 1941, eleven months before the Japanese attack on Pearl Harbor. Because his father had died in 1929 and his grandfather Hom Fook's age lessened his ability to provide for the extended family, Wing Hong Hom became the primary breadwinner for his mother and siblings struggling to survive in war-torn southern China. For this reason, Wing Hong Hom appealed to the local draft board for a deferment based on the claim that his dependents needed his financial support. The draft board recognized his role as providing for dependents and granted his appeal.[31] A decade later, the government questioned if these same dependents were in fact family, erecting obstacle after obstacle to their entry to America to join Wing Hong Hom.

Wing Hong Hom's family benefited from his increased earnings but worried about the dangers of his new job. Cousin Hom Tong wrote: "We have received your letter from America. We are all happy with your job mining. Under these circumstances working, though, one has to be very careful. Is your health good?"[32] Family members were right to worry. The dangerous conditions in the mines, worsened by increased needs of wartime production, resulted in numerous accidents.[33] Though work in the mines in Butte was dangerous, the benefit to the Allied war effort must have been on Wing Hong Hom's mind as his family felt the suffering from the war firsthand.

By 1943 the Japanese occupied Taishan, destroying the Hom family's home village. Wing Hong Hom's grandmother, Lee Shee, died during the Japanese occupation of the village. Key documents were destroyed as well, which had important implications years later when family members worked to prove relationships as they sought entry to the United States.

About the other documents: regarding the certificate of us rescuing children that you reported to the Department of Enlistment Service, please use the child photo that I took and write an explanation for it. The actual photo of us rescuing the child was in our house in the old village but our house, including the photo and other family pictures, was burned to the ground by the Japanese army when they invaded. A destroyed family photograph [from the late 1920s] had Grandmother, Father, Mother, Third Uncle, you, me, Brother Soong, Brother Tong, Sister, in total of nine people on it.[34]

Back in Montana, Wing Hong Hom worked long hours to support family members in China. During this time, he became more integrated into Butte's non-Chinese community, forming friendships and even being allowed to join the union. He later explained:

At first I thought the work at the mines would be hard, but I was surprised to find that the "Piece" method meant each man had his special job. He waited around until he was needed. Once, I was put on a job laying railroad tracks. I was working there with another fellow, an American. When he left to get some supplies, I worked as hard as I could. When he came back, he found I had dug two big tracks and laid the tracks in. He looked at it and said, "Don't work so hard. That's too much work for one day." The men often take over an hour for lunch; they sleep on the timber boards. We all take turns; the others are all very friendly to me. I eat their lunches and they eat some of mine. I go to union meetings and I can vote just like the rest of them. I have a lot of friends up there now.[35]

These relationships, made possible by the wartime need for workers, allowed Wing Hong Hom to move outside the traditional Chinese community, establish friendships with non-Chinese Montanans, and integrate into mainstream American life. Photos show Wing Hong Hom hunting and fishing with white friends, enjoying time in the mountains around Butte, decorating his apartment for Christmas, and proudly displaying his new car. Mirroring this transition on a national level, the wartime alliance between the United States and China against the Japanese caused a rethinking of policy.[36]

With the partnership between America and China in the war against Japan, Chinese officials worked to end the unequal relationship between the two countries that had persisted since the 1882 Chinese Exclusion Act. They viewed exclusion, based on racial assumptions of inferiority, along with the practice of extraterritoriality, in which foreigners were not held to Chinese laws while in China, as embarrassing evidence of continued inequality. The exclusion era ended in 1943 with the passage of the Magnuson Act, which finally allowed Chinese to become naturalized citizens.[37] In terms of changing flow of people, this effort was largely symbolic. The act established a quota that allowed 105 Chinese immigrants per year to enter the United States. Furthermore, in contrast to migrants from other nations who were assessed on the nation from which they sought to migrate, not on their ethnicity, the Chinese quota applied to anyone of Chinese ethnicity no matter which country they currently inhabited. The continued racial identification of the Chinese and the small quota reinforced the persistent perception of the Chinese as less desirable immigrants and as an unassimilable group within America.[38]

As the war continued, Japanese advances in China interrupted remittances and communications from abroad. Many families relied on remittances for as much as 70 to 80 percent of their income. With remittances interrupted, these families suffered greatly. The human cost of war was high in Taishan, with more than 200,000 deaths both from combat and due to starvation caused by the conflict. Hundreds of thousands more fled, complicating continued communication with family members abroad. The war's end in September 1945 allowed communications to resume between overseas Chinese people and their family members in Taishan. A letter arrived in Butte from a village elder in southern China, the first communication the city's Chinese community had received since before the attack on Pearl Harbor. The elder instructed "that the contents be shared with all the Chinese residents in Butte." The letter passed along news of individual families and the general suffering from the war, noting that "starvation had killed off half the inhabitants of one area; others had been killed during the Japanese invasion . . . Farm lands remain untilled from lack of manpower and energy."[39] Separated from relatives for years due to the disruption caused by the war, men returned in great numbers to find families scattered by the fighting. Many hoped to marry and start families of their own.[40]

Wing Hong Hom followed this path. While he had formed close friendships outside traditional Chinese circles in Butte, several factors limited his possibilities for marriage in Montana. Decades of immigration restriction combined with Chinese cultural traditions meant that very few Chinese women resided there. Additionally, as assimilated as Wing Hong Hom was becoming, Montana law limited his marriage prospects. Passed in 1909, Montana's anti-miscegenation law—fully titled "An Act Prohibiting Marriages between White Persons, Negroes, Persons of Negro Blood, and between White Persons, Chinese and Japanese, and making such Marriage Void, and prescribing punishment for Solemnizing such Marriages"—remained in effect until 1953.[41] Few options existed for Wing Hong Hom to start a family other than to return to China to marry.

Wing Hong Hom and thousands of others returned to China to meet brides chosen for them by family members. Arranged marriages were not only in keeping with Chinese traditions, but also necessitated by decades of American immigration restrictions designed to bar Chinese women from entry. As Congressman Albert Johnson of Washington State indicated during debates that led to the tightening of restrictions on immigration in the 1920s, "The necessity arises from the fact that we do not want to establish additional Oriental families here."[42] The outcome of these policies limited the Chinese population both by controlling who could enter and restricting the growth of the community once within the United States.

With the disruption of the Second World War over, large numbers of Chinese American men sought brides through the traditional system. In 1947 twenty-seven thousand Chinese people returned from the United States to south China.[43] The possibility of arranged marriages resulting in large numbers of Chinese immigrants being allowed into the United States alarmed some consular officials who retained the exclusionary mindset. George D. Hopper, writing from the American consulate in Hong Kong, suspected arranged marriages of being a ploy to circumvent immigration restrictions. Hopper brought his concerns to the State Department in 1947, noting, "in many cases pending here parties have never met. Engagement arranged by families or third parties in accordance [with] Chinese customs."[44] Hopper asked for guidance in dealing with such cases. The State Department initially agreed with Hopper's sentiment, questioning how people who had never met could enter into a legitimate marriage. Realizing that cultural traditions differed significantly from standard Western views on marriage, however, the State Department advised Hopper that the fact of a marriage being arranged was not enough evidence to reject the claims of a union and the admission of the bride through her husband's status as an American citizen. Unsatisfied with this response, Hopper continued to reject these claims feeling that he was on the front lines of fraud and knew better than his superiors in Washington. Consular officials in other Chinese locations agreed with Hopper, going farther to assert that these marriages were not in fact consensual unions and that the women, if allowed entry, were then sold into prostitution, echoing earlier rationales of barring Chinese women from entry such as the Page Act of 1875.[45] Later consular officials, notably Everett Drumright, revived and amplified these concerns but with an added Cold War reasoning. Drumright worried that infiltration of Communist agents through arranged marriages was a major threat to U.S. security, presenting the problem that "male Americans of Chinese origin who are proceeding to Hong Kong in ever increasing numbers, marrying Chinese women who have recently arrived from Communist China, and bringing them to the U.S. as non-quota immigrant wives."[46] The earlier exclusionary sentiments persisted, growing with added ideological justification as the struggle between the Nationalists and the Communists for control of China played out in the late 1940s.

It was during this transition that Wing Hong Hom returned to China for the first time since early 1933. In addition to reconnecting with family members after the suffering caused by war, Wing

Hong Hom also went home to start his own family. He married Mei Lai Lee, a woman selected for him by relatives in advance of his return, and children soon followed. He fathered two children while staying in China from May 1947 through July 1949. With the weight of supporting extended family and his newly enlarged immediate family, Wing Hong Hom returned to Montana by the time his second son was born. His aunt wrote to give him good news: "I hope you are prosperous and things are well. Your mother is well. I congratulate you—yesterday, your wife had a baby boy! Everyone in the family is happy and I wholeheartedly congratulate you! Your son is very cute and your wife is well."[47] From Hong Kong, Wing Goon also wrote to let his brother know of the good news: "At home, your wife received the blessing of giving birth to a child! The baby is lively and it grows very fast. Everyone at home is happy and I wrote especially to inform you of the good news."[48] These letters also contained reports of new disruptions and political circumstances far outside the control of family members that would have direct impact on the family's life.

> Aug. 1: Recently the war intensified. The Great Battle of Chang Sha spread violently. The security of the south relies on this battle. Fortunately, there were no riots in Taishan. Ten days ago, eight communists and some suspects were captured in the lower valley.[49]

> Sept. 6: Yesterday, Communist troops entered Taishan . . . Waterways to Hong Kong are not open. . . . We can get rice for 60–70 yuan, but there is a tax. The village chief says its 10 baskets of raw rice. The farmers need five baskets. Civil servants need two baskets. Landlords need three baskets. Shopkeepers need the same. These, the rich, need an amount equal to a poor person's house. . . . From my childhood, life has been very difficult and I can't find the spirit to face the world. I hope we can get some help soon.[50]

> Sept. 29: The situation is desperate! Under these circumstances, being Chinese is difficult, especially for the common man. All disasters come unprompted. If you don't fear theft, then you fear the draft. In Guangzhou, the Nationalists are drafting 'piglet soldiers'—it's insane!

Nº 61529 G. R.

HONG KONG

Port Health Office,
Hong Kong.

種　痘　證　書

INTERNATIONAL CERTIFICATE OF VACCINATION AGAINST SMALLPOX

This is to certify that (Name) 姓名 .... *Hom Wing Hung* ....
年齡 (age) ...22... 性別 sex ...*H.*...), whose photograph appears below/whose passport

number and signature appear below, has this day been vaccinated by me against

smallpox, (Origin and Batch No. of vaccine: ...*P.l. (4)20)*...............................)

PHOTOGRAPH

Signature of vaccinator:— ....

PUBLIC VACCINATOR

Official position:— ....

Place: HONG KONG. Date: .... 9 APR 1949 ....

Signature of person vaccinated: ....

OFFICIAL SEAL

IMPORTANT: In the case of primary vaccination, the person vaccinated should be
warned to report to the Port Health Officer between the 8th and 14th day, in order
that the result of the vaccination may be recorded on this certificate. In the case
of revaccination, the person should report within 48 hours for first inspection in order
that any immune reaction which has developed may be recorded.

This is to certify that the above vaccination was inspected by me on the date(s)
and with result(s) shown hereunder:

Date of inspection:

11 APR 1949

Result: *Reaction of Immunity*

Signature of Doctor ....

Official position:— PORT HEALTH OFFICER HONG KONG

Place:—HONG KONG. Date:— 11 APR 1949

Use one of the following terms in stating the result, viz.—"Reaction of Immunity"
"Accelerated Reaction (Vaccinoid)", "Typical primary vaccinia"

N.B.—This certificate is not valid for more than 3 years from date of issue.

FEE: 50 Cents.

26. Record of Wing Hong Hom's vaccination, 1949. Wing Hong Hum Papers,
UPMC 87:2–4, Montana Historical Society Research Center Archives, Helena MT.

This is the extent of society's instability! The common man shoulders the crisis between the clashing heads of the Communists and Nationalists. We're under pressure from both sides. It's unbearable! The Chinese living in China have a hard life. From this I admire the overseas Chinese—money earned by the sweat of their brow: what they give is what they get, and they can raise a big family. This is a life better than in China ten-thousand times. In the future one simply must leave the country.[51]

The Chinese Civil War created new urgency for the Homs to get as many family members out of China as possible. Unfortunately for them, some American officials saw the Cold War in Asia as an opportunity to a reassert exclusion under claims of preventing Communist infiltration.

With Cold War-anxieties high in the early 1950s, officials saw subversives and spies everywhere; they were ever-vigilant but produced little proof. Fears of Communist agents blackmailing Chinese Americans, stories of marriage scams that sought to infiltrate the United States with Communist-trained brides, and the realization that the individuals seeking entry were men of military age came together in the minds of some to form a potential fifth column within the United States. These worries consumed officials in Hong Kong and politicians at home.[52]

Immigration reform complicated the situation. With the realization that restrictive policies could be used as propaganda by Communist states, American leaders ended the last vestiges of exclusion. This resulted in a debate in American political circles about whether policies should promote a generous, welcoming attitude, thus gaining good will in the eyes of the world, or if immigration policies should selectively restrict who could enter with emphasis on national security concerns. Senator Pat McCarran, a Democrat from Nevada, and Representative Francis Walter, a Democrat from Pennsylvania, proposed a bill to constrain immigration for national security purposes. Opponents argued that restrictive, race-based quotas hurt America's standing abroad, a key factor in the rhetorical battles of the Cold War.[53] From this stance, President Harry S. Truman vetoed the bill, stating that it would "perpetuate injustices of long standing against many other nations of the world, hamper the efforts we are making to rally the men of East and West alike to the cause of freedom, and intensify the repressive and inhumane aspects of our immigration procedures."[54] Proponents of the bill, citing national security needs, easily voted to override the veto. The McCarran-Walter Act of 1952 ended exclusion and bans on naturalization for Asians; however, the actual result was complicated. The act retained the quota system established during the 1920s, expanding this system to all nations. Ethnic preferences were apparent, with 70 percent of slots allotted to the United Kingdom, Ireland, and Germany. The act created the Asia-Pacific Triangle; each nation in this triangle was permitted one hundred immigrants per year. For Asians, the quotas were based on race, not nationality. Therefore, a person of Chinese descent who resided in France, or Canada, or Australia who sought to come to America counted against the quota for all Chinese people world-wide. Additionally, the 1952 act gave consular officials final authority to grant or deny visas, eliminating judicial review for rulings on status of alleged citizens, such as Wing Goon Hom.[55]

Thousands of requests from alleged derivative citizens overwhelmed the consulate in Hong Kong, which was committed to investigating every case so that "we will not be inundated with a flood of illegal Chinese."[56] The sheer number of applicants threatened to grind the process to a halt. The State Department offered Drumright a considerable increase in the number of investigative staff members in Hong Kong, but he argued the cost would be too high.[57] Drumright claimed that "it has been the experience of the Consulate General that bona fide applicants seldom have serious trouble in establishing their identities."[58] In reality, applicants' claims were seldom accepted. Drumright and his team looked for any reason to deny requests, with applicants challenged to provide mountains of irrefutable evidence to verify their identity. Whereas previously a key determination of the validity of an applicant's claims was an interview conducted under oath, Drumright believed the Chinese were culturally inclined to fraud and perjury and were a people who "lack a concept equivalent to the Western concept of an oath."[59] The American consulate at Hong Kong pioneered the use of blood tests to determine relations in 1951 and during his initial tenure at the consul Drumright put great faith in these results, which exposed a large number of fraudulent claims. By 1955, however, he began to suspect that positive matches also indicated fraud, believing that news of how to beat the blood tests had leaked and that applicants worked with nurses and doctors to conduct pre-tests in order to confirm blood type markers.[60] This pattern of using tests to deny but not affirm applicants' claims persisted beyond blood tests. Regarding x-rays of bones and physical examinations to determine age, Drumright noted, "radiological and clinical examinations only confirm the fact that a discrepancy in age exists."[61] If answers given during extensive questioning under oath matched with family records and the testimony of others, Drumright assumed coaching and, therefore, fraud. If answers differed even slightly it was evidence enough to deny the claim. Documents including family photographs, records of remittances, marriage certificates, and birth records were also viewed as easily forged and likely evidence of fraud. Discrepancies in evidence was proof of fraud. Evidence that fit too neatly into the category requested was proof of coaching, and thus, fraud. Drumright's policy was that "identity cases could be refused on the simple grounds: identity not established."[62] In December 1955 Drumright released a "Report on the Problem of Fraud at Hong Kong" detailing the history of attempts to circumvent immigration restrictions and the present crisis he faced in Hong Kong as a result. Viewing claims of all applicants with extreme suspicion, the work of investigating and processing cases foundered. By 1956 more than fourteen hundred cases lingered in waiting.[63]

Still trapped in Hong Kong, Wing Goon pressed his brother and his lawyer to keep working. Wing Hong Hom and his lawyer elevated their appeals to higher offices, calling on the assistance of Senator Mike Mansfield. Mansfield's office worked to facilitate Wing Goon Hom's case, but efforts like this had been tried before by elected officials in other instances.[64] Drumright had grown frustrated with interference from "members of Congress with constituents' problems in mind." He urged the State Department to use "firmness in resisting outside pressure" and follow his suggestions detailed in his lengthy "Report on the Problem of Fraud."[65] Practicing his own policy, Drumright received many requests from members of Congress about specific cases and simply refused to respond.

Tensions emerged between Drumright's group and the State Department in early 1956. An inspection team visited the American Consul General in Hong Kong to look into its operations, possibly prompted by complaints from constituents in America about long delays in processing requests and the abundance of denials of claims to enter the United States. In his response to a critical inspection report, Drumright noted "that the present abyss that separates the Department's thinking from [the American Consulate General in Hong Kong] can be bridged," but only if the State Department read his report on fraud and acted according to his suggestions. Drumright expressed that he and his consular team understood the situation more fully because of their proximity to the problem, whereas American policymakers and politicians were disconnected from the rampant fraud he dealt with on a daily basis. The inspection team expressed concern that Drumright generalized his impressions of all Chinese. They argued that "in order to place the whole question of Chinese fraud in its proper perspective, it does not seem amiss to observe here that, while there are no doubts as to the incredibly high ratio of fraud, the majority of those involved . . . are not basically immoral people." Drumright disagreed, reaffirming his belief that "most of the Chinese seeking immigration here are experts at lying, cheating and circumventing laws and regulations and have no scruples about their action to circumvent those of the United States." Chastised by the State Department, Drumright pledged to soften his intransigence in not responding to requests from members of Congress and promised that his office would "redouble its efforts to improve both quality and content, with particular care given to correspondence originating from members of Congress."[66] In other communications from the same time, however, Drumright urged new methods of detection, including fingerprinting, polygraphs, and listening devices that would surveil conversations and detect if interpreters were coaching applicants during interviews. He also contacted departments of anthropology and genetics at American universities to explore new scientific advances to detect fraud.[67] While rejecting offers to hire more consular staff to help clear the backlog of cases, arguing that the expense was too high, Drumright requested a budget increase to pay informants to infiltrate suspected fraud circles in Hong Kong.[68] These efforts, from Drumright's perspective, could expose fraudulent claims, but never positively affirm and approve identity.

Those believing that Drumright's approach was too severe kept up their pressure. Secretary of State John Foster Dulles pushed back at Drumright's inflexible mindset and the attitude of extreme suspicion toward every application. Dulles acknowledged that the burden of proof for establishing identity did rest on the applicant but noted that this did not give consular officials unlimited power:

> The consul is not to assume automatically at the outset that each and every Chinese nonquota visa case is fraudulent. . . . If the Consulate General's view is fully understood, the Department is of the opinion that were such a view adopted, documentation would be automatically refused in practically all cases except those where evidence of entitlement was so complete and well documented that no doubt whatsoever could be raised in the mind of the issuing officer. . . . Moreover, the possibility would also exist if this method were adopted and all petitions denied on the basis of "identity not established" without investigation, legitimate applicants for documentation might be unnecessarily delayed or perhaps even denied the right to come to the United States.[69]

Drumright was convinced that he and his office could end the decades of fraud that characterized the exclusion era. He believed the system of circumventing the law had to be "destroy[ed] . . . once and for all, thus bringing to an end a unique history of illegal immigration and of resisting Americanization while buying and selling the rights of American citizenship before Communist China is able to bend that system to the service of her purposes alone."[70] Even though there was little evidence that Communist China actively sought to "bend that system . . . to her purposes," Drumright took vigorous action before it could happen.

Drumright's suspicions of the connections between immigration fraud and Communist infiltration brought together departments devoted to the same concerns. Collaborating with the Immigration and Naturalization Service (INS), the Federal Bureau of Investigation (FBI) began efforts to find Communists suspected of operating in the nation's Chinatowns. Systems of informants developed to share information with INS and FBI agents who sought connections between suspected immigration fraud and Communist cells. Though maintaining strict secrecy regarding the identity of informants, rumors of surveillance and suspicion ran throughout Chinese communities.[71] With general fears of infiltration during these peak years of Cold War tensions, other agencies eagerly joined the efforts to expose suspected Communists. In 1956 an agent of Montana's Alcohol Tax Unit reported that an informant knew of a passport forging operation in Helena. The identity of the alleged forger was not certain initially, only that he was "one of the Wong family who operates the Chinese Cafes in Helena, Billings, Great Falls and Missoula." Investigators eventually learned that Fred Wong was the man suspected of forging passports. The surveillance and investigative apparatus of several agencies mobilized, setting the task of "locating informants and possibly witnesses, securing a forged document if possible, and locating pharaphernelia [*sic*] used in making the forgeries."[72]

To learn if the allegations were true and to try to catch Wong and his associates in the act, "The Post Office Department had been contacted and a 30 day check is being made of all mail received at and sent from this address with particular attention as to whether size and shape of mail may indicate passports being received or sent. The mail carrier who delivers mail at this address will be contacted as soon as possible. . . . Discreet inquiries will be made as to the occupation of Fred Wong, means of support, associates, habits, whether he has a bank account, amount of deposits, etc."[73] The findings of the surveillance are not contained in the file, indicating that the investigations turned up little evidence to corroborate the informant's claims. The Cold War tensions that fostered such suspicions and the existence of informants making claims against Montana's Chinese residents either from within the community itself or from their non-Chinese neighbors certainly weighed heavily on them.

Wing Hong Hom continued his efforts on behalf of his brother. At the same time, he set on an additional goal of bringing his wife and children to America. His lawyer advised against this act, arguing that opening a new request would complicate and possibly weaken his brother's case, under review since 1949. Indeed, starting procedures on a new case must have been daunting. Records show the government's repeated requests for ever more documents, payments, and proof of identity connected with the claims of his family members. For instance, in May 1955 the INS office in Seattle requested a blood test to determine the truth of the claim of paternity for his children. Though he had submitted a blood test years before through a physician in Butte, this new test required that he travel to Seattle and appear in person. Repeated requests such as this pulled Wing Hong Hom in many directions, making his continued residence in Montana difficult. Economic changes also disrupted his life in Butte. As historian Brian Leech notes in his work on Butte's mining history: "The price of copper dropped from about 42 cents a pound in 1956 to around 30 cents a pound in 1957. Faced with a national recession and claiming that the cost of copper production was excessive, the Anaconda Company took action. Chairman Roy Glover closed the Belmont and Mountain Con underground mines. . . . [The] Anaconda [Company] had nearly 5,200 employees in 1955, but by 1959 three thousand miners and a few hundred craftspeople would be gone."[74]

Coupled with these changes to employment opportunities and continual calls to appear in person to facilitate his family's case, Wing Hong Hom left Butte by 1957, relocating to Seattle. In the last recorded communication between the brothers, Wing Goon wrote:

> My humble brother, you are away from home, but are lucky and healthy, holding stable work and earning well. Your brother here is still safe, luckily . . . From last August when I went to U.S. Consulate to give the materials and wait for the investigating process for approval to come to America, I have heard nothing. I really don't know the reason. This makes me have the feeling of waiting eagerly

without a clear target! I heard that four consuls of U.S. Consulate went back to their country. Now there are only four here so the process is even slower than it was. There were several fellow countrymen like me, none got the letter or notice. . . . I hope you, dear brother, can instruct the office as fast as possible to help me get the chance to go to America. I am deeply thankful for all the efforts you make and the precious time you spend. Later when we meet again in America, I will thank you directly.[75]

Stuck in Hong Kong for almost ten years, Wing Goon Hom's case eventually disappeared from the record. After providing every record requested, multiple layers of testimony from family members and friends in Hong Kong and Montana, and submitting to physical examinations and blood tests, it is likely that Drumright's office rejected the case outright with a stamp of "identity not established." In such instances, Wing Goon and others who claimed to be American citizens were not given access to the American legal system to press their claim any further. Unable to leave Hong Kong for America, Wing Goon returned to Taishan. Life in China over the next several decades was no easier than before, with the Great Leap Forward from 1958 to 1961 resulting in more than forty million deaths and the Cultural Revolution from 1966 to 1976 causing extensive societal disruption. It is likely that the Hom family's foreign ties made life even more difficult for them during the Cultural Revolution due to its attack on western influences.

In effect, Drumright and others like him reasserted Chinese exclusion based on their fears of Chinese Communist infiltration. Looking more closely at Drumright's rhetoric and ideological reasonings, his efforts were based on cultural suspicions and racial animosity reminiscent of the treatment that Chinese people in America had experienced for decades. He viewed the Chinese as inclined to fraud and deceit, incapable of understanding the bond of an oath, racially unassimilable, and resistant to Americanization. While Wing Hong Hom became fully Americanized, even fully Montanan, while working in Butte's mines, joining the union, hunting, and fishing, Wing Goon Hom never had an opportunity to accept or reject assimilation. In a larger sense, the barriers faced by the Hom family echoed throughout Montana's Chinese community. Once forming as much as 10 to 15 percent of Montana's total population, during the 1950s the Chinese community dipped to its lowest numbers in state history, just over two hundred in total.[76] By bending the Cold War fears to his purposes, Drumright and others like him kept out many who had legitimate claims to enter America.

Conclusion

From the earliest days of non-Native settlement of Montana, the Chinese were present. Also from these earliest days, they faced animosity. As Thomas Dimsdale, the editor of Montana's first newspaper, noted in 1865, "A Chinese can never be made into a citizen and we say get rid of any human animal that is not susceptible of improvement."[1] Assumptions abounded, including that every Chinese woman was a prostitute and that the Chinese brought decay and pestilence to white society. Fourteen years after Dimsdale equated the Chinese to leeches, opponents of the Chinese deepened the comparisons to pests, parasites, and vermin:

> No one objects to the Chinese because of their color, race or creed. The objection to them is that they remain to the end what they were when they landed—Chinese. Europeans are welcome here because they assimilate and become a part of the nation. . . . But it is different with the Asiatics. Whatever territory they occupy they convert into a little strip of Asia, filled with Asiatic slavish customs, moral and physical filth and disease. . . . Shall we continue to invite this tapeworm into our entrails? . . . [W]hen an immigrant comes to this country, he must come to be an American, and if he doesn't intend to become one, he ought to be made to stay away.[2]

In truth, no amount of acculturation would have placated this anti-Chinese element. Nearly thirty years after Dimsdale's assessment, an 1893 editorial extended the dehumanizing comparison: "The Chinaman is no more a citizen than a coyote is a citizen, and never can be."[3] As ugly as these statements are, they capture the legal reality as it stood for almost eight decades.

Yet the Chinese came, contributed, paid taxes, built the infrastructure of the state, and tried to build lives under the Big Sky. The raw numbers attest to the Chinese presence throughout Montana, whether in large communities of close to 650 in Helena in 1870, or in isolated pockets, with thirteen in Boulder in 1880, four in White Sulphur Springs in 1894, eleven in Pony in 1900, two in Wibaux in 1905, and five in Scobey in 1930. Through complex transnational networks of support, communication, politics, and evolving family structures, Chinese Montanans persevered and adapted key cultural practices to survive in hostile environments. They worked hard, supported families back in China, and contributed to the development and functioning of Montana. Chinese residents of Helena noted this fact in 1866, expressing a sentiment that persisted across time in Montana: "We pay our taxes and assessments, and only ask that the good people of Montana may let us earn an honest living by the sweat of our brow."[4]

The long history of animosity and racism, combined with laws intentionally designed to preclude the establishment of self-sustaining Chinese communities, prevented the very assimilation that critics argued they should embrace. Even when Chinese Montanans earned citizenship, it proved tentative. The daughters of Lee Sam Fong, born in Helena in the 1890s, became some of the first women to vote in Montana and were productive members of the workforce. Yet others continually saw them as Chinese, not American. Rose Hum Lee, a citizen by virtue of her birth in Butte, lost that status through marriage to a noncitizen and was initially unable to reclaim it following her divorce because Chinese were "aliens ineligible for citizenship." Wing Goon Hom, a citizen by his birth to an American father, was barred entry to America through persistent racist fears amplified by Cold War anxieties. Regardless of how acculturated and Americanized Chinese Montanans became, to many they remained forever foreign.

Though not achieved as quickly as intended, the combination of restrictive laws and persistent animosity did, in essence, finally realize Senator Wilbur Fisk Sanders's goal "that they shall be diminished to extinction."[5] By the time that Chinese people could become naturalized citizens in 1943 fewer than 250 remained in the state. Many accounts of Montana's Chinese history describe this population decline in general terms, noting that the Chinese once comprised a large portion of Montana's populace but faded away, leaving behind few traces of their presence. A closer examination of their experiences in their own words clarifies the reasons for the exodus. In 1901 Lee Bet, a Chinese man from Butte, described this process in detail: "Some have gone to places where the picking is better, some have gone to their old homes in China and others have gone to the cemetery south of town, and will go to China later on. . . . In this country we have little or no protection from assault, and no one can blame us for going back to China to spend the balance of our days." Lee added that eighty-eight members of Butte's Chinese community had returned to China over the previous six months "and as many more will go in the next six." Alluding to the ongoing Boxer Rebellion, which had whites concerned that race wars in China would spill over to America, Lee observed, "There are lots of Boxers in Butte—white Boxers, I mean. They throw stones at us whenever they get a chance, and would kill us if an opportunity offered."[6] Lee's point about the only "Boxers" in Butte being white rowdies was true—Montana's Chinatowns demonstrated very little sympathy for the Boxer movement. Yet Montana's Chinese were deeply connected to global events. Realizing they could never change the minds of those who portrayed them as less than human, Montana's Chinese residents ignored these detractors and worked for personal, communal, and national empowerment.

As Montana's Chinese population declined throughout the twentieth century, animosity toward its remaining Chinese residents softened. Towns across the state often noted when the last Chinese resident died or returned to China, with non-Chinese residents seeing off the departing neighbor with farewell banquets and gifts. In 1927 Bozeman restauranteur Chin Au Ban threw a banquet the day before his departure that featured two dozen of the city's non-Chinese elite, including the mayor. Newspaper reports illustrate the increasing acceptance of Chin on the eve of his departure, noting that he was "not just an ordinary oriental as he bore the distinction of being a solid citizen."[7] In Choteau in 1933, a U.S. senator, a state senator, and the mayor celebrated the departure of Soo Son, a resident of the town for forty-four years, praising him for his honesty, fairness, charity, law-abiding nature, and "his citizenship—though he could never claim that privilege."[8] It seems that as the Chinese population declined and became less of a threat in the minds of white Montanans, nostalgia for Chinese Montanans grew. This trend was noted earlier by Lewis Den, who became an interpreter for the government in 1915. Den noted the declining Chinese population of the state and offered the following prediction: "A few years more and the Chinaman of the frontier days of the west will be only a reminiscence of the past. . . . [S]ince Chinese immigration has ceased, there is a very pronounced change of feeling toward my people. In fact, I think the old antagonism, among some people, has given place to a positive feeling of kindliness."[9] As Montana's Chinese population declined, nostalgia replaced hostility and the memory of the region's diversity became more accepted than the actual Chinese pioneers themselves. Montana's laws followed the same trend. An overwhelming majority in the state legislature repealed Montana's anti-miscegenation law in 1953, though the Chinese population had declined to around two hundred by that time.

It is likely that the Chinese Montanans who returned to China remained politically active, emboldened to contribute to their home country's development through their experiences abroad. They had played key roles in state, national, and global affairs. They had the ear of Confucian scholars one step removed from the Chinese Emperor. They stood up to oppressive restrictions designed to diminish them to extinction. They advocated for family members tossed about by global affairs and ever-changing legal barriers. Even those forced from the state against their will through the execution of the Geary Act and the raids of the special census of 1905 noted their transnational political mindfulness. Chen Bow, who was deported from Billings even though he believed he had a right to remain in Montana, promised that he would inform his countrymen of his mistreatment and fight on through his support for the boycott of 1905.

Seen through the lenses of Chinese culture and history and by hearing of their experiences through their own words, Chinese Montanans emerge as far more complex and fully formed than the anonymous "Chinaman" of the 1870 census. Instead, they come to us with vibrancy, complexity, and agency, shaped by and shaping events in Montana and in China. By recovering the voices of Montana's Chinese residents and by seeing their experiences in the context of Montana, Chinese, and world history, we see them as they saw themselves—as hardworking family members with responsibilities that stretched thousands of miles, as activists seeking to build bridges between white and Chinese workers, and as reformers engaged in a global struggle to remake their homeland and themselves through their experiences in the American West.

Anti-Chinese Actions in Montana, 1866–1909

1866	Anti-Chinese boycott against Chinese laundries in Helena
1881	Chinese workers contracted to gather lumber attacked by mob from Butte
1885 (April)	Explosion in Chinese laundry in Anaconda, three Chinese men killed
1885 (September)	Anti-Chinese boycott in Anaconda
1885 (September)	Anti-Chinese boycott in Butte
1885 (October)	Anti-Chinese boycott in Dillon
1885 (November)	Anti-Chinese boycott in Deer Lodge
1885 (November)	Anti-Chinese forces attempt arson at Butte Chinese Temple
1885 (November)	Chinese workers fired from hotels in Glendale
1885 (December)	Anti-Chinese boycott in Neihart
1885–1938	Chinese people prohibited from settling in Great Falls
1886	Residents of Maiden drive out Chinese settlers
1887	Chinese residents of Livingston ordered to leave
1891–92	Anti-Chinese boycott in Missoula
1892	Chinese laundry burned in Meaderville (Butte)

1893	Anti-Chinese boycott in Anaconda
1893	Anti-Chinese boycott in Butte
1896	Attempted arson against Chinese neighborhood in Anaconda
1896	Chinese man murdered in Quigley
1896–97	Anti-Chinese boycott in Butte
1902	Anti-Chinese forces attack Chinese Temple in Butte
1902–3	Anti-Chinese boycott in Kalispell
1908	Residents of Harlowton object to Chinese people settling in the town, attack Chinese man, vandalize property
1909	Anti-Chinese forces attack Chinese temple in Billings

Note: Actions taken against Chinese residents in attempts to intimidate, exclude, or expel them from Montana.

Sources: "Celestials in Helena," *Montana Radiator* (Helena), February 10, 1866; Chung, *Chinese in the Woods*, 105; "War in the Woods: Chinese Wood Choppers Dispersed Sunday," *Butte Weekly Miner*, December 27, 1881; "A Fatal Explosion: A Chinese Laundry in Anaconda Blown Up and three Chinamen Killed," *Helena Weekly Herald*, April 23, 1885; "The Chinese Must Go," *River Press* (Fort Benton), September 23, 1885; "The Chinese Question," *Semi-Weekly Miner*, September 19, 1885; "The Chinese Must Go," *Dillon Tribune*, October 10, 1885; "Boycotting in Deer Lodge: An Edict by the Knights of Labor to Boycott Those Employing Chinese," *Helena Weekly Herald*, November 12, 1885; "The Chinese Have Been Fired from the Glendale hotels," *Rising Sun* (Sun River), November 5, 1885; "Incendiary Attempt: The Chinese Joss House Comes Very Near Going Up in Smoke," *Semi-Weekly Miner*, November 28, 1885; "The Chinese Must Go," *River Press*, December 23, 1885; "Laboring Man's Home: Resolutions Adopted at Mass Meeting of the Workingmen of Great Falls," *Great Falls Weekly Tribune*, November 4, 1892; *Rising Sun*, January 28, 1886; History Museum (Great Falls); "Citizens of Livingston Order Chinese to Leave," *Glendive Independent*, January 29, 1887; "Missoula Mélange," *Anaconda Standard*, August 31, 1891; "What Montana's Governor Has to Say Regarding Alleged Chinese Outrages in Butte," *Helena Independent*, February 25, 1892; "Against the Heathen: Fight of the Honest Laborer for His Rights and Privileges," *Anaconda Standard*, February 6, 1893; Morris, *Anaconda, Montana*, 113–24; "Chinese Must Go: Resolutions Adopted by the Citizens' Committee," *Anaconda Standard*, February 14, 1893; "In Old Chinatown: An Attempt to Burn a Block of the Celestial Landmarks, But It Is Still Intact," *Anaconda Standard*, October 21, 1896; "The Quigley Killing," *Daily Missoulian*, June 3, 1896; Flaherty, "Boycott in Butte," 34–47; "Vandals Invade Chinese Joss House," *Butte Inter Mountain*, May 3, 1902; "Question Is Serious: Chinese Restaurants Detrimental to All Classes," *Kalispell Bee*, January 6, 1903; "Wage War on China: Harlowton People Object to Invasion of the 'Yellow Peril,'" *Fergus County Democrat* (Lewistown), December 29, 1908; "Broke Up Worship to Chinese Gods," *Billings Gazette*, July 20, 1909.

1. Telling the History

1. "Self Preservation the First Law of Nature," *Montana Post* (Virginia City MT), August 19, 1865, italics in original.

2. *Montana Post*, June 9, 1866.

3. "Chinese Servants vs. White Girls," *Montana Post*, April 21, 1866.

4. The role of Chinese labor in mining and railroad work in the American West and Montana specifically has been thoroughly examined by other authors. As such, the present work does not seek to add to these topics. For information on Chinese miners in the Rocky Mountain West, see Swartout, "From Guangdong to Big Sky," 94–120; Zhu, *A Chinaman's Chance*; Zhu, "No Need to Rush," 43–57. For coverage of railroad work in Montana and the West more broadly, see Merritt, *The Coming Man from Canton*; Dixon, et al., "Landscapes of Change"; Chang, *Ghosts of Gold Mountain*.

5. Zhu, "No Need to Rush," 42–57.

6. Fisk quoted in *Not in Precious Metals Alone*, 151. Exactly how many Chinese residents were present in settlements across Montana is difficult to accurately assess. This is particularly true with regard to Butte. Frequently, a number for the total size of Butte's Chinese community is given as 2,532, often rounded down to 2,500. This comes from the work of sociologist Rose Hum Lee (referenced in detail in chapter 7), who claims in her 1960 work *The Chinese in the United States of America*: "It should be noted that between 1870 and 1910, the Chinese population of Butte varied from 1,265 to 2,532 inhabitant, so that these families constituted a very minute segment of the total." The context of the sentence and the fact that the number she cites—2,532—is the highest number of Chinese recorded for Montana indicates that she meant "Montana" but wrote "Butte." The reference that she gives for the statistic is her own earlier dissertation, which gives 2,532 as the statewide total, not the total for Butte. The most accurate data available, from an 1891 Health Officer's Report, suggests the highest number ascribed to Butte is 841. Some claim that the 2,532 number must still be accurate because the Chinese were often undercounted in official tallies. While it is true that the Chinese often avoided government officials, likely leading to undercounting, this difference is too large to account for such a large discrepancy. Given the inconsistency in Lee's sourcing, the 1891 Health Officer's Report, and the total number for Montana's Chinese pop-

ulation being a high of 2,532, it is inaccurate to state that Butte's Chinese population was this high at any point in the city's history. Taking all factors into consideration, it is likely that Butte's Chinese community reached a high of just under 1,000 in 1890.

7. Baumler, et al., "Forgotten Pioneers," 7.

8. "Celestials in Helena," *Montana Radiator* (Helena), February 10, 1866.

9. "Good Chinamen," *Montana Radiator*, February 17, 1866.

10. Allen, *A Decent, Orderly Lynching*, 349–50.

11. Allen, *A Decent, Orderly Lynching*, 365–66.

12. *Helena Daily Herald*, January 25, 1870.

13. "Search for the Murderer," *Rocky Mountain Gazette* (Helena), January 21, 1870.

14. *Helena Daily Herald*, January 21, 1870.

15. "Chinese New Year," *Montana Post*, February 12, 1869.

16. "All the Same Pickles," *Helena Weekly Herald*, January 21, 1875.

17. "The Chinese New Year," *Helena Weekly Herald*, February 15, 1872.

18. "Citizens' Meeting at Court House," *Helena Weekly Herald*, January 15, 1874.

19. *Acts, Resolutions and Memorials of the Territory of Montana*, 178.

20. "A Peculiar Case," *Montana Post*, September 18, 1868.

21. "A Celestial Applicant for Citizenship," *Montana Post*, May 18, 1867.

22. For a detailed analysis of the status of Chinese before the law in the American West, see Wunder, *Gold Mountain Turned to Dust*.

23. "Received the Rewards," *Helena Herald*, January 27, 1870.

24. Sanders, *History of Montana*, 193n1.

25. "Broadwater County Pioneer Recalls Early-Day Hangings," *Helena Independent Record*, news inserts, September 5, 1937.

26. For full coverage of the Chinese cultural beliefs on women staying behind as men migrated for work, see Chan, *Diaspora's Homeland*, 107–45.

27. "Broadwater County Pioneer Recalls Early-Day Hangings."

28. Wright and Hunt, *History and Growth of the United States Census*, 156.

29. *Ninth Census of the United States, 1870*.

30. Email correspondence between the author and the owner of the bed and breakfast and blog in question, January–March 2012.

31. For an excellent discussion debunking the myth of "Chinese Tunnels" purported to be in many western towns, see Wegars, "Exposing Negative Chinese Terminology and Stereotypes," 83–108. For an exploration of reports of "Chinese tunnels" in Montana, specifically Missoula, see Manning, "The 'Chinese Underground': Chinese Immigrants in the American West," in *Historic Underground Missoula*. Also see Baumler and Axline, *Hidden History of Helena*, 84.

32. For a scholarly approach to the secret societies and Tong Wars, see Arata, "Beyond the 'Mongolian Muddle'" 23–35.

33. *Helena Daily Herald*, January 18, 1870.

34. Louie, "Surnames as Clues to Family History," 101–8; Chang, *Ghosts of Gold Mountain*, 84, 142; Wegars, "Exposing Negative Chinese Terminology and Stereotypes," 85.

35. *Tenth Census of the United States, 1880*.

36. "Chinese Census, District of Montana and Idaho, June 30, 1905," United States Bureau of Immigration, District of Montana and Idaho, MF 510, MHS.

37. Spaulding, *Benton Avenue Cemetery*, 18, 289–90.

2. Pressures on Butte's Chinese Residents

1. Merritt, "Toward a Historical Archeology of the Chinese in Montana and a Transnational Lens," 212, 228.

2. While several of the envelopes in the collection are addressed to Quong Tuck Wing and Kim Chong Tai and these individuals do appear in the historic record, it seems that these prominent Butte businessmen served as community leaders, collecting and distributing letters meant for others.

3. For the tendency of Chinese migrants to maintain two identities, one that accorded with their official paperwork and their "paper" identity, and one known to friends and family, see Lew-Williams, "Paper Lives of Chinese Migrants and the History of the Undocumented," 1–22.

4. Wong, "East Asian Immigrants," 105.

5. McKeown, "Conceptualizing Chinese Diasporas," 306–31.

6. Chew and Liu, "Hidden in Plain Sight," 71.

7. Quoted in Mei, "Socioeconomic Origins of Emigration," 474.

8. Chan, *Diaspora's Homeland*, 17–47.

9. The only other copy of the map known to exist is housed at the National Archives Records Administration at San Francisco (San Bruno). Thank you to Sik-Lee Dennig of Stanford University for consultation and collaboration on this map.

10. A3 4–2 Chinese Map, Chinese Collection UPMC 157, MHS.

11. Hsu, *Dreaming of Gold, Dreaming of Home*, 21–23.

12. Quoted in Hsu, *Dreaming of Gold, Dreaming of Home*, 42.

13. Letter to De Quan, file Ac 87–5.28, Chinese Collection UPMC 157, MHS.

14. Hsu, "Migration and Native Place," 311.

15. Quoted in Chan, *Diaspora's Homeland*, 135.

16. Letters to De Quan, file Ac 87–5.28, Ac 87–5.3, Chinese Collection UPMC 157, MHS.

17. Letter to De Quan, file Ac 87–5.21, Chinese Collection UPMC 157, MHS.

18. Hsu, *Dreaming of Gold, Dreaming of Home*, 111.

19. Letter to De Quan, file Ac 87–5.31, Chinese Collection UPMC 157, MHS.

20. Letter to De Quan, file Ac 87–5.4, Chinese Collection UPMC 157, MHS.

21. Letter to De Quan, file Ac 87–5.4, Chinese Collection UPMC 157, MHS.

22. Letter to De Quan, file Ac 87–5.1, Chinese Collection UPMC 157, MHS.

23. Hsu, *Dreaming of Gold, Dreaming of Home*, 35–38.

24. Letter to De Quan, file Ac 87–5.21, Chinese Collection UPMC 157, MHS.

25. Sinn, *Pacific Crossing*, 163–64.

26. Letter to De Quan, file Ac 87–5.18, Chinese Collection UPMC 157, MHS.

27. Yuan and Hsu, "Overseas Remittances of Chinese Laborers in North America," 78–79.

28. Letter to De Quan, file Ac 87–5.31, Chinese Collection UPMC 157, MHS.

29. Letter to De Quan, file Ac 87–5.7, Chinese Collection UPMC 157, MHS.

30. Letter to De Quan, file Ac 87–5.44, Chinese Collection UPMC 157, MHS.

31. Letter to De Quan, file Ac 87–5.28, Chinese Collection UPMC 157, MHS.

32. Letter to De Quan, file Ac 87–5.31, Chinese Collection UPMC 157, MHS.

33. McKeown, "Conceptualizing Chinese Diasporas," 314–15; Hsu, *Dreaming of Gold, Dreaming of Home*, 91–92.

34. Letter to De Quan, file Ac 87–5.20, Chinese Collection UPMC 157, MHS.

35. Hsu, *Dreaming of Gold, Dreaming of Home*, 102–3.

36. "Married a Chinawoman," *Helena Weekly Herald*, November 20, 1873.

37. Merritt, *Coming Man from Canton*, 128. On the Page Act see Daniels, *Not Like Us*, 12. For a very detailed examination of the Page Act and issues relating to Chinese women in the American West, see Peffer, *If They Don't Bring Their Women Here*.

38. Winans and Wu, "Not Adding and Stirring," 472.

39. *Hearings Before the Committee on Immigration and Naturalization*, 68th Cong., 1st sess., December 27, 1923, 104.

40. Merritt, *Coming Man from Canton*, 128.

41. Kennedy and Rose, *Chinese Diaspora*, 3–5.

42. Letter to De Quan, file Ac 87–5.4, Chinese Collection UPMC 157, MHS.

43. Letter to De Quan, file Ac 87–5.31, Chinese Collection UPMC 157, MHS.

44. Letter to De Quan, file Ac 87–5.4, Chinese Collection UPMC 157, MHS.

45. Letters to De Quan, files Ac 87–5.4, Ac 87–5.31, Chinese Collection UPMC 157, MHS.

46. Letter to De Quan, file Ac 87–5.7, Chinese Collection UPMC 157, MHS.

47. Letter to De Quan, file Ac 87–5.3, Chinese Collection UPMC 157, MHS.

48. Letter to De Quan, file Ac 87–5.28, Chinese Collection UPMC 157, MHS.

49. Letter to De Quan, file Ac 87–5.28, Chinese Collection UPMC 157, MHS.

50. Quoted in Swartout, "Guangdong to Big Sky," 109.

51. Chang, *Ghosts of Gold Mountain*, 46–48.

52. Baumler, et al., "Forgotten Pioneers," 14.

53. Chung, "Zhigongtang in the United States," 231–49; Arata, *Race and the Wild West*, 90–92.

54. Quoted in Gardiner, "Chee Kung Tong 'Chinese Freemasons,'" 15.

55. "Chinese Celebration," *River Press* (Fort Benton MT), September 5, 1888.

56. "Chinese Masonry: A Brief History of the Chee Kung Tong, A Secret Organization," *New Northwest* (Deer Lodge MT), October 22, 1886.

57. Wei, *Asians in Colorado*, 80; Chung, *In Pursuit of Gold*, 25–26, 97–100.

58. Chung, *In Pursuit of Gold*, 101–3.

59. Chinese Masonic Temple banner, 1876 (Virginia City), MHS, Translated by Fr. John Wang, University of Montana.

60. "Chinese Masonry: A Brief History of the Chee Kung Tong, A Secret Organization," *New Northwest*, October 22, 1886.

61. "The Chinese Six Companies," *Philipsburg (MT) Mail*, March 28, 1888.

62. Qin, *The Diplomacy of Nationalism*, 44–47.

63. Zhu, *Road to Chinese Exclusion*, 258–71.

64. Lew-Williams, *The Chinese Must Go*, 113–28.

65. Quoted in Lee, "Defying Exclusion," 1.

66. Lee, *Making of Asian America*, 95, 98.

67. Qin, *The Diplomacy of Nationalism*, 112–15.

3. Chinese Resistance to Geary Act

1. Qin, *The Diplomacy of Nationalism*, 121.

2. *Compilation from the Records of the Bureau of Immigration* (1906), 71.

3. *Tenth Census of the United States, 1880; Eleventh Census of the United States, 1890.*

4. *Congressional Record Proceedings and Debates of the Fifty-Second Congress*, 3569.

5. *Congressional Record Proceedings and Debates of the Fifty-Third Congress*, 1159.

6. Pegler-Gordon, *In Sight of America*, 32–37.

7. *Congressional Record Proceedings and Debates of the Fifty-Second Congress*, 3569.

8. "More Money Demanded," *Helena Independent*, April 25, 1893.

9. "Doesn't Like Haskell," *Helena Independent*, April 27, 1893.

10. It is interesting to note that the Zhigongtang (Chinese Masons) urged members to comply with the initial Geary Act. This division between the Zhigongtang and the Six Companies widened during this period due to this difference in approaches to exclusion; Chung, *In Pursuit of Gold*, 26–27. As previously noted in Chapter 2, though Montana had several Zhigongtang branches, the group was considerably less powerful than native-place *huiguan* and the Six Companies.

11. "Chinese Defiance," *Helena Daily Independent*, September 30, 1892.

12. While most of the Chinese in America were in the western part of the country, the fight against the Geary Act mobilized Chinese communities across the nation. Notably, Wong Chin Foo formed the Chinese Equal Rights League, based largely in Philadelphia, New York, and Boston. Seligman, *The First Chinese American*, 209–19.

13. *Congressional Record Proceedings and Debates of the Fifty-Third Congress*, First Session, House of Representatives, 1893, 1369.

14. It is likely that Representative Hitt faced less pressure from the anti-Chinese lobby than politicians in the western United States.

15. "Doesn't Like Haskell," *Helena Daily Independent*, April 27, 1893.

16. *Congressional Record Proceedings and Debates of the Fifty-Second Congress*, 3923.

17. "Doesn't Like Haskell," *Helena Daily Independent*, April 27, 1893.

18. "He Scares the Chinese," *Helena Daily Independent*, September 19, 1893.

19. "But Ten Registered," *Helena Daily Independent*, April 7, 1893.

20. *Butte Bystander*, February 11, 1893.

21. *Butte Bystander*, February 11, 1893.

22. "Down with the Chinese," *Anaconda Standard*, March 5, 1893.

23. *Butte Bystander*, April 22, 1893.

24. "They'll Not Register," *Anaconda Standard*, April 15, 1893.

25. "Doesn't Like Haskell," *Helena Daily Independent*, April 27, 1893.

26. "Fong Yue Ting v. United States," *Reports of Cases Argued and Decided in the Supreme Court of the United States*, Book 37, 1894, 909.

27. Salyer, *Laws Harsh as Tigers*, 48–50.

28. Hernández, *City of Inmates*, 79.

29. Hernández, *City of Inmates*, 79.

30. *Fong Yue Ting v. United States*, 149 U.S. 762–763 (1893).

31. Salyer, *Laws Harsh as Tigers*, 52–53.

32. Wunder, *Gold Mountain Turned to Dust*, 135.

33. Salyer, *Laws Harsh as Tigers*, 55.

34. Hernández, *City of Inmates*, 86.

35. "Chinese Will Register" *Helena Independent*, April 1, 1893.

36. "Terms of the Treaty," *Anaconda Standard*, March 25, 1894.

37. "Chinese Must Register," *Anaconda Standard*, December 16, 1893.

38. "All Tintypes Barred," *Anaconda Standard*, December 27, 1893.

39. "Chinese Census, District of Montana and Idaho, June 30, 1905," United States Bureau of Immigration, District of Montana and Idaho, MF 510, MHS.

40. Quoted in Pegler-Gordon, *In Sight of America*, 98.

41. "Toy Can Tarry," *Great Falls Weekly Tribune*, August 2, 1895.

42. "Will Hold Chinese for Proof of His Identity," *Butte Inter Mountain*, September 12, 1903.

43. *Anaconda Standard*, August 6, 1899.

44. *Eleventh Census of the United States, 1890*; *Twelfth Census of the United States, 1900*; *Thirteenth Census of the United States, 1910*.

45. Lee Sam Fong Papers, SSC 2747, MHS.

46. "They Do Not Stop Long: Mongolians Tarry Little in the City of Great Falls," *Anaconda Standard*, December 17, 1899.

47. "Clothier—Nate Wertheim," *Daily Tribune* (Great Falls), April 21, 1892, clipping at the History Museum, Great Falls MT.

48. "They Do Not Stop Long: Mongolians Tarry Little in the City of Great Falls," *Anaconda Standard*, December 17, 1899.

49. "A Chinese Merchant: He Arrives from Portland and Soon Finds that He is in Trouble," *Great Falls Tribune*, January 22, 1898.

50. "Not So Easy," *Billings Gazette*, December 9, 1902.

51. "They Do Not Stop Long: Mongolians Tarry Little in the City of Great Falls," *Anaconda Standard*, December 17, 1899.

52. "Chinese Census, District of Montana and Idaho, June 30, 1905," United States Bureau of Immigration, District of Montana and Idaho, MF 510, MHS.

53. Sue Nam; application for duplicate certificate of residence, June 18, 1904, no. 12343, Bureau of Commerce and Labor, Immigration Service, Chinese General Correspondence, RG 85, NARA, Washington DC.

54. *Compilation from the Records of the Bureau of Immigration*, (1906), 143.

55. "Inspector Eby [*sic*] Here," *Fergus County Argus* (Lewistown MT), April 19, 1905.

56. "Chinese Immigration," *Butte Inter Mountain*, April 3, 1902.

4. Chinese Empire Reform Association

1. Daniels, *Asian America*, 59–63.

2. Vohra, *China's Path to Modernization*, 85–86; Hsu, *Rise of Modern China*, 366.

3. Mishra, *From the Ruins of Empire*, 143–46.

4. Kang Youwei, "Comprehensive Consideration of the Whole Situation," 269–70.

5. Headland, *Court Life in China*, 137–39, 355–56.

6. "Advocacy of Complete Westernization," 158–60.

7. "Chinese Reformer Flees to America," *Butte Inter Mountain*, June 30, 1900.

8. Note that the Chinese Empire Reform Association is known in Chinese as the Baohuanghui (The Society to Protect the Emperor). Key sources of new scholarship on the Chinese Empire Reform Association are found at "Baohuanghui Scholarship," http://baohuanghui.blogspot.com and the Chinese in Northwest America Committee (CINARC) at www.cinarc.org.

9. Larson, "Association to Save China."

10. Larson, "The United States as a Site for Baohuanghui Activism;" Merritt, *Coming Man from Canton*, 171–72.

11. From email correspondence with Jane Leung Larson.

12. *Not in Precious Metals Alone*, 164–65.

13. Flaherty, "Boycott in Butte," 34–47.

14. *Not in Precious Metals Alone*, 164–65.

15. Quoted in Lee, *Growth and Decline of Chinese Communities*, 123.

16. "The Real Issue," *Butte Semi-Weekly Miner*, October 30, 1886.

17. *Congressional Record Proceedings and Debates of the Fifty-Second Congress*, 3569.

18. Flaherty, "Boycott in Butte," 34–47.

19. Quoted in Lee, *Growth and Decline of Chinese Communities*, 123.

20. Wunder, *Gold Mountain Turned to Dust*, 159–76.

21. Long Ka Tien (Liang Qitian) was the cousin of Liang Qichao and student of Kang Youwei.

22. "Chinamen Are Aroused: Those in Butte Have Organized a Reform Society," *Anaconda Standard*, August 12, 1901.

23. "Gong Hee Is a Wizard: Chinese Masters Electrician's Trade in Portland," *Morning Oregonian* (Portland), February 12, 1903.

24. "New Chinese Electrical Book," *Electrical Review* 39, December 1901, 915.

25. "Gong Hee Is a Wizard: Chinese Masters Electrician's Trade in Portland," *Morning Oregonian*, February 12, 1903.

26. "Chinamen are Aroused," *Anaconda Standard*, August 12, 1901.

27. "Chinese Enter into Politics: Mongolians of Montana Will Campaign for Young Kwang Hsu and Pay Their Own Expenses," *Butte Inter Mountain*, August 12, 1901.

28. *Articles of Incorporation of the Chinese Empire Reform Society of Butte, Montana*, August 12, 1901, D003563, MHS; *Articles of Incorporation of the Chinese Empire Reform Society of Montana*, June 25, 1901, D003526, MHS.

29. The Articles of Incorporation for both the Helena and Butte branches are identical, obviously having been drafted from the same original source. Upon close examination of the documents, a possible interpretation emerges. On the "Articles of Incorporation of the Chinese Empire Reform Society of Montana" the names of Ting Fong, F. Kahn, and Wong Sing Won, who all served as the original officers, appear. Wong Sing Won could not write in English and instead wrote his name in Chinese characters. To attest to his true identity, a witness was needed. Written twice on the

document is "Witness to mark or Chinese signature of Wong Sing Won, Gong Hee." Clearly, Gong Hee was at the official meeting in which the Articles were presented to the county clerk to be notarized and submitted. This document was filed in Helena on June 25, 1901. The *Anaconda Standard* article of August 12, 1901 proves that Gong Hee, with Long Ka Tien, arrived in Butte on August 11. The "Articles of Incorporation of the Chinese Empire Reform Society of Butte, Montana," were filed on August 19. It appears that the original source from which the Helena and Butte branches' documents either was brought with Long and Gong, serving as the template, or emerged during the reformers extensive time in Montana. Long and Gong provided the external leadership that, combined with the leadership in both Helena and Butte, moved the CERA branches forward to the next stage of organization and official status.

30. "Good-Bye to Pigtails: Society of Chinese Who Will Include It in Their Reforms," *Anaconda Standard*, August 22, 1901.

31. "Chinamen in Meeting: They Are Holding Sessions Nearly Every Night," *Anaconda Standard*, December 3, 1901.

32. "Club Life Among the Chinese of Helena," *Anaconda Standard*, June 30, 1901.

33. "They Are Reformers: Local Chinese Organize School in Aid of Good Cause," *Billings Gazette*, November 15, 1901.

34. For more information on the regional nature of Chinese affiliation, see Lai, *Becoming Chinese American*, 143–76.

35. Ma, *Revolutionaries, Monarchists and Chinatowns*, 48–49; Chen, "Understanding Chinese American Transnationalism," 160–61.

36. "Great Reforms Are Being Urged: Chinese Agitators Finish Campaign in Butte and Go to Helena," *Butte Inter Mountain*, August 18, 1903.

37. "Progress in Chinese Empire," newspaper clipping from vertical file on Chinese, Butte-Silver Bow Public Archives (BSBPA), Butte MT.

38. "The Committee of the Chinese Empire Reform Association, Marysville, Mont.," PAC 85–27 MS, MHS.

39. Non-Chinese reporters from across the state noticed the trend of shaving the queue and adopting Western styles. The *Rosebud County News* (Forsyth MT) of November 14, 1902 noted that "Charley Kam, a Chink restaurateur at Livingston, has joined the Chinese Reform society, since which, consequently, he hasn't any more queue than a rabbit."

40. "The Committee of the Chinese Empire Reform Association, Butte, Mont., 1901," PAC 95–22 MMI, MHS.

41. Liang Qichao, "His Trip to America," 335–40.

42. Huang, *Liang Ch'i-ch'ao and Modern Chinese Liberalism*, 78.

43. "Two Chinese Diplomats: They Are In Town on Their Mission of Reform," *Anaconda Standard*, August 16, 1903.

44. Gao, *Activities of Kang Youwei*, 52–55, 308–11.

45. Shortly before his visit to Montana, Kang presided over a meeting of Chinese Empire Reform Association (CERA) leaders in New York City's Chinatown. The group formed a new constitution for the organization. One aspect dealt with proof of membership. Not all Chinese in North America supported the effort to reinstate the Guangxu

Emperor. Sun Yat-sen worked to build support in overseas Chinese communities to topple the Qing dynasty. Thus, with rival political groups competing for limited resources and working at cross purposes, proving membership was key in maintaining the integrity of the organization's efforts. The constitution of 1905 clarified the issue with its "Section 10: Proof of Membership," which read, "A membership certificate (*huipiao*) has been issued to all who have joined the Baohuanghui. . . . For the sake of convenience, a membership badge (*huipai*) can be used instead of a membership certificate. On the upper left side of the badge is the national flag and, on the right, the Baohuanghui flag, and a portrait of the emperor. All the members must wear the badge at Baohuanghui meetings or gatherings to show they are comrades. And, any member traveling to other Baohuanghui locations should wear the badge as proof of membership without which comradely reception will be denied." Following the establishment of this 1905 constitution and the standardization of proof of membership, Kang visited Montana, likely bringing this huipai, which was found during a 2008 dig in Butte's former Chinatown led by archaeologist Mitzi Rossillon and her team with Renewable Technologies, Inc. Photograph credit: Richard Gibson, Mai Wah Society, Butte, Montana, 24SB765.

46. An exceptionally interesting character named Homer Lea convinced Kang that he could equip and train a Chinese army abroad for a triumphant return to China to militarily defeat the forces of the Dowager Empress and reinstate the Guangxu Emperor. Lea was a white man who stood just over five feet tall, weighed about one hundred pounds, and had a hunchback. He also suffered from multiple severe health issues. Though he had no formal military training and little experience that seemed relevant for his grand claims, he convinced CERA leaders that he was the man to lead the newly formed "Chinese Imperial Army" from exile to a glorious return. Most of Lea's efforts were focused in California, but the militarization of the movement did spread to Montana as well. For more on Homer Lea and the military efforts of the CERA, see Kaplan, *Homer Lea*.

47. "Chinese Are Drilling Like Old Hands At It: Members Fully Equipped," *Anaconda Standard*, August 25, 1905.

48. One possible theory is that the person who took the photograph, Joseph Hervey, was involved in training the Chinese militia. Hervey served in the Philippines during the Spanish-American War. After his service in the Philippines, "[Hervey] re-enlisted with the regulars, during which time he was in the Chinese campaign and participated in the famous march on Pekin, where he was among the first to scale the wall of the Sacred City" during the suppression of the Boxer Rebellion (*Butte Daily Post*, August 8, 1906). It appears that Hervey sought out opportunities while in China. "While at Canton, Mr. Hervey was employed by the American-China Developing company, which had a contract to build the Canton & Hankow railway, which will be 750 miles long when completed. He worked during the larger part of this year on the railroad. Then the company and the Chinese government got into a quarrel and work on the road was suspended." Hervey returned to Butte, but his interest in China persisted: "If the Canton & Hankow railroad resumes building, Mr. Hervey will return to China to his former employment" (*Butte Inter Mountain*, December 2, 1904). Some accounts report Hervey actually serving with the Chinese military: "Lieutenant Her-

vey has seen service in the Philippines, and was also for a time in the imperial Chinese army" (*Anaconda Standard*, October 20, 1906). These extensive connections to events in China while he was abroad, his geographic proximity to large Chinese communities while home in Montana, and the photograph of the banquet coming from his collection strongly indicate that Hervey had some role in the military training of the cera troops in Montana.

49. "Butte City Gancheng School's Opening Ceremony," *New York China Reform News*, April 20, 1905, translated by Chi Jeng Chang.

50. "Chinese Are Drilling Like Old Hands At It: Members Fully Equipped," *Anaconda Standard*, August 25, 1905.

51. Kang's visit to Livingston was cut short due to the length of their tour of Yellowstone Park. Yellowstone Gateway Museum.

52. "Chinese Reform Party Going to Spokane: President Kang Yu Wei Reviews Soldier Boys," *Anaconda Standard*, September 30, 1905.

53. "Chinese Reform Party Going to Spokane: President Kang Yu Wei Reviews Soldier Boys," *Anaconda Standard*, September 30, 1905.

54. Larson, "1905 Anti-American Boycott."

55. "Reform Army a Dream: The Chinese Wake Up," *Anaconda Standard*, January 8, 1906.

5. Anti-American Boycott of 1905

1. Quoted in McKeown, *Melancholy Order*, 217–19.

2. Salyer, *Laws Harsh as Tigers*, 102.

3. Powderly, *Thirty Years of Labor*, 421.

4. Quoted in McKeown, *Melancholy Order*, 217.

5. Ng, "Treatment of the Exempt Classes of Chinese," 109–17; Wong, "Liang Qichao and the Chinese of America," 3–24. For an excellent analysis of the use of the Bertillon system and other aspects of photographic evidence as applied to the Chinese, see Pegler-Gordon, *In Sight of America*.

6. "Table 39. Aliens Removed or Returned: Fiscal Years 1892 to 2016," U.S. Department of Homeland Security.

7. "To Deport Two Chinese," *Butte Inter Mountain*, November 2, 1903.

8. "They Must Go Away Back," *Western News* (Stevensville mt), February 17, 1904.

9. *River Press*, March 2, 1904.

10. *River Press*, April 29, 1903; *River Press*, May 27, 1903.

11. Quoted in Wong, "Liang Qichao and the Chinese of America," 3–24.

12. "Chinese Census, District of Montana and Idaho, June 30, 1905," United States Bureau of Immigration, District of Montana and Idaho, mf 510, mhs; Smith, "Immigration and Naturalization Service," 127–47.

13. "Inspector Eby [*sic*] Here," *Fergus County Argus*, April 19, 1905.

14. *Western News* (Stevensville, mt), May 17, 1905.

15. *River Press*, May 17, 1905.

16. *Havre (mt) Herald*, February 2, 1906.

17. "Still in Custody," *Billings Gazette*, May 26, 1905.

18. Tom Sin (Hom You Sin), Chinese Exclusion Case Files, 1895–1943, file 4/193, RG 85, NARA, Seattle WA.

19. Coolidge, *Chinese Immigration*, 324.

20. *Kalispell (MT) Bee*, August 3, 1900.

21. "Had a Chinese Holiday," *Anaconda Standard*, August 20, 1900.

22. Larson, "Articulating China's First Mass Movement," 6–10; McKeown, *Melancholy Order*, 222, 300.

23. McKee, "Chinese Boycott of 1905–1906 Reconsidered," 176.

24. Yue, *Shanghai at the Edges of Empire*, 120–25.

25. Judge, "Factional Function of Print: Liang Qichao, *Shibao*," 120–22; Judge, *Print and Politics*, 32–33.

26. Zhu, *Shanghai Historic Days*, 117–18; Larson, "A Galvanizing Issue," 3.

27. Quoted in Larson "Articulating China's First Mass Movement," 11.

28. John Endicott Gardner, "Chinese Boycott on American Goods," August 7, 1905, Chinese General Correspondence, RG 85, NARA, Washington DC.

29. Larson, "An Association to Save China;" Kramer, "Imperial Openings," 317–47.

30. "Leaflet opposing the Exclusion Treaty—manuscript from Chinese living in America," June 1905, in Zhiqin and Huiyao, eds., *Kang Liang yu Baohuanghui*, 379–83. Translation checked by Renqiu Yu, SUNY Purchase. UCLA Digital online document: http://digital2.library.ucla.edu/viewItem.do?ark=21198/zz00253t3n.

31. Quoted in Larson, "Articulating China's First Mass Movement," 1.

32. Quoted in Dong, *Shanghai*, 83.

33. *Rosebud County News*, February 8, 1906.

34. "Late News Items," *Western News*, August 2, 1905.

35. McKee, "Chinese Boycott of 1905–1906 Reconsidered," 177; Meissner, "China's 1905 Anti-American Boycott," 175.

36. *Havre Herald*, November 30, 1905.

37. Wong, "Mobilizing a Social Movement in China," 381.

38. Meng, *Shanghai at the Edges of Empire*, 120–25; Wong, "Mobilizing a Social Movement in China," 387–95.

39. "Wu and the Boycott," *Billings Gazette*, August 22, 1905.

40. Wang, *In Search of Justice*, 89.

41. J.H. Arnold, "Chinese placards against American goods in Shanghai," August 17, 1905, Dispatches from U.S. Consuls in Shanghai, China 1847-1906, RG 59, NARA, College Park MD.

42. James L. Rodgers, "Boycott Situation," August 12, 1905, Dispatches from U.S. Consuls in Shanghai, China 1847–1906, RG 59, NARA, College Park MD.

43. Dondlinger, *Book of Wheat*, 197.

44. "Crops and Prosperity," *Billings Gazette*, August 22, 1905; Hill's thoughts on the impact of the boycott received widespread coverage in newspapers of the American West. Often Hill brought up the boycott unprompted, which showed readers the seriousness of the topic. For instance, a reporter noted, "The fact that the Chinese boycott enters into his interview on the subject [the general status of the region's wheat crop in 1905]

is evidence that the Chinese situation is causing grave concern among the handlers of the northwest's wheat crop." "Hill Fears Chinese Boycott," *River Press*, August 23, 1905.

45. *Billings Gazette*, August 22, 1905.

46. *Billings Gazette*, December 29, 1905.

47. "Boycott Stops Flour Trade," *New York Times*, August 27, 1905.

48. Quoted in Wang, *In Search of Justice*, 163.

49. Meissner, "China's 1905 Anti-American Boycott," 179, 182.

50. Meissner, "China's 1905 Anti-American Boycott," 193.

51. *Western News*, January 10, 1906.

52. "Exports to China," *Fergus Country Argus*, January 19, 1906.

53. Meissner, "China's 1905 Anti-American Boycott," 194.

54. John Endicott Gardner, "Chinese Boycott on American Goods," August 7, 1905, Chinese General Correspondence, RG 85, NARA, Washington DC.

55. *River Press*, February 14, 1906.

56. *Western News*, February 14, 1906; *Billings Gazette*, August 18, 1905; "Fear Attacks on Americans," *Western News*, August 16, 1905.

57. Thomas Bowen, Letter to President Roosevelt, August 7, 1905, Chinese General Correspondence, RG 85, NARA, Washington DC.

58. Wong, "Mobilizing a Social Movement in China," 399–401; Wang, *In Search of Justice*, 117–18.

59. "New Troubles Brewing with China," *Literary Digest* XXXI, No. 20, 1905.

60. "Shooting of Chinese is Nothing Unusual," *Anaconda Standard*, November 1, 1905.

61. "New Troubles Brewing with China," *Literary Digest* XXXI, No. 20, 1905.

62. William Rockhill letter to John Hay, August 17, 1905, Dispatches from U.S. Consuls in China, 1843–1906, M 92, NARA, College Park MD.

63. Letter from Washington State Millers Association to Theodore Roosevelt, July 12, 1905; Letter from Scharlin & Co. to Theodore Roosevelt, September 26, 1905; Letter from Howard Elliot, President of Northern Pacific Railway Company to Theodore Roosevelt, August 26, 1905; Letter from President of Cotton Goods Export Association of New York to Theodore Roosevelt, June 22, 1905; Letter from Theodore Wilcox, President of Trans-Mississippi Commercial Congress to Theodore Roosevelt, August 31, 1905; Letter from William D. Wheelwright President of Portland, OR Chamber of Commerce to Theodore Roosevelt, June 23, 1905; Telegram from Tacoma Chamber of Commerce to Theodore Roosevelt, July 12, 1905, file 12264, Chinese General Correspondence, RG 85, NARA, Washington, DC; Beth Lew-Williams, *The Chinese Must Go*.

64. Larson, "A Galvanizing Issue," 19.

65. "What the Chinese Think about the Chinese Exclusion Act," *Spokane (WA) Press*, May 23, 1905.

66. McKeown, *Melancholy Order*, 242.

67. Thompson, *Great Power Rising*, 103.

68. "Enforcement of the Chinese-Exclusion Laws—General Instructions: Department Circular No. 81—Bureau of Immigration," *Congressional Record Senate Documents, 59th Cong., 2nd sess.*, December 3, 1906–March 4, 1907 (Washington DC: Government Printing Office, 1907), 55.

69. Theodore Roosevelt, "State of the Union Address," December 5, 1905.

70. "Chinese Are Drilling Like Old Hands," *Anaconda Standard*, August 25, 1905.

71. "Chinese Census, District of Montana and Idaho, June 30, 1905," United States Bureau of Immigration, District of Montana and Idaho, MF 510, MHS.

72. "Chinaman Deported," *Billings Gazette*, April 3, 1906.

73. Letter from Kang Yu Wei to Theodore Roosevelt, January 30, 1906, file 12264–78, Chinese General Correspondence, RG 85, NARA, Washington DC.

74. Salyer, *Laws Harsh as Tigers*, 164–66; McKeown, *Melancholy Order*, 242–43.

75. *Compilation from the Records of the Bureau of Immigration*, (1906), 155.

76. *Fergus County Argus*, May 29, 1906.

77. Lew-Williams, *The Chinese Must Go*, 209.

78. McKeown, *Melancholy Order*, 250.

6. Religious and Burial Practices

1. "A Chinese Funeral," *Montana Post*, May 11, 1867.

2. "Funeral of Chinese," *Helena Daily Independent*, December 27, 1918.

3. *Montana Post*, October 28, 1865; "Guards the Joss House," *Anaconda Standard*, December 17, 1899.

4. "A Chinese Funeral: An Almond-eyed Celestial Buried with the Usual Ceremony," *Anaconda Standard*, August 9, 1897.

5. "Murdered Chinese Given Regulation Funeral," *Helena Independent*, January 13, 1928.

6. Baumler, et al., "Forgotten Pioneers," 14.

7. For the synthesis of the Chinese belief systems of Confucianism, Daoism, Buddhism, and folk traditions, see Lum, "Religion on the Road," 160, 167, 171, 176–78; Chang, *Ghosts of Gold Mountain*, 116–17; Rouse, "'What We Didn't Understand,'" 19–45; Pasacreta, "White Tigers and Azure Dragons," 5–36.

8. The term "joss" or "josh" is a corruption of the Portuguese word "deos" or God. It is likely due to the influence of Portuguese traders and missionaries working in southern China in the 16th century. Interactions with Chinese, discussions of religion, and the evolution of languages brought the term Joss to the Chinese experience in North America. The term applies to incense burned for ritual occasions ("Joss sticks"), temples used for worship ("Joss houses"), and the statues of gods featured in temples (referred to as "Joss").

9. "All the Dead Quiet: The Anaconda Chinamen Celebrated their New Years," *Anaconda Standard*, January 31, 1895.

10. "Guards the Joss House," *Anaconda Standard*, December 17, 1899.

11. Interview with Richard Gibson, Mai Wah Society and Museum, Butte MT, September 26, 2019.

12. Chung, Frampton, and Murphy, "Venerate These Bones," 112; Chace, "On Dying American," 62.

13. "Chinese Census, District of Montana and Idaho, June 30, 1905," United States Bureau of Immigration, District of Montana and Idaho, Montana Historical Society, MF 510.

14. Quoted in Lee, *Growth and Decline of Chinese Communities*, 262–64.

15. "Vandals Invade Chinese Joss House," *Butte Inter Mountain*, May 3, 1902.

16. "Broke Up Worship to Chinese Gods," *Billings Gazette*, July 20, 1909.

17. *Neihart (MT) Herald*, March 4, 1889.

18. Watson and Rawski, *Death Ritual in Late Imperial and Modern China*, 9, 133.

19. "The Chinese Funeral," *Benton Weekly Record* (Fort Benton MT), June 2, 1881.

20. *Montana Post*, October 28, 1865.

21. Watson and Rawski, *Death Ritual in Late Imperial and Modern China*, 112.

22. Pasacreta, "White Tigers and Azure Dragons," 32.

23. "Woman Took Poison," *Helena Weekly Herald*, October 9, 1873.

24. Quoted in Lee, *Growth and Decline of Chinese Communities*, 262–64, 355.

25. The gender imbalance worsened throughout the end of the nineteenth century. In 1870 there were 14.2 Chinese men for every Chinese woman in Montana. The ratio was 20.5/1 by 1880 and 40.3/1 by 1900. Merritt, *Coming Man from Canton*, 98.

26. Watson and Rawski, *Death Ritual in Late Imperial and Modern China*, 113; Pasacreta, "White Tigers and Azure Dragons," 33.

27. Quoted in McGlashan, *Buried in Butte*, 122–23.

28. Chace, "On Dying American," 55, 68–69.

29. "Chinaman Dies," *Billings Gazette*, March 26, 1907; "Posterity May Worship: Dead Chinaman will be Buried in Native Country, Where His Descendants May Pay Tribute at His Grave," *Billings Gazette*, April 16, 1907; "Chinese Graveyard," *Billings Gazette*, May 28, 1907.

30. Hermann and Company Records, 1883–1967, MF 183, MHS.

31. "Chinese Graveyard," *Billings Gazette*, May 28, 1907.

32. Watson and Rawski, *Death Ritual in Late Imperial and Modern China*, 123–24.

33. Similar trends for Chinese mourners to use non-Chinese musicians were noted in funeral processions in Colorado and elsewhere. Zhu, *Road to Chinese Exclusion*, 86.

34. "Woman Took Poison," *Helena Weekly Herald*, October 9, 1873.

35. Museum label for Chinese in Butte exhibit, Mai Wah Society, Butte, Montana, 20 September 2019.

36. Bik, "China Row."

37. Pasacreta, "White Tigers and Azure Dragons," 178.

38. "A Chinese Funeral," *Montana Post*, May 11, 1867.

39. "Chinese Funeral," *Age-Sentinel* (Boulder), November 5, 1902, clipping from the Heritage Center, Boulder MT.

40. "A Chinese Funeral," *Montana Post*, May 11, 1867.

41. WPA *Guide to Montana*, 182.

42. *Weekly Avant Courier (Bozeman MT)*, October 28, 1899.

43. "A Chinese Funeral," *Montana Post*, May 11, 1867.

44. McGlashan, *Buried in Butte*, 122–23.

45. Merritt, *Coming Man from Canton*, 130–33.

46. Author interview with Bob Morgan, Helena MT, June 2014.

47. Pasacreta, "White Tigers and Azure Dragons," 34.

48. "Chinese Bones," *Helena Daily Independent*, October 14, 1881.

49. Rouse, "'What We Didn't Understand,'" 24; Pasacreta, "White Tigers and Azure Dragons," 34.

50. *Montana Post*, October 28, 1865.

51. "Feeding the Dead," *Helena Weekly Herald*, April 9, 1869.

52. *Great Falls Leader*, April 6, 1901.

53. Rouse, "'What We Didn't Understand,'" 28.

54. "Chinese Penance Day," *Helena Independent Weekly*, October 11, 1883.

55. Quoted in Lee, *Growth and Decline of Chinese Communities*, 267.

56. *Helena Weekly Herald*, September 24, 1885.

57. *Missoula Pioneer*, June 22, 1871.

58. "John Chinaman, My Jo John," *New Northwest*, March 28, 1879.

59. *Butte Bystander*, February 11, 1893.

60. Papers Relating to the Foreign Relations of the United States, 115.

61. Sinn, *Pacific Crossing*, 270.

62. *Anaconda Standard*, April 27, 1893.

63. Pasacreta, "White Tigers and Azure Dragons," 47–48.

64. Sinn, *Pacific Crossing*, 270.

65. Sinn, *Pacific Crossing*, 266–70; Yip, "Institutionalizing Charity," 1–11.

66. *Helena Weekly Herald*, September 24, 1885.

67. Yip, "Institutionalizing Charity," 3.

68. Quoted in Yip, "Institutionalizing Charity," 2.

69. Zhu, *A Chinaman's Chance*, 90; Sinn, *Pacific Crossing*, 280.

70. Quoted in Yip, "Institutionalizing Charity," 2–3.

71. "A China Funeral," *Helena Weekly Herald*, September 19, 1867.

72. Helterline, *Horse Plains*, 19–20, 134.

73. "Chinese Graves," Neil Fullerton research collection, 1932–1968 MC 76 (4:5–1).

74. "Bones of Bozeman Chinks Sent Home," May 13, 1913, clipping from the Gallatin History Museum, Bozeman MT.

75. "The Chinese Funeral," *Fort Benton Weekly Record*, June 2, 1881.

76. *The WPA Guide to Montana*, 182.

77. "A Chinese Funeral," *Montana Post*, May 11, 1867; Pasacreta, "White Tigers and Azure Dragons," 55.

78. "Ah Hong is Dead," *Daily Inter Mountain (Butte MT)*, January 26, 1901.

79. "Condensed Heathen," *New Northwest*, October 17, 1874.

80. "Chinese Bones: Several Bags of them Prepare for an Excursion and Enjoy a Grand Feast by Proxy," *Helena Daily Independent*, October 14, 1881.

81. "Bones of Chinaman Sent from Anaconda to Flowery Kingdom," *Great Falls Tribune*, February 13, 1921.

82. "All the Same Pickles," *Helena Weekly Herald*, January 21, 1875.

83. "Chinese Graveyard," *Billings Gazette*, May 28, 1907.

84. "No Longer a Mystery: Where the Bones Found in a Central Avenue Cellar Came From," *Great Falls Weekly Tribune*, October 21, 1892.

85. "A Brief Historical Review," *Great Falls Weekly Tribune*, July 4, 1891.

86. "A Sensational Find," *Great Falls Daily Leader*, August 11, 1892.

87. "The Story of the Skeleton," *Great Falls Daily Leader*, August 11, 1892.

88. Interestingly, there is another instance of bones being found in a strange place in Montana. A 1903 article in the *Butte Inter Mountain* newspaper claims that a construction crew unearthed a skeleton of a Chinese woman in the basement of the Eagle Saloon on Bozeman's Main Street. Clues from the jewelry led the coroner to consult the Chinese community, and a representative corroborated the theory that the skeleton was of a Chinese woman. The remains were thought to have been in the basement for more than twenty-five years. Little more is known about the story. "Ghastly Find in Cellar: Excavators at Bozeman Unearth Remains of Chinese." *Butte Inter Mountain*, March 30, 1903.

89. Yip, "Institutionalizing Charity," 1–11.

90. Grebenkemper and Morris, "China Row."

91. Quoted in Wong, *Long Way Home*, 202–3.

7. Changing Status of Chinese Women

1. "Self Preservation the First Law of Nature," *Montana Post*, August 19, 1865.

2. As noted previously, the majority of Chinese migrants to the United States were men. However, some scholars note that before the Chinese Exclusion Act banned laborers, many of the women who joined Chinese communities were wives of laborers. This was especially the case in the late 1860s and early 1870s and is relevant to Montana in light of the experiences of Ah Choy, whose husband Ah Chow was executed in Helena in 1870. Yung, *Unbound Feet*, 42–43.

3. *The Page Act: An Act Supplementary to the Acts in Relation to Immigration*, 18 Stat. 477, 43rd Congress, 2nd sess. (Washington, DC: Government Printing Office, 1875), 141, 477–78.

4. Yung, *Unbound Feet*, 41.

5. *Ninth Census of the United States, 1870; Tenth Census of the United States, 1880*. Specific information is unavailable for the 1890 census as it was destroyed by fire in 1921. For details, see Blake, "'First in the Path of the Firemen.'" By 1900, Montana's female Chinese population was 36, with seven noted to be working as prostitutes.

6. Wright and Hunt, *History and Growth of the United States Census*, 169.

7. Baumler, *Helena*, 22–23.

8. For excellent analysis of the topic of prostitution and Chinese women in the nineteenth century, see Hirata, "Free, Indentured, Enslaved," 3–29; Tong, *Unsubmissive Women*.

9. Peffer, *If They Don't Bring Their Women Here*, 12–27.

10. *Congressional Record Proceedings and Debates of the Fifty-Second Congress*, 3569.

11. Quoted in Lee, *At America's Gates*, 92–96

12. Quoted in Lee, *Growth and Decline of Chinese Communities*, 249; for another account marriage arranged across the Pacific, see Wong, *Long Way Home*.

13. Lee, *At America's Gates*, 96.

14. Mrs. Wo Hop, "Chinese Exclusion Act," vf1052, bsbpa.

15. Quoted in Lee, *Growth and Decline of Chinese Communities*, 252–53.

16. Quoted in Mei, "Socioeconomic Origins of Emigration," 474.

17. Quoted in Yung, *Unbound Feet*, 37.

18. Ngai, *The Lucky Ones*, 15–19.

19. "Received Their Diplomas," *Herald* (Los Angeles), June 5, 1896.

20. Chinn, *Other Side of Paradise*, chapter 2.

21. Quoted in Pascoe, "Gender Systems in Conflict," 639.

22. Pascoe, "Gender Systems in Conflict," 631–640.

23. Some accounts claim detailed knowledge about Ah Oie's (Alice Lamb's) circumstances and path to the Mission Home. Indeed, an "Ah Oie" was rescued from dire conditions as a young girl, having been sold as a *mui tsai*, brought to San Francisco to work in brothels, and rescued through the efforts of the Presbyterian Mission Home and the Society for the Prevention of Cruelty to Children. The story of this "Ah Oie" is grounded in the 1880s, includes specific claims about the amount exchanged for purchase of the girl, specific mistreatments the girl suffered, and aspects of the story of her rescue. Some claim that this is the same "Ah Oie" who later married Dr. Wah Jean Lamb. The documents relating to "Ah Oie's" tribulations in San Francisco, however, are from a considerably earlier time period, noting the girl as fourteen in 1884. Records from the Presbyterian Mission Home indicate that this woman married a man named Low Ah Fook in 1889. The Ah Oie (Alice) who married Lamb appears on the 1910 census as twenty-six years old. This woman resided at the Mission Home in 1902 and was matched in marriage at that time. While their lives as mui tsai and rescue through the Mission Home may have been similar for the two women, it seems that they are two different people with the same name. Morgan, *Wanton West*, 96–98; "Ah Oie," *Log Book of Presbyterian Occidental Board Mission Home*, 1884, 79, 141; Woman's Foreign Missionary Society, "Woman's Work for Woman," 364–65; Lettieri, "'Maximize Our Missions,'" 157.

24. "Mission Ladies Give Dr. Lamb a Bride," *San Francisco Examiner*, April 5, 1901.

25. "Occidental Mission in Annual Convention," *San Francisco Chronicle*, April 5, 1901.

26. Pascoe, "Gender Systems in Conflict," 637.

27. For thorough analysis of the Quong Tuck Wing case, see Fong, "Establishing and Maintaining," 39–51.

28. Quoted in Fong, "Establishing and Maintaining," 42.

29. "Denies Story of Kidnapping," *San Francisco Call*, September 26, 1902.

30. "Butte Police Overstep Their Authority," *Butte Inter Mountain*, September 24, 1902.

31. "Woman and Child Held for Ransom," *Butte Inter Mountain*, September 23, 1902.

32. "Butte Police Overstep Their Authority," *Butte Inter Mountain*, September 24, 1902.

33. "The Chinese in Butte," *Anaconda Standard*, December 8, 1899; *Annual Report of the Woman's American Baptist Home Mission Society*, 1897, 128.

34. "Chinese Problem is a Hard One to Solve," *Butte Miner*, September 29, 1902.

35. "Rescued from a Life of Slavery," *San Francisco Chronicle*, September 26, 1902.

36. "Chinese—Long Ying Story," VF 1057, BSBPA.

37. Fong, "Establishing and Maintaining," 39–45.

38. Quoted in Pascoe, "Gender Systems in Conflict," 639.

39. Fong, "Establishing and Maintaining," 39–52.

40. Na Loy was also known as Na Lay or as Annie Cum Chee/Annie Kum Chee in more recent retellings.

41. *Compilation from the Records of the Bureau of Immigration* (1906), 145.

42. *Anaconda Standard*, May 7, 1897.

43. "A Chinese Marriage," *Wichita Daily Eagle*, October 4, 1903. The article appeared across the nation throughout 1904 under the headline: "Marriage of Wong Wa Foy: The True Story of a Stolen Bride," authored by J. H. Emery.

44. "Chinese Murderer Executed at an Early Hour," *Butte Inter Mountain*, April 9, 1906.

45. "Butte Scaffold is in Demand," *Butte Miner*, April 10, 1906.

46. Indeed, if Tom was a member of the Zhigongtang and if Na Loy had been claimed by another member, Tom's assassination might have been in keeping with the rules of the society, as described in chapter 2, that noted members must not "covet the wife or sisters of brethren because of their beauty."

47. "Pity Felt for Woman: Court Orders Deportation of Murdered Man's Wife," *Evening Statesman* (Walla Walla wa), April 3, 1906.

48. Ham Hung Wah, Chinese Exclusion Case Files, 1895–1943, Case RS653, Box RS019, File 1507, RG 85, NARA, Seattle wa.

49. *Compilation from the Records of the Bureau of Immigration*, (1906), 143.

50. "The Deportation of Na Lay," *Billings Gazette*, February 21, 1908.

51. Senator Thomas H. Carter was an advocate for the state's Chinese residents. Most notably, Carter supported Billy Kee, who worked for him for several years. Carter assisted Kee's education while he attended night school in Helena. Kee went on to run the High Point Inn in Lombard, Montana, and was popularly regarded as the "mayor of Lombard." Kee brought a wife to America and had several children. In the early twentieth century Kee returned to China. Several Montana newspapers report that in 1916 Billy Kee ran afoul of the government, run by Yuan Shikai at the time, and was tried for treason and beheaded. "Patriot's End for Billie Kee," *Glasgow (MT) Courier*, October 13, 1916.

52. *Compilation from the Records of the Bureau of Immigration*, (1906), 144.

53. Quoted in Lee, *Growth and Decline of Chinese Communities*, 252–53.

54. "An Early Morning Arrival: The First Chinese Baby Born in Lawful Wedlock in Helena," *Helena Independent*, January 20, 1893.

55. "Helena Has Two Chinese Stenos," *Powder River County Examiner* (Broadus MT), March 11, 1921.

56. "First Women of Their Race in Montana to Secure Ballot," newspaper clipping from May 23, 1916, Lee Sam Fong Papers, SSC 2747, MHS.

57. Malone, Roeder, and Lang, *Montana*, 262–64.

58. "All Samee Melican: Chinese Woman Asks Court to Give Her Divorce," *Billings Gazette*, September 3, 1901.

59. "Fame Thrust Upon Annie: Erstwhile Mrs. Art Tin Highly Honored," *Billings Gazette*, November 11, 1902.

60. "Montana's Strangest Social Reformer: A Chinese Girls who thinks the American Way is the Right Way," *Anaconda Standard*, November 9, 1902.

61. "Chinese Woman Has Ideas," *Meridian (MS) Evening Star*, November 28, 1902.

62. Gao, "Soo Yong: Hollywood Celebrity and Cultural Interpreter," 379–80.

63. Quoted in Gao, "Soo Yong," 382.

64. Melvin, "Sounds of Distinction."

65. "Chinese Actor Welcomed by City Officials," *San Francisco Chronicle*, April 21, 1930.

66. "Chinese Coming Back?" *Montana Oil and Mining Journal*, September 19, 1931.

67. "Wealthy New York Start Alder Gulch Mine," *Helena Independent Record*, October 16, 1931.

68. "Chinese Play an Important Part in Western Mining," *Ka Leo O Hawai'i* (Honolulu), December 3, 1931.

69. "Winnetka Prepares for Golden Harvest," *Montana Oil and Mining Journal*, March 5, 1932.

70. Quoted in Gao, "Soo Yong," 389–90. The story of Ah Hee Yong/Soo Yong is reminiscent of Anna May Wong, a Chinese American actress of the same time period who struggled to gain leading roles due to discrimination in Hollywood. For more information, see Hodges, *Anna May Wong*.

71. "Chinese Play an Important Part in Western Mining," *Ka Leo O Hawai'i*, December 3, 1931.

72. "Soo Yong, Motion Picture and Stage Actress," *Billings Gazette*, April 16, 1939.

73. For more on Lee's views on assimilation, see Yu, *Thinking Orientals*.

74. Nicolosi, "'We Do Not Want Our Girls to Marry Foreigners,'" 1–4. Similarly, views in American law tracked the status of children with the father, not the mother. As described in the next chapter, the concept of "derivative citizenship" meant that children born abroad to fathers who were American citizens became citizens themselves. This same status was not accorded to children born abroad to a mother who was an American citizen. Volpp, "Divesting Citizenship," 420.

75. *Relative to Citizenship of American Women*, 5.

76. Cott, "Marriage and Women's Citizenship," 1464.

77. Rose Hum Lee was part of a trend of second-generation Chinese Americans going to southern China in the late 1920s and 1930s. With the onset of the Great Depression causing jobs in America to be scarce, many second-generation Chinese Americans moved to China where their dual language abilities and knowledge of both cultures opened opportunities. For more on this topic, see Brooks, *American Exodus*.

78. Lee, "Madame Chiang Kai-Shek's Children," 136–37.

79. Letter to Elaine Lee, November 14, 1960, Rose Hum Lee papers (Collection 1002), Department of Special Collections, Charles E. Young Research Library, UCLA.

80. "Chinese Woman Tells of War," *Montana Oil and Mining Journal*, January 7, 1939.

81. For thorough coverage of Rose Hum Lee, her thoughts on assimilation, and her personal and professional life, see Ng, "Fitting in Space," 1–13.

82. Various sources in Rose Hum Lee's personal papers illustrate her growing paranoia throughout the late–1950s and early–1960s. She reached out to government officials informing them of her theories and suspicions, but her claims appear less grounded in reality and apparently were never corroborated by external sources. Rose Hum Lee papers.

83. Letter to Elaine Lee, November 14, 1960, Rose Hum Lee papers.

8. Cold War Fears

1. The subject of this chapter, Wing Hong Hom, is alternatively referred to as Hom Wing Hung. He is of the Hom/Hum family, with the given name Wing Hong. I refer to him as Wing Hong Hom as that was how he most often gave his name in official documents in Montana. His shift to placing his family name last may indicate his increasing assimilation to American culture. When referring to Wing Hong Hom and his brother Wing Goon Hom, given names are referenced to avoid confusion between the brothers. The collection of documents providing information on him at the Montana Historical Society is titled "The Wing Hong Hum Papers, 1935–1954," and I have left that unchanged in the citations.

2. Letter from Wing Goon Hom to Wing Hong Hom, July 28, 1949, file 89.30.3, "Wing Hong Hum Papers, 1935–1954," MHS.

3. Wing Goon Hom to Wing Hong Hom, November 28, 1949, file 89–30.12, "Wing Hong Hum Papers, 1935–1954," MHS.

4. Wing Goon Hom to Wing Hong Hom, November 28, 1949, file 89–30.134, "Wing Hong Hum Papers, 1935–1954," MHS.

5. English language file in "Wing Hong Hum Papers, 1935–1954," MHS.

6. English language file in "Wing Hong Hum Papers, 1935–1954," MHS.

7. Wing Goon Hom to Wing Hong Hom, August 10, 1953, file 89–30.194, "Wing Hong Hum Papers, 1935–1954," MHS.

8. English language file in "Wing Hong Hum Papers, 1935–1954," MHS.

9. Madokoro, *Elusive Refuge*, 116.

10. Ngai, *Impossible Subjects*, 206–8; Oyen, *Diplomacy of Migration*, 109.

11. Hsu, *Dreaming of Gold, Dreaming of Home*, 3.

12. Quoted in Lee, "Defying Exclusion," 1.

13. Quoted in Lee, *Making of Asian America*, 95.

14. McKeown, *Melancholy Order*, 278.

15. Glenn Ginn, the attorney who assisted Wing Hong Hom, was known for careful adherence to American laws when working to facilitate entry for applicants. "[Ginn] represents the Amer[ican] Law which the Chin[ese] do not like to uphold but spend their time getting around. . . . [Ginn] was anxious to get a method that permitted people to come in legally on their own rightful status and name. . . . They're not coming under false pretenses." Letter from Rose Hum Lee to Elaine Lee, January 22, 1958, Rose Hum Lee papers (Collection 1002). Department of Special Collections, Charles E. Young Research Library, UCLA.

16. Drumright, "Report on the Problem of Fraud at Hong Kong," Dispatch 931, December 9, 1955, file 122.4732/1–755, NARA, College Park MD.

17. Drumright, "Report on the Problem of Fraud at Hong Kong," Dispatch 931, December 9, 1955, file 122.4732/1–755, NARA, College Park MD.

18. Immigration file for Hom Hong, Chinese Exclusion Act case files, file 7030/5251, RG 85, NARA, Seattle WA.

19. Ngai, "Legacies of Exclusion," 4.

20. Immigration file for Hom Wing Hung, Chinese Exclusion Act case files, file 7030/5252, RG 85, NARA, Seattle WA.

21. Immigration file for Hom Wing Hung, Chinese Exclusion Act case files, file 7030/5252, RG 85, NARA, Seattle WA.

22. Immigration file for Hom Hong, Chinese Exclusion Act case files, file 7030/5251, RG 85, NARA, Seattle WA.

23. Quoted in Lee, "Defying Exclusion," 5.

24. Takaki, *Strangers from a Different Shore*, 239.

25. Lee, "Occupational Invasion," 53.

26. Wing Goon Hom to Wing Hong Hom, nd, file 89–30.194, "Wing Hong Hum Papers, 1935–1954," MHS.

27. Konitz, *Alien and the Asiatic in American*, 195.

28. Lee, "Occupational Invasion," 50–58.

29. Quoted in Lee, *Growth and Decline of Chinese Communities*, 215–16.

30. Takaki, *Strangers from a Different Shore*, 372.

31. English language file in "Wing Hong Hum Papers, 1935–1954," MHS.

32. Hom Tong to Wing Hong Hom, June 6, 1951, file 89–30.113, "Wing Hong Hum Papers, 1935–1954," MHS.

33. Two incident reports from 1943 note Wing Hong Hom being involved in accidents while working at the Mountain Con Mine. In one accident, Hom was the miner injured. In the other, his mining partner was injured and he served as a witness to describe what happened. "Chinese Exclusion Act," VFI052, BSBPA.

34. Wing Goon Hom to Wing Hong Hom, August 10, 1953, file 89–30.194, "Wing Hong Hum Papers, 1935–1954," MHS.

35. Quoted in Lee, *Growth and Decline of Chinese Communities*, 214–16.

36. For a detailed study of the impact World War II had on Chinese Americans, see Wong, *Americans First*.

37. Wong, "East Asian Immigrants," 109.

38. Oyen, *Diplomacy of Migration*, 13–41.

39. Quoted in Lee, *Growth and Decline of Chinese Communities*, 330n2.

40. Hsu, *Dreaming of Gold, Dreaming of Home*, 179–81.

41. Montana, *Laws, Resolutions and Memorials of the State of Montana Passed at the Eleventh Regular Session of the Legislative Assembly*, 57–58.

42. *Hearings Before the Committee on Immigration and Naturalization*, 68th Cong., 1st sess., December 27, 1923, 104.

43. Oyen, *Diplomacy of Migration*, 87.

44. Quoted in Oyen, *Diplomacy of Migration*, 81.

45. Oyen, *Diplomacy of Migration*, 82.

46. Drumright, "Proposals to Better Cope with Problem of Fraud at Hong Kong," Foreign Service Dispatch 942, December 13, 1955, file 122.4732/1–755, NARA, College Park MD.

47. Yi Mei to Wing Hong Hom, September 6, 1949, file 89–30.143, "Wing Hong Hum Papers, 1935–1954," MHS.

48. Wing Goon Hom to Wing Hong Hom, September 23, 1949, file 89–30.11, "Wing Hong Hum Papers, 1935–1954," MHS.

49. Wing Goon Hom to Wing Hong Hom, August 1, 1949, file 89–30.1, "Wing Hong Hum Papers, 1935–1954," MHS.

50. Yi Mei to Wing Hong Hom, September 6, 1949, file 89–30.143, "Wing Hong Hum Papers, 1935–1954," MHS.

51. Wing Soong Hom to Wing Hong Hom, September 29, 1949, file 89–30.9, "Wing Hong Hum Papers, 1935–1954," MHS.

52. Cheng, *Citizens of Asian America*, 150.

53. Oyen, *Diplomacy of Migration*, 101–3.

54. Harry Truman, "Veto of Bill to Revise the Laws Relating to Immigration, Naturalization, and Nationality, June 25, 1952," Harry S. Truman Presidential Library and Museum.

55. Lee, *Making of Asian America*, 270–71; Zhao, *Remaking Chinese America*, 158.

56. Quoted in Ngai, *Impossible Subjects*, 207.

57. Ngai, "Legacies of Exclusion," 12.

58. Drumright, "Report on the Problem of Fraud at Hong Kong," Dispatch 931, December 9, 1955, file 122.4732/1–755, NARA, College Park MD.

59. Drumright, "Report on the Problem of Fraud at Hong Kong." Drumright's views on Chinese people not understanding the bond of an oath or being trusted to give true testimony echo earlier sentiments from the American West. Throughout the western states, Chinese individuals were restricted at times from serving on juries or providing testimony against whites. At times, they could testify, but only after having first been scrutinized as to their religious and cultural beliefs concerning an afterlife and the impact on one's soul for lying. Non-Chinese residents were not subjected to such questioning. For more on legal issues relating to the Chinese in the American West, see Wunder, *Gold Mountain Turned to Dust*.

60. Ngai, "Legacies of Exclusion," 13.

61. Drumright, "Report on the Problem of Fraud at Hong Kong," Dispatch 931, December 9, 1955, file 122.4732/1–755, NARA, College Park MD. The radiological and physical exams reminded Chinese of the hated Bertillon System, originally developed for identifying convicted criminals, used from 1903–1906 to physically identify Chinese immigrants.

62. Drumright, "Report on the Problem of Fraud at Hong Kong," Dispatch 931, December 9, 1955, file 122.4732/1–755, NARA, College Park MD.

63. Oyen, *Diplomacy of Migration*, 112.

64. Records of Senator Mansfield's efforts to aid entry for constituents and their family members are housed at the Mansfield Library, University of Montana, Missoula.

65. Drumright, "Report on the Problem of Fraud at Hong Kong," Dispatch 931, December 9, 1955, file 122.4732/1–755, NARA, College Park MD.

66. "Report on Action Taken on Inspection Recommendations," From Dispatch. No. 1041, January 10, 1956, file 122.4732/1–1056, NARA, College Park MD.

67. Drumright, "Report on the Problem of Fraud at Hong Kong," Dispatch 931, December 9, 1955, file 122.4732/1–755, NARA, College Park MD.

68. Budget Request for 1956, October 5, 1955, Dispatch 545, file 122.4732/1–755, NARA, College Park MD.

69. Department of State Instruction, A-503 Response to Drumright's "Proposals to Better Cope with the Problem of Fraud at Hong Kong," May 7, 1956, file 122.4732/1–1056, NARA, College Park MD.

70. Drumright, "Report on the Problem of Fraud at Hong Kong," Dispatch 931, December 9, 1955, file 122.4732/1–755, NARA, College Park MD.

71. Zhao, *Remaking Chinese America*, 160–68.

72. Otto Engen, Lead Investigator, to James M. Sweet, Acting District Director, Helena, Mont. "Forged Passports," October 10, 1956, file 56364/51.6, RG 85, NARA, College Park MD.

73. James M. Sweet, Acting District Director, Helena, Mont. to G.S. Remington, Deputy Regional Commissioner, St. Paul, Minn., "Re Item 6 Monthly Intelligence Report," November 14, 1956, file 56364/51.6, RG 85, NARA, College Park MD.

74. Leech, *The City That Ate Itself*, 112, 113.

75. Wing Goon Hom to Wing Hong Hom, February 3, year unintelligible, file 8930.81, "Wing Hong Hum Papers, 1935–1954," MHS.

76. Swartout, "Guangdong to Big Sky," 107; U.S. Federal Census, 1870–2000.

Conclusion

1. "Self Preservation the First Law of Nature," *Montana Post*, August 19, 1865.

2. *Benton Record* (Fort Benton MT), February 8, 1878.

3. *Butte Bystander*, February 11, 1893.

4. "Good Chinamen," *Montana Radiator*, February 17, 1866.

5. *Congressional Record Proceedings and Debates of the Fifty-Second Congress*, 3569.

6. "Chinese Are Disappearing from Butte," *Butte Inter Mountain*, November 5, 1901.

7. "China Alley: Historians Unearth Mysteries of the Disappearance of Bozeman's Chinese Community," *Bozeman Daily Chronicle*, August 2, 2014.

8. "Ancient Chinaman Honored at Dinner Given at Choteau," *Helena Independent Record*, August 16, 1933.

9. "Lewis Den Visits Old-Time Scenes and Friends," *Missoulian*, January 17, 1915.

Archives and Manuscript Materials

Butte-Silver Bow Public Archives (BSBPA), Butte, Montana
    "Chinese in the Northwest," VF1055
    "Chinese Exclusion Act," VF1052
    "Chinese: Long Ying Story," VF 1057
    C. Owen Smithers Photo Collection, Acc. 2014.204
The Gallatin History Museum, Bozeman, Montana
Harry S. Truman Presidential Library and Museum, Independence, Missouri
The Heritage Center, Boulder, Montana
The History Museum, Great Falls, Montana
Joel F. Overholser Historical Research Center, Fort Benton, Montana
Mai Wah Society, Butte, Montana
Mansfield Library, University of Montana, Missoula, Montana
Montana Historical Society, Helena, Montana (MHS)
    Articles of Incorporation of the Chinese Empire Reform Society of Butte, Montana, 1901 (D003563)
    Articles of Incorporation of the Chinese Empire Reform Society of Montana (D003526)
    Bik, Patricia. China Row: A Report on the Chinese Burial Ground at Forestvale Cemetery, 1993
    Chinese Altar, Robert F. Morgan, Watercolor, 1993, 1995.78.01
    Chinese Census, District of Montana and Idaho, June 30, 1905. United States Bureau of Immigration, District of Montana and Idaho (MF 510)
    Chinese Collection UPMC 157 (87:2–6)
    Chinese Map, Chinese Collection UPMC 157 (A3; 4–2)
    Committee of the Chinese Empire Reform Association, Butte, Montana, 1901 (PAC 95–22 MMI)
    Committee of the Chinese Empire Reform Association, Marysville, Montana, 1901 (PAC 85–27 MS)
    Lee Sam Fong Papers (SSC 2747)
    Neil Fullerton Research Collection, 1932–1968 MC 76 (4:5–1)
    Hermann and Company Records, 1883–1967 (MF 183)

Virginia City's Chinese Masonic Temple Banner Canvas, ink, March 3, 1876, Translated by Fr. John Wang (x1982.01.46)

The Wing Hong Hum Papers, 1935–1954, UPMC 156 (87:2–4)

Montana Masonic Library and Museum, Helena, Montana

National Archives and Records Administration (NARA), College Park, Maryland

Dispatches from U.S. Consuls in China, 1843–1906, M 92

Dispatches from U.S. Consuls in Shanghai, China 1847–1906, Record Group 59

Records of the Department of State, Record Group 59

National Archives and Records Administration (NARA), Seattle, Washington

Chinese Exclusion Act Case Files, Record Group 85

Records of the U.S. Circuit Courts, Record Group 21

National Archives and Records Administration (NARA), Washington DC

Chinese General Correspondence, Record Group 85

University of California–Los Angeles Charles E. Young Research Library

Rose Hum Lee Papers, Department of Special Collections (Collection 1002)

Yellowstone Gateway Museum, Livingston, Montana

Published Works

Acts, Resolutions and Memorials of the Territory of Montana: Passed by the First Legislative Assembly, Convened at Bannack, December 12, 1864. Virginia City MT: D.W. Tilton, 1866.

"Advocacy of Complete Westernization." In *China's Response to the West: A Documentary Survey, 1839–1923*, edited by Ssu-yu Teng and John King Fairbank, 158–60. Cambridge MA: Harvard University Press, 1978.

Allen, Frederick. *A Decent, Orderly Lynching: The Montana Vigilantes*. Norman: University of Oklahoma Press, 2009.

Annual Report of the Woman's American Baptist Home Mission Society. Boston: C. H. Simonds, 1897.

Arata, Laura J. "Beyond the 'Mongolian Muddle': Reconsidering Virginia City, Montana's China War of 1881." *Montana: The Magazine of Western History* 62, no. 2 (Spring 2012): 23–35.

———. *Race and the Wild West: Sarah Bickford, the Montana Vigilantes, and the Tourism of Decline, 1870–1930*. Norman: University of Oklahoma Press, 2020.

Baumler, Ellen. *Helena: The Town that Gold Built, The First 150 Years*. San Antonio: HPN, 2014.

Baumler, Ellen and John Axline. *Hidden History of Helena, Montana*. Charleston SC: History Press, 2019.

Baumler, Ellen, Rowena Harrington, Roberta Jones-Wallace, Deb Mitchell, and Todd Saarinen. "Forgotten Pioneers: The Chinese in Montana." *Montana: The Magazine of Western History* (Summer 2015): 1–16.

Blake, Kellee. "'First in the Path of the Firemen': The Fate of the 1890 Population Census." *Prologue* 28, no. 1 (1996).

Brooks, Charlotte. *American Exodus: Second-Generation Chinese Americans in China, 1901–1949*. Berkeley: University of California Press, 2019.

Chace, Paul G. "On Dying American: Cantonese Rites for Death and Ghost-Spirits in an American City." In *Chinese American Death Rituals: Respecting the Ancestors*, edited by Sue Fawn Chung and Priscilla Wegars, 47–80. New York: Altamira, 2005.

Chan, Shelly. *Diaspora's Homeland: Modern China in the Age of Global Migration*. Durham NC: Duke University Press, 2018.

Chang, Gordon. *Ghosts of Gold Mountain: The Epic Story of the Chinese Who Built the Transcontinental Railroad*. Boston: Houghton Mifflin Harcourt, 2019.

Chang, Gordon and Shelley Fisher Fishkin, eds. *The Chinese and the Iron Road: Building the Transcontinental Railroad*. Stanford CA: Stanford University Press, 2019.

Chen, Yong. "Understanding Chinese American Transnationalism During the Early Twentieth Century: An Economic Perspective." In *Chinese American Transnationalism: The Flow of People, Resources, and Ideas between China and America during the Exclusion Era*, edited by Sucheng Chen, 156–73. Philadelphia: Temple University Press, 2006.

Cheng, Cindy I-Fen. *Citizens of Asian America: Democracy and Race during the Cold War*. New York: New York University Press, 2013.

Chew, Kenneth S.Y., and John M. Liu. "Hidden in Plain Sight: Global Labor Force Exchange in the Chinese American Population, 1880–1940." *Population and Development Review* 30, no. 1 (March 2004): 57–78.

Chinn, Bob. *The Other Side of Paradise: The Uncensored Memoirs of Bob Chinn*. Los Angeles: Rare Bird, 2017.

Chung, Sue Fawn, Fred P. Frampton, and Timothy W. Murphy. "Venerate These Bones: Chinese American Funerary and Burial Practices as Seen in Carlin, Elko County, Nevada." In *Chinese American Death Rituals: Respecting the Ancestors*, edited by Sue Fawn Chung and Priscilla Wegars, 107–46. New York: Altamira, 2005.

Chung, Sue Fawn. *The Chinese in the Woods: Logging and Lumbering in the American West*. Urbana: University of Illinois Press, 2015.

———. *In Pursuit of Gold: Chinese American Miners and Merchants in the American West*. Urbana: University of Illinois Press, 2011.

———. "The Zhigongtang in the United States." In *Empire, Nation, and Beyond: Chinese History in Late Imperial and Modern Times*, edited by Joseph W. Esherick, Wen-hsin Yeh, and Madeleine Zeling, 231–49. Berkeley: University of California Berkeley, 2006.

Compilation from the Records of the Bureau of Immigration of Facts Concerning the Enforcement of the Chinese-Exclusion Laws, Doc. 847, *Congressional Record 59th Cong., 1st sess*. Washington DC: Government Printing Office, 1906.

Congressional Record Proceedings and Debates of the 52nd Cong., 1st sess. Washington DC: Government Printing Office, 1892.

Congressional Record Proceedings and Debates of the 53rd Cong., 1st sess., also Special Session of the Senate, Volume 25. Washington DC: Government Printing Office, 1893.

Congressional Record Relative to Citizenship of American Women Married to Foreigners: Hearings Before the Committee on Immigration and Naturalization. 65th Cong., 2nd sess. Washington DC: Government Printing Office, 1917.

Congressional Record Senate Documents, 59th Cong., 2nd sess. Washington DC: Government

Printing Office, 1907.

Coolidge, Mary Roberts. *Chinese Immigration*. New York: Henry Holt, 1909.

Cott, Nancy F. "Marriage and Women's Citizenship in the United States, 1830–1934." *American Historical Review* 103, no. 5 (December 1998): 1440–74.

Daniels, Roger. *Asian America: Chinese and Japanese in the United States since 1850*. Seattle: University of Washington Press, 1992.

———. *Not Like Us: Immigrants and Minorities in America, 1890–1924*. Chicago: Ivan R. Dee, 1997.

Dixon, Kelly J. with contributions by Gary Weisz, Christopher W. Merritt, Robert Weaver, and James Bard, "Landscapes of Change: Culture, Nature, and the Archeological Heritage of Transcontinental Railroads in the North American West." In *The Chinese and the Iron Road: Building the Transcontinental Railroad*, edited by Gordon H. Chang and Shelley Fisher Fishkin, 126–38. Stanford CA: Stanford University Press, 2019.

Dondlinger, Peter Tracy. *The Book of Wheat: An Economic History and Practical Manual of the Wheat Industry*. New York: Orange Judd, 1908.

Dong, Stella. *Shanghai: The Rise and Fall of a Decadent City*. New York: Harper Perennial, 2000.

Fang Zhiqin and Cai Huiyao, eds. *Kang Liang yu Baohuanghui—Tan Liang zai Meiguo suocang ziliao huibian* [*Kang Youwei, Liang Qichao, and the Baohuanghui: A Compilation of Materials Collected by Tom Leung in the U.S.A.*]. Hong Kong: Xianggang Yinhe Chubanshe, 2008.

Federal Writers' Project. *The WPA Guide to Montana: The Big Sky State*. San Antonio: Trinity University Press, 1939.

Flaherty, Stacy. "Boycott in Butte: Organized Labor and the Chinese Community, 1896–1897." *Montana: The Magazine of Western History* 37, no. 1 (Winter 1987): 34–47.

Fong, Colleen. "Establishing and Maintaining a Family in the Shadow of Chinese Exclusion: A Case Study of the Fong Family of Santa Barbara County, California." *Chinese America: History & Perspectives* (2013): 39–51.

"Fong Yue Ting v. United States." *Reports of Cases Argued and Decided in the Supreme Court of the United States*. Book 37, 1894.

Gao Weinong. [*Activities of Kang Youwei and the Baohuanghui Among the Chinese in the United States in the First Part of the 20th Century*]. Beijing: Beijing Academy Press, 2009.

Gao, Yunxian. "Soo Yong (1903–1984): Hollywood Celebrity and Cultural Interpreter." *Journal of American-East Asian Relations* 17 (2010): 372–99.

Gardiner, Reid. "The Chee Kung Tong 'Chinese Freemasons' Helena, Montana." *Montana Freemason* 94, no. 6 (August 2018): 14–17.

Grebenkemper, John and Adela Morris. "China Row, Forestville [*sic*] Cemetery MT." Report Prepared for the Montana History Foundation, 2018.

Headland, Isaac Taylor. *Court Life in China: The Capital, Its Officials and People*. New York: F. H. Revell, 1909.

Hearings Before the Committee on Immigration and Naturalization, 68th Cong., 1st sess., Dec. 27, 1923.

Helterline, Maurice. *Horse Plains, Montana Territory*. Plains MT: Printery, 1984.

Hernández, Kelly Lytle. *City of Inmates: Conquest, Rebellion, and the Rise of Human Caging in Los Angeles, 1771–1965*. Chapel Hill: University of North Carolina Press, 2017.

Hirata, Lucie Cheng. "Free, Indentured, Enslaved: Chinese Prostitutes in Nineteenth-Century America." *Signs* 5, no 1 (1979): 3–29.

Hodges, Graham Russell Gao. *Anna May Wong: From Laundryman's Daughter to Hollywood Legend*. London: Palgrave Macmillan, 2004.

Hsu, Immanuel C. Y. *The Rise of Modern China*, 6th ed. Oxford: Oxford University Press, 1999.

Hsu, Madeline Y. "Migration and Native Place: *Qiaokan* and the Imagined Community of Taishan County, Guangdong, 1893–1993." *Journal of Asian Studies* 59, no. 2 (May 2000): 307–31.

———. *Dreaming of Gold, Dreaming of Home: Transnationalism and Migration Between the United States and South China, 1882–1943*. Stanford CA: Stanford University Press, 2000.

Huang, Philip C. *Liang Ch'i-ch'ao and Modern Chinese Liberalism*. Seattle: University of Washington Press, 1972.

Judge, Joan. "The Factional Function of Print: Liang Qichao, *Shibao*, and the Fissures in the Late Qing Reform Movement." *Late Imperial China* vol. 16, no. 1 (June 1995): 120–40.

———. *Print and Politics: 'Shibao' and the Culture of Reform in Late Qing China*. Stanford CA: Stanford University Press, 1996.

Kang Youwei. "Comprehensive Consideration of the Whole Situation." In *Sources of Chinese Tradition: From 1600 Through the Twentieth Century*, edited by William Theodore DeBary and Lufrano, Richard, 2nd ed., vol. 2, 269–70. New York: Columbia University Press, 2000.

Kaplan, Lawrence M. *Homer Lea: American Soldier of Fortune*. Lexington: University Press of Kentucky, 2010.

Kennedy, J. Ryan and Chelsea Rose. "Charting a New Course for Chinese Diaspora Archeology in North America." In *Chinese Diaspora Archeology in North America* edited by J. Ryan Kennedy and Chelsea Rose, 1–34. Gainesville: University of Florida Press, 2020.

Konitz, Milton R. *The Alien and the Asiatic in American Law*. Ithaca: Cornell University Press, 1946.

Kramer, Paul A. "Imperial Openings: Civilization, Exemption, and the Geopolitics of Mobility in the History of Chinese Exclusion, 1868–1910." *Journal of the Gilded Age and Progressive Era* 14 (2015): 317–47.

Lai, Him Mark. *Becoming Chinese American: A History of Communities and Institutions*. Lanham MD: Altamira, 2004.

Larson, Jane Leung. "The 1905 Anti-American Boycott as a Transnational Chinese Movement." *Chinese America: History & Perspectives* (2007): 191–98.

———. "An Association to Save China, the Baohuang Hui: A Documentary Account." *China Heritage Quarterly* no. 27 (September 2011).

———. "A Galvanizing Issue for the Baohuanghui: American Exclusion Policy and Chinese Nationalism." Forthcoming.

———. "Articulating China's First Mass Movement: Kang Youwei, Liang Qichao, the Baohuanghui, and the 1905 Anti-American Boycott." *Twentieth-Century China* 33, no. 1 (2007): 4–26.

———. "The United States as a Site for Baohuanghui Activism." In *World Confederation of Institutes and Libraries in Chinese Overseas Studies*, proceedings of Fifth International Conference of Institutes and Libraries in Chinese Overseas Studies. Vancouver BC (2011).

Laws, Resolutions and Memorials of the State of Montana Passed at the Eleventh Regular Session of the Legislative Assembly. Helena MT: Independent, 1909.

Lee, Erika. *At America's Gates: Chinese Immigration During the Exclusion Era, 1882–1943.* Chapel Hill: University of North Carolina, 2003.

———. "Defying Exclusion: Chinese Immigrants and Their Strategies During the Exclusion Era." In *Chinese American Transnationalism: The Flow of People, Resources, and Ideas between China and America during the Exclusion Era*, edited by Sucheng Chan, 1–21. Philadelphia: Temple University Press, 2006.

———. *The Making of Asian America.* New York: Simon & Schuster, 2016.

Lee, Rose Hum. *The Chinese in the United States of America.* Hong Kong University Press, 1960.

———. *The Growth and Decline of Chinese Communities in the Rocky Mountain Region.* New York: Arno, 1978.

———. "Madame Chiang Kai-Shek's Children." *Survey Graphic* 32 (January 1943): 136–44.

———. "Occupational Invasion, Succession, and Accommodation of the Chinese of Butte, Montana." *American Journal of Sociology* 55, no. 1 (July 1949): 50–58.

Leech, Brian J. *The City That Ate Itself: Butte, Montana and Its Expanding Berkeley Pit.* Reno: University of Nevada Press, 2018.

Lettieri, Michelle A. "'Maximize Our Missions!' Mui Tsai, Missionaries, and Material Representation." Master's thesis, University of Nevada, Las Vegas, 2004.

Lew-Williams, Beth. *The Chinese Must Go: Violence, Exclusion, and the Making of the Alien in America.* Cambridge MA: Harvard University Press, 2018.

———. "Paper Lives of Chinese Migrants and the History of the Undocumented." *Modern American History* (2021): 1–22.

Liang Qichao. "Liang Qichao on His Trip to America." In *Chinese Civilization: A Sourcebook*, edited by Patricia Buckley Ebrey, 335–40. New York: Free Press, 1993.

Louie, Emma Woo. "Surnames as Clues to Family History." In *Chinese America: History & Perspectives*, edited by Marlon K. Hom, 101–8. San Francisco: Chinese Historical Society of America, 1991.

Lum, Kathryn Gin. "Religion on the Road: How Chinese Migrants Adapted Popular Religion to an American Context." In *The Chinese and the Iron Road: Building the Transcontinental Railroad*, edited by Gordon H. Chang and Shelley Fisher Fishkin, 159–78. Stanford CA: Stanford University Press, 2019.

Ma, L. Eve Armentrout. *Revolutionaries, Monarchists and Chinatowns: Chinese Politics in the Americas and the 1911 Revolution.* Honolulu: University of Hawaii Press, 1990.

Madokoro, Laura. *Elusive Refuge: Chinese Migration in the Cold War.* Cambridge MA: Harvard University Press, 2016.

Malone, Michael P., Richard B. Roeder, and William T. Lang. *Montana: A History of Two Centuries.* Seattle: University of Washington Press, 1991.

Manning, Nikki M. *Historic Underground Missoula.* Charleston SC: History Press, 2015.

McGlashan, Zena Beth. *Buried in Butte.* Butte MT: Wordz and Ink, 2010.

McKee, Delber L. "The Chinese Boycott of 1905–1906 Reconsidered: The Role of Chinese Americans." *Pacific Historical Review* 55, no. 2 (May 1986): 165–91.

McKeown, Adam. "Conceptualizing Chinese Diasporas, 1842 to 1949." *Journal of Asian Studies* 58, no. 2 (May 1999): 306–31.

———. *Melancholy Order: Asian Migration and the Globalization of Borders.* New York: Columbia University Press, 2008.

Mei, June. "Socioeconomic Origins of Emigration: Guangdong to California, 1850–1882." *Modern China* 5, no. 4 (October 1979): 463–501.

Meissner, Daniel T. "China's 1905 Anti-American Boycott: A Nationalist Myth?" *Journal of American-East Asian Relations* 10, no. 3–4 (Fall-Winter 2001): 175–96.

Melvin, Sheila. "Sounds of Distinction: Peking Opera Idol Mei Lanfang May Be Best Remembered for His Overseas Tour of the U.S." *China File,* 2014.

Merritt, Christopher W. "Toward a Historical Archeology of the Chinese in Montana and a Transnational Lens." In *Chinese Diaspora Archeology in North America,* edited by Chelsea Rose and J. Ryan Kennedy, 209–33. Gainesville: University of Florida Press, 2020.

———. *The Coming Man from Canton: Chinese Experience in Montana, 1862–1943.* Lincoln: University of Nebraska Press, 2017.

Mishra, Pankaj. *From the Ruins of Empire: The Intellectuals Who Remade Asia.* New York: Farrar, Straus, and Giroux, 2012.

Morgan, Lael. *Wanton West: Madams, Money, Murder, and the Wild Women of Montana's Frontier.* Chicago: Chicago Review Press, 2011.

Morris, Patrick F. *Anaconda, Montana: Copper Smelting Boom Town on the Western Frontier.* Bethesda MD: Swann, 1997.

Ng, Katharine. "Fitting in Space: Rose Hum Lee's Negotiation of Assimilation and Citizenship in America." *Chinese America: History & Perspectives: The Journal of the Chinese Historical Society of America* (2006): 1–13.

Ng Poon Chew. "The Treatment of the Exempt Classes of Chinese in the U.S. (1908)." In *Chinese American Voices,* edited by Judy Yung, Gordon H. Chang, and Him Mark Lai, 109–17. Berkeley: University of California Press, 2006.

Ngai, Mae M. "Legacies of Exclusion: Illegal Chinese Immigration during the Cold War Years." *Journal of American Ethnic History* 18, no. 1 (Fall 1998): 3–35.

———. *The Lucky Ones: One Family and the Extraordinary Invention of Chinese America.* Boston: Houghton Mifflin Harcourt, 2010.

———. *Impossible Subjects: Illegal Aliens and the Making of Modern America.* Princeton NJ: Princeton University Press, 2004.

Nicolosi, Ann Marie. "'We Do Not Want Our Girls to Marry Foreigners': Gender, Race, and American Citizenship." *NWSA Journal* 13 no. 3 (Autumn 2001): 1–21.

Not in Precious Metals Alone: A Manuscript History of Montana. Helena: Montana Historical Society, 1976.

Oyen, Meredith. *The Diplomacy of Migration: Transnational Lives and the Making of U.S. China Relations in the Cold War.* Ithaca NY: Cornell University Press, 2015.

Pasacreta, Laura J. "White Tigers and Azure Dragons: Overseas Chinese Burial Practices in the Canadian and American West (1850s to 1910s)." Master's thesis, Simon Fraser University, 1998.

Pascoe, Peggy. "Gender Systems in Conflict: The Marriages of Mission-Educated Chinese American Women, 1874–1939." *Journal of Social History* 22, no. 4 (Summer 1989): 631–52.

Peffer, George Anthony. *If They Don't Bring Their Women Here: Chinese Female Immigration before Exclusion.* Urbana: University of Illinois Press, 1999.

Pegler-Gordon, Anna. *In Sight of America: Photography and the Development of U.S. Immigration Policy.* Berkeley: University of California Press, 2009.

Powderly, Terence. *Thirty Years of Labor: 1859–1889.* Columbus OH: Excelsior, 1889.

Qin, Yucheng. *The Diplomacy of Nationalism: The Six Companies and China's Policy Toward Exclusion.* Honolulu: University of Hawaii Press, 2009.

Quinn, Larry D. "'Chink Chink Chinaman': The Beginnings of Nativism in Montana." *Pacific Northwest Quarterly* 58, no. 2 (April 1967): 82–89.

Rohe, Randall E. "After the Gold Rush: Chinese Mining in the Far West, 1850–1890." *Montana: The Magazine of Western History* 32, no. 4 (Autumn 1982): 2–19.

Rouse, Wendy L. "'What We Didn't Understand': A History of Chinese Death Ritual in China and California." In *Chinese American Death Rituals: Respecting the Ancestors,* edited by Sue Fawn Chung and Priscilla Wegars, 19–46. New York: Altamira, 2005.

Salyer, Lucy. *Laws Harsh as Tigers: Chinese Immigrants and the Shaping of Modern Immigration Law.* Chapel Hill: University of North Carolina Press, 1995.

Sanders, Helen F. *History of Montana.* Vol. 1. Chicago: Lewis, 1913.

Seligman, Scott D. *The First Chinese American: The Remarkable Life of Wong Chin Foo.* Hong Kong: Hong Kong University Press, 2013.

Sinn, Elizabeth. *Pacific Crossing: California Gold, Chinese Migration, and the Making of Hong Kong.* Hong Kong: Hong Kong University Press, 2013.

Smith, Marian. "The Immigration and Naturalization Service (INS) at the US-Canadian Border, 1893–1993: An Overview of Issues and Topics." *Michigan Historical Review* 26, no. 2 (Fall 2000): 127–47.

Spaulding, Charleen. *Benton Avenue Cemetery: A Pioneer Resting Place.* Helena MT: Pioneer Tales, 2010.

Swartout, Robert J., Jr. "From Guangdong to Big Sky: The Chinese in Montana, 1864–1900." In *Montana: A Cultural Medley,* edited by Robert J. Swartout, Jr., 94–120. Helena MT: Farcountry, 2015.

Takaki, Ronald. *Strangers from a Different Shore: A History of Asian Americans.* Boston: Back Bay, 1998.

Thompson, John M. *Great Power Rising: Theodore Roosevelt and the Politics of U.S. Foreign Policy.* Oxford: Oxford University Press, 2019.

Tong, Benson. *Unsubmissive Women: Chinese Prostitutes in Nineteenth-Century San Francisco.* Norman: University of Oklahoma Press, 1994.

U.S. Department of Commerce, Bureau of the Census, *Ninth Census of the United States, 1870.*

———. *Tenth Census of the United States, 1880.*

———. *Eleventh Census of the United States, 1890.*

———. *Twelfth Census of the United States,1900.*

———. *Thirteenth Census of the United States, 1910.*

———. *Fifteenth Census of the United States, 1930.*

U.S. Department of State. *Papers Relating to the Foreign Relations of the United States.* Washington DC: Government Printing Office, 1902.

U.S. House of Representatives. *Relative to Citizenship of American Women Married to Foreigners: Hearings Before the Committee on Immigration and Naturalization.* 65th Cong., 2nd sess. December 13–14, 1917.

Vohra, Ranbir. *China's Path to Modernization: A Historical Review from 1800 to the Present.* 3rd ed. New York: Pearson, 1999.

Volpp, Leti. "Divesting Citizenship: On Asian American History and the Loss of Citizenship Through Marriage." UCLA *Law Review* 53, no. 405 (2005): 404–83.

Wang, Guanhua. *In Search of Justice: The 1905–1906 Chinese Anti-American Boycott.* Cambridge MA: Harvard University Press, 2001.

Watson, James L. and Evelyn S. Rawski. "Funeral Specialists in Cantonese Society: Pollution, Performance, and Social Hierarchy." In *Death Ritual in Late Imperial and Modern China*, edited by James L. Watson and Evelyn S. Rawski, 109–34. Berkeley: University of California Press, 1988.

Wegars, Priscilla. "Exposing Negative Chinese Terminology and Stereotypes." In *Chinese Diaspora Archeology in North America*, edited by Chelsea Rose and J. Ryan Kennedy, 83–108. Gainesville: University of Florida Press, 2020.

Wei, William. *Asians in Colorado: A History of Persecution and Perseverance in the Centennial State.* Seattle: University of Washington Press, 2016.

The WPA Guide to Montana: The Big Sky State. San Antonio: Trinity University Press, 2012.

Winans, Adrienne Ann and Judy Tzu-Chun Wu. "Not Adding and Stirring: Women's, Gender, and Sexuality History and the Transformation of Asian America." In *The Oxford Handbook of Asian American History*, edited by David K. Yoo and Eiichiro Azuma, 468 488. Oxford: Oxford University Press, 2016.

Woman's Foreign Missionary Society of the Presbyterian Church. "Woman's Work for Woman." February 1882.

Wong, Flora. *Long Way Home: Journeys of a Chinese Montanan.* Helena MT: Sweetgrass, 2011.

Wong, K. Scott. *Americans First: Chinese Americans and the Second World War.* Cambridge: Harvard University Press, 2005.

———. "Liang Qichao and the Chinese of America: A Re-Evaluation of His 'Selected Memoir of Travels in the New World.'" *Journal of American Ethnic History* 11, no. 4 (Summer 1992): 3–24.

———. "East Asian Immigrants." In *The Oxford Handbook of Asian American History*, edited by David K. Yoo and Eiichiro Azuma, 104–15. Oxford: Oxford University Press, 2016.

Wong Sin-Kiong. "Mobilizing a Social Movement in China: Propaganda of the 1905 Boycott Campaign." *Chinese Studies* 19, no. 1 (2001): 375–408.

Wright, Carroll D. and William C. Hunt. *The History and Growth of the United States Census*. Washington DC: Government Printing Office, 1900.

Wunder, John R. *Gold Mountain Turned to Dust: Essays on the Legal History of the Chinese in the Nineteenth-Century American West*. Albuquerque: University of New Mexico Press, 2018.

Yip, Hon-ming. "Institutionalizing Charity: Hong Kong and the Homebound Burial of Chinese Americans, 1900–1949." *Chinese America: History & Perspectives: The Journal of the Chinese Historical Society of America* (2018): 1–11.

Yu, Henry. *Thinking Orientals: Migration, Contact, and Exoticism in Modern America*. Oxford: Oxford University Press, 2002.

Yuan Ding and Roland Hsu. "Overseas Remittances of Chinese Laborers in North America." In *The Chinese and the Iron Road: Building the Transcontinental Railroad*, edited by Gordon H. Chang and Shelley Fisher Fishkin, 76–89. Stanford CA: Stanford University Press, 2019.

Yue, Meng. *Shanghai at the Edges of Empire*. Minneapolis: University of Minnesota Press, 2006.

Yung, Judy. *Unbound Feet: A Social History of Chinese Women in San Francisco*. Berkeley: University of California Press, 1994.

Zhao, Xiaojian. *Remaking Chinese America: Immigration, Family, and Community, 1940–1965*. New Brunswick NJ: Rutgers University Press, 2002.

Zhu, Minyan, ed. *Shanghai Historic Days*. Shanghai: Shanghai Brilliant Publishing House, 2009.

Zhu, Liping. "No Need to Rush: The Chinese, Placer Mining, and the Western Environment." *Montana: The Magazine of Western History* 49, no. 3 (Autumn 1999): 43–57.

———. *A Chinaman's Chance: The Chinese on the Rocky Mountain Mining Frontier*. Boulder: University Press of Colorado, 1997.

———. *The Road to Chinese Exclusion: The Denver Riot, 1880 Election, and the Rise of the West*. Lawrence: University of Kansas Press, 2013.

Page numbers in italics indicate figures.

Chinese experience, xi, xiv, 2, 3, 5, 8, 20, 21, 33–34, 85, 213; geographical/chronological scope of, 19; interpreting, xii, xiii; story of, 17

Chinese immigrants, 4, 42, 43, 45, 61, 65, 184, 195; burden of proof and, 46; criticism of, 2, 203; exclusion of, 17, 53, 54, 147; hardships for, 96, 116; illegal, 201; marriages and, 196–97; treatment of, 113, *113*, 146; work for, 172–73

Chinese Imperial Army, 225n46

Chinese language, 19, 20, 80, 153

Chinese laundries, 22, 52, 61, 96, 172, 191; boycott of, 5, 8; taxes on, 17

Chinese Lodge, 38

Chinese Masonic temple, banner from, *40*

Chinese New Year, 10, 11, 157

Chinese population, 2, *6*, *17*, 18, 52, 91, 97, 208, 212, 217n6; aging of, 123; decline of, 99, 126, 154, 211, 212; ill treatment of, 19–20, 59, 120; increase in, 154

Chinese Revolution (1911), 157, 170

Chinese Service of Bureau of Immigration, 97

Chinese women, *151*; assumptions about, 209; criticism of, 151; exclusion of, 34, 152; impropriety and, 157; kidnapping/retribution against, 160; role of, 175; scarcity of, 169–70; status of, 13–14; work for, 172, 175–76

Chinese Women National War Relief Society, 177

Chinese workers, 42, 65, 90, 118, 120; attracting, 103, 120; criticism of, 1–2, 3; economic niche of, 5; exclusion of, 24, 94, 116–17, 121; goals of, 101; mistreatment of, 102, 116; pressures on, 24, 41, 59, 101; registration and, 56; role of, 192; sympathy for, 118

Choteau, 212

Choy Gay, 162, 163, 164

Christianity, 124, 163

citizenship, 65, 122, 155, 170, 182, 184, 204, 212; birthright, 177; Chinese and, 3, 12, 34, 51, 179, 209–10; claiming, 187, 188; derivative, 187, 235n74; forfeiting, 176, 177; naturalized, 178; split, 176–77; women and, 34, 179

Cixi, Dowager Empress, 68, 69–70, 86, 90, 100–101, 225n46

clan affiliations, 18, 19

Cold War, 149, 178, 182, 187, 197, 205, 208; anxieties of, 210; immigration and, 200

Committee of Safety, 11

Committee on Immigration and Naturalization, 48

communication, 3, 32, 55, 96, 102, 115, 122, 147, 195, 203

Communism: fears of, 183; turn to, 181

Communists, xii, 197, 205; infiltration by, xiv, 185, 200; Nationalists and, 178, 181, 200; schemes by, 178

Confucianism, 11, 29, 68, 107, 124, 139

Confucius, 124

Cooper, Gary, 175

copper, 22, 89, 192, 206

Cornet Band, 132

corpse handlers, 129, 131

Cotton Goods Export Association, 115

cultural adaptations, 141, 170

cultural expectations, 32–33, 43

cultural practices, 20, 22, 128, 210

Cultural Revolution, 207

culture, 103, 127, 236n1; foreign, 69; patriarchal, 157; western, 102. *See also* Chinese culture

Daoism (Taoism), 124, 130, 136, 139

death insurance, 140, 143, 147

Deer Lodge MT, 5, *6*, 38, 215; registering in, 56

Den, Lewis, 212

De Nu, 28, 31

Department of Enlistment Services, 194

deportation, 19, 54, 56, 93, 96, 98, 99, 118, 155, 168; decrease in, 115; threat of, 64

De Quan, 29, 31, 33, 37, 41, 43; Butte merchants and, 32; family conditions and, 28; identity of, 42; letter to, *23*; life of, 22; question about, 23–24; return of, 35, 36; Taishan and, 25

De Xiu, 31, 35, 36, 37

Dillon MT, 5, *6*, 215

Dimsdale, Thomas, 8; anti-Chinese forces and, 3–4; Chinese women and, 151; on Chinese workers, 1–2, 3; on citizenship, 209; multicultural workforce and, 1; vigilante actions and, 2

CPSIA information can be obtained
at www.ICGtesting.com
Printed in the USA
LVHW100716240822
726740LV00002B/29